PACIFIC SALMON FISHING

PACIFIC SALMON FISHING

Allen Bonenko

Illustrations by
G. Thomas Henderson

SAN DIEGO • NEW YORK
A.S. BARNES & COMPANY, INC.
IN LONDON
THE TANTIVY PRESS

Pacific Salmon Fishing text copyright © 1980 by
A. S. Barnes and Co., Inc.

The Tantivy Press
Magdalen House
136-148 Tooley Street
London, SE1 2TT, England

First Edition
Manufactured in the United States of America
For information write to A. S. Barnes and Company, Inc.,
P.O. Box 3051, San Diego, CA 92038

Library of Congress Cataloging in Publication Data

Bonenko, Allen 1944-
  Pacific salmon fishing.

    Bibliography: p.
    Includes index.
    1.   Pacific salmon fishing — Northwest Pacific.
I.   Title.
SH686.B66   799.1'7'55   78-75298
ISBN 0 — 498-02326-5

1 2 3 4 5 6 7 8 9   84 83 82 81 80

For David and Andy, my better sides

CONTENTS

PREFACE

As this is written, a brilliant summer sun casts long afternoon shadows across the bank in front of my study window and sends up dazzling light-bursts from the water, part of Puget Sound. Squinting to filter the glare, I count three boats—two "kickers" and a small cruiser—between the point of land to my right and the Seattle skyline. They are moving slowly, trolling or drift-mooching, and I can make out the human forms aboard. They are salmon fishermen, and while I have no way of knowing if they have taken fish, they are lucky anglers indeed, for it is Tuesday afternoon.

We of the Pacific Northwest are fortunate to have such prime waters at our doorstep. We are further blessed in that our waters hold some of the most coveted and famed of all sport fish—Pacific salmon. For the sportsman inclined to sample the fishing, success is not guaranteed. Yet what salmon enthusiast doesn't relish even a fruitless day on the water? If fish are caught, fine; if not—well, that's okay, too.

But it's better if fish *are* caught. At least, such is the thinking of most salmon anglers, even those ardent few who do not plan on keeping their catches but will release them instead, satisfied in having done battle with a fish of such stature. While there may indeed be a few fishermen who really do *not* care if they score, scoring is the name of the game; it is the logical conclusion of the hunt, and few among us would argue otherwise.

Precisely because successful fishing is more enjoyable than unsuccessful fishing, most anglers are keen to learn how they can improve their odds. For better or worse, "odds" are virtually synonymous with knowledge and experience when it comes to tricking Pacific salmon. While experience may be gained only firsthand, knowledge may be assimilated in a variety of ways. In fact, knowledge is best gained through firsthand experience, and the former is usually a poor substitute for the latter.

It is the purpose of this book to impart knowledge to the reader, but only as a supplement for actual experience. There is nothing quite like getting "skunked" a few times or failing to hook a half dozen gently biting Chinook or losing a fine fish at the side of the boat to make the novice cry out for help. Even the veteran salmon fisherman who is normally successful but falls into a slump is likely to look for answers when others, lacking a great deal of angling experience, continue to take fish after fish.

Granted, luck plays a part in fishing, as it does in most of life's other arenas. But it is truly the ignorant angler who, failing to connect as consistently as he should, pronounces in earnestness that he simply isn't as "lucky" as others. This is usually the same guy who makes hard way bets at the Vegas craps tables or who instructs his broker to select "investments" for him by throwing darts at the Wall Street Journal. It has been said that luck is a lady; still, not everyone would take that lady for a wife. In fact, there are those who, through bitter experience, proclaim the lady best suited for a one-night stand.

The most successful salmon fishermen—those who do not always score but who take fish consistently—are those who apply their knowledge of salmon habits and salmon fishing techniques *on the fishing grounds*. For them, knowledge is not an abstract notion; it is a very real and helpful asset. Used properly, it will result in more fish. It's that simple.

It requires months, sometimes years, to acquire all the experience needed to score consistently on Pacific salmon. This book covers the subject broadly but at the same time focuses on those details which are frequently omitted in most material published on the subject. If this volume extends to the reader a shortcut here and there and a knowledge of salmon and salmon fishing just beyond what is required to take a brace of fish, it will have served its purpose.

I would like to stress that, in those sections of the book which deal with where and when the best salmon fishing may be found, the reader is strongly urged to compare information found here with the current angling regulations in effect in each geographical area. Because situations may change rapidly and radically, and because seasonal closures

—as well as those prompted by various emergencies —are possible, the individual agency responsible for the management of each particular fishery is the final authority. *Dates and places outlined here are intended as a guide only*, and such specifics should not be construed to imply that certain fisheries are, in fact, legal. It is always a good idea to check for closures with the responsible agency, and this writer does not wish to assume responsibility for fish which may be taken illegally.

The reader will find scattered throughout the book a number of notes. These notes merely cite material sources and are outlined at the ends of the chapters. Thus, the reader may—without short-changing him/herself—skip the notes so as not to interrupt the flow of reading. Those interested in the specific source of such notes may turn immediately to the end of the chapter.

Allen Bonenko

ACKNOWLEDGMENTS

I am indebted to a number of individuals without whose aid and guidance this book would not have materialized. I would especially like to thank Frank Woolner, longtime Editor-in-Chief of *Salt Water Sportsman* and (though he will deny it) the grand old man of the sea, and Henry Lyman, publisher of the magazine. It was Frank who bought—and Hal who paid for—my first feature article on salmon fishing a number of years ago. Frank, with whom I have exchanged scurrilous letters over the years, has been kind enough to offer his valuable advice on countless occasions, and he has read the proofs of this manuscript.

Special thanks are also due Frank Haw, Deputy Director of the Washington State Department of Fisheries and a master salmon angler, as well as a biologist. This Frank, too, was kind enough to read over my manuscript proofs and offer professional advice.

I would also like to thank those diligent officers of the various agencies under which falls the responsibility of salmon management: a host of biological and supervisory personnel with the Washington State Department of Fisheries; the Oregon Department of Transportation, Travel Information Section; the Oregon Department of Fish and Wildlife, Fish Division; the Sport Fish Division of the Alaska Department of Fish and Game; the State of California, Department of Fish and Game; the Fisheries and Marine Division, Environment Canada; the British Columbia Department of Fish and Wildlife; and the Idaho Fish and Game Department.

Special kudos are due Mr. Robert C. Cumbow, Chief of the Information and Education Division of the Washington Department of Fisheries. Bob rose above and beyond the call of duty in supplying me with information and photographs on a number of occasions and is to be commended for his extraordinary promptness on all counts. Others who went out of their way to provide me with information and to answer specific questions are Mr. Brian Jubinville, Information Officer, and Mr. Lyle Freeman, District Supervisor, of Canada's Fisheries and Marine office. Mr. Dave Ortmann, Anadromous Fisheries Manager with the Idaho Fish and Game Department, was also kind enough to allow me to query him exhaustively about salmon and salmon fishing in that inland state.

My thanks also go to a stable of knowledgeable writers who have passed on many of their experiences and observations. A book of this sort requires both live and library research; it is through no faults of these authors that the former is more enjoyable.

I am further indebted to an army of salmon fishermen—both sport and commercial—who have instilled in me a respect for the various Pacific species and who have provided me with the joys of comradeship possible only among anglers. Not all sport salmon fishermen are inclined to lie, but find one who says he doesn't thoroughly enjoy a day on the water and I'll show you a real Tom Pepper.

Allen Bonenko
Bainbridge Island, Washington

SPECIAL NOTE TO READERS

The date—May 18, 1980—is one which Pacific salmon fishermen are not likely to forget for years, perhaps for decades. At approximately 8:30 on that fateful morning, something happened which will doubtless have severe and far-reaching consequences for both sport and commercial salmon anglers, as well as for fisheries managers. Mt. St. Helens erupted in a violent explosion, spelling immediate doom for millions of Pacific salmon—and uncertainty for large segments of the resource.

At the time of the eruption, this book had been completed and was due to go to press. Because the blast—and the resulting damage to salmon stocks—is so intricately related to certain sections of this book, it is necessary that the impact of the volcano's wrath on Pacific salmon species be included here.

The titanic explosion—estimated at 500 times the force of the bomb which devastated Hiroshima—rocked southwest Washington that Sunday morning, spreading death, destruction and panic. By far the most destructive of modern American eruptions, St. Helens' explosion was the first to occur in the continental United States in 65 years. Not since northern California's Lassen Peak erupted in 1914-15 had there been a volcanic disturbance of this magnitude. Emitting nearly as much material—chiefly ash, mud and debris—as had Mt. Vesuvius in A.D. 79, the Mt. St. Helens blast of May 18 caused an enormous mudflow which reached speeds of at least 30 miles per hour and sent ash, gas, steam and debris to the dizzying height of 63,000 feet. The various phenomena associated with the exploson brought tens of confirmed deaths; still more were reported missing and presumed dead.

But humans were not alone in suffering. Among the other victims were fish, wildlife and enormous expanses of the most magnificent forests and streams. The eruption—fortunately not as lethal as the one which buried Pompeii and Herculaneum and killed at least 2,000—leveled all trees and standing objects within some 10 miles to the north, east and west of the blast. While some 36,000 perished as a result of giant tidal waves caused by the 1883 eruption of Krakatoa, and some 30,000 died in the 1902 explosion of Mt. Pelée on the island of Martinique, the St. Helens eruption produced mudflows which reached heights of at least 50 feet and raced down the major river valleys leading from the blast area. Not since the 1912 eruption of Alaska's Mt. Katmai (which geologists estimate was roughly 10 times as powerful as the May 18 St. Helens blast), had an American volcano caused such widespread damage to habitat.

While on assignment to cover the impact of St. Helens' eruption on nature and the environment for *National Wildlife* magazine, this writer was awed by the magnitude of the damage. A first-hand inspection of the blast area from a small, single-engine aircraft produced only bewilderment. The northern flank of the mountain lay exposed like some vulnerable, defeated opponent. Yet the mountain itself had delivered defeat to the formerly pristine land which surrounds it—once idyllic lakes, streams and great stands of old timber. Where once these had inspired, their remnants left only a deep and painful regret, bitter as the odor of sulphur which hung in the air.

Before the ash produced by the May 18 explosion had settled, state and federal officials were preparing preliminary estimates of the damage. Nature's wrath had destroyed some 240 square miles of prime fish and wildlife habitat, including 150 square miles of timber estimated at over $200 million. It had "moderately"

11

damaged no less than 27 lakes and "heavily damaged or destroyed" another 26 lakes—at least two of which, it was believed, had been literally blown dry by the initial blast. These lakes, Crane and Hoo Hoo, had a total surface area of six acres and were located in the vicinity of Smith Creek and Muddy River. Popular Spirit Lake, 1,262 surface acres and lying in the path of the blast, was severely damaged and probably lost all aquatic life. A subsequent flight over the lake approximately one month after the May 18 explosion, disclosed to this writer that the lake was indeed unrecognizable. Its shoreline was almost completely hidden by mud, debris, and fallen timber.

Nor were lakes the only casualties. Numerous streams were also impacted. An assessment prepared only 10 days after the May 18 blast indicated that in excess of 2,000 miles of stream may have sustained moderate to light damage. In addition, severe damage probably occurred to the headwaters of Coldwater Creek and the lower reaches of Spirit Lake tributaries. The U.S. Forest Service estimated that these waters are "undoubtedly almost devoid of aquatic life." This includes approximately 152 miles of streambed, counting the damage to the Toutle River's north and south forks, Pine Creek and Muddy River. A Gifford Pinchot National Forest spokesman said that "probably only scattered bits of aquatic life survived in the approximately 297 miles of heavily damaged streams."

Wildlife biologists feared that some 2,000 black-tailed deer, 300 elk, 30 black bear, 12 mountain goats and 15 cougars were lost in the blast, mudflows and ashfall. Added to this figure were small game and furbearing animals, as well as non-game species, small birds, reptiles, amphibians and other wildlife.

Game Department spokesmen said that the state's economy would lose $102 million during 1980 alone as a direct result of fish and wildlife losses. They also estimated that they would lose $4.5 million in revenue during the 1981-83 biennium. Still another depressing figure was cited by officials who estimated wildlife habitat and recovery costs over the 1980-90 period at $22.5 million. Because sportsmen and other wildlife enthusiasts contribute millions of dollars annually to the state's economy, the recreational losses were expected to have a wide and severe economic impact. In the end, the Game Department estimated that the eruption and its aftermath will cost the state no less than $522 million before the fish, wildlife and habitat populations are replenished.

Both fresh and salt water angling opportunities were thrown into havoc by the explosion. While hunters and fishermen whose quarry includes trout, bass and other spinyrays or panfish were hard-hit by the volcano, salmon anglers were especially gloomy. Initial estimates of the damage to Pacific salmon stocks were staggering: an immediate loss of approximately 11.6 million fish—and the loss of perhaps many millions more yet unborn.

No less than 11,590,000 salmon were killed outright at the Toutle River's Green River Hatchery and at Beaver Slough Rearing Pond. This figure represents over seven per cent of Washington State's recent annual hatchery production. In short, immediate salmon mortalities total roughly one thirteenth of what the state can produce artificially each year—a substantial loss for Washington's salmon anglers, both sport and commercial. Fisheries spokesmen said that commercial anglers would almost certainly lose at least $2.5 million; sportsmen, however, may feel the impact far into the future.

In addition to the 11.6 million salmon lost outright, about 66,000 "wild" or naturally-produced (nonhatchery-reared) salmon were killed by siltation and soaring water temperatures which reportedly rose to over 100 degrees F. Anadromous fish like salmon and steelhead cannot survive in water over 70 degrees F., so there was little question that these 66,000 fish had been lost. These wild stocks were a combination of adults, upstream migrants and juveniles at various stages of growth. All told, the *immediate* loss came to about 12 million salmon.

But this figure represents only the proverbial iceberg tip. Perhaps more important than the immediate loss, despite the staggering magnitude, are the long-range effects on future salmon stocks. At this writing, the Toutle River—all of the north fork, and a substantial portion of the south fork—is unable to support salmon runs. Also heavily impacted is the lower Cowlitz River. And these rivers are not the only southwest Washington salmon streams to be affected. Because the Toutle dumps into the Cowlitz, and the Cowlitz into the stem Columbia, it's not unreasonable to speculate that fisheries problems could be felt as far away as the Pacific Ocean.

"I don't think that a person could expect to do too much freshwater salmon fishing in the Toutle River for a few years," said Frank Haw, Deputy Director of the Washington Department of Fisheries. "I guess that's pretty safe to say. I'd imagine the lower Cowlitz is going to be difficult to support fish for a while."

The primary problems for Toutle River system salmon are related to temperature, siltation, volcanic ash and stream flow volumes. Of these, the high water temperatures are likely to be the most short-lived, and thus, the least hazardous. There is little chance—barring additional super-heated volcanic flows into the Toutle system—that temperatures will remain too high for long. Biologists worry, however, that reduced stream flow volumes could raise temperatures dangerously high later. Without sufficient glacial runoff, temperatures could still prove inhospitable to salmon.

Siltation may be detrimental to salmon for years to come. At this writing, fisheries biologists have already begun experiments related to siltation and the U.S. Army Corps of Engineers has planned relief. For example, the Corps has begun dredging operations on the Columbia and plans to remove debris from the Cowlitz and Toutle systems.

"We have 25 million cubic yards of material to remove," said Mary Portner, information specialist with the Corps' Portland District Office. "It's really an awesome quantity of material, and they have to get it all out in such a short period of time. And they're just really looking for what seems to be the very best way to do it."

The Corps is discussing the use of what they call "debris restraining structures"—essentially temporary, small dams designed to catch the debris. It would be easier, they say, to collect debris from these locations than to scour the riverbanks for years.

Fisheries biologists were quick to begin their assessment of the situation. Within a matter of days following the May 18 eruption, biologists were running tests in key areas. One such test involved the use of "live boxes"—underwater cages used to hold fish—into which juvenile salmon were placed. Fifty juveniles were placed into each of four live boxes and the boxes submerged at four different points along the Columbia-Cowlitz-Toutle system. One group, the control group, was placed in the Cowlitz, *upstream* from its confluence with the mud- and ash-filled Toutle. A second group was placed in the Cowlitz River at Kelso, several miles downstream from the Toutle's confluence with that river. A third box was submerged in the Columbia River *above* its confluence with the Cowlitz, and the fourth group was placed a short distance *below* the Colitz's entrance into the Columbia.

"We had zero mortality in the control box," explained Dave Hubert, information and education specialist with the Washington Department of Fisheries, "one hundred percent mortality at Kelso, and zero mortality at both places in the Columbia." The experiment, completed shortly after the major eruption of May 18, confirmed biologists' fears that the enormous amount of mud, debris, and volcanic ash which inundated the Toutle's north and south forks would cause serious problems for salmon.

What about the ash? "The pathology of it all is that this stuff, this silt, the ash," said Hubert, "is very sharp. It has a high silica content and sharp edges, and they're physically abrading the gill structure where the gas/blood exchange takes place. And these fish, as they process the stuff, are actually bleeding to death. Whether or not that stuff is as dangerous to adult fish as to juveniles, we won't know until we run further experiments."

It wasn't long before biologists began those experiments, initiating a similar test on adult salmon. Four groups of adults, which had already returned to the Cowlitz River Hatchery, were re-planted in approxi-

mately the same spots as were the juveniles in the live box test. "We're planting them again," said Hubert. "One group in the upper Cowlitz at Interstate 5. The second fifty we put in the Cowlitz at Kelso, which is about 11 miles downstream from where the Toutle runs into the Cowlitz. We put another group of 50 in the Columbia River at the port of Kalama. The control group is the I-5 Bridge. They won't be exposed to any of that stuff."

While the jury is still out on the test results at this writing, it seems logical to speculate that biologists may find results which are similar to those found in the juvenile experiment. At this early date, only two salmon—tagged for identification—have returned to the hatchery; the pair was part of the control group.

Still another problem facing our salmon populations is that stream flow volumes may be reduced in the future. Because large segments of the glaciers which fed Spirit Lake and the Toutle River were destroyed by recent eruptive activity, experts fear that the Toutle—and to a certain extent, other streams in the area surrounding St. Helens—will be reduced to a shadow of their former magnitude. Glacial runoff may produce mere trickles.

"When and if the Toutle comes back," said Jay Stockbridge of the Washington State Game Department, "it may not come back to anywhere near what it had been before if these glaciers aren't there to feed it. Volume would be down and temperatures would be up. And it may be that it would be up enough to make it useless as a stream for anadromous species. It's not really even going to be the same river, it looks like. Even assuming that you could find a way to preserve those strains of fish in the hope that someday you'd have a Toutle to put them back into, it may be—in fact, it's even probable—that it won't even be able to support a major fishery like that."

Still another major concern is that the loss of certain insect populations will have a serious impact on the food chain. Most of the insects within the immediate blast zone are presumed to have been lost, and heavy volcanic fallout has apparently hurt insect populations in other areas, as well.

"Of course, insects are a *major* food supply for most kinds of fish and wildlife," explained John Gilstrom, a biologist for the Washington Game Department and one of three appointed to write an assessment of the eruption and what it will take to recover from it. "If you look at just the biological world, insects are a critical food supply for a majority of the things that live on earth. Because, if the animals don't feed directly on them, then they probably feed on animals that *do* feed on them—both fish and wildlife. The single largest biomass, the most successful and adaptive group of animals on earth are insects. They're so adaptive that they're going to come back, there's no doubt about it. It's just that in some places, it'll take longer than others."

The U.S. Forest Service is also concerned about the effects of the ashfall, especially as it relates to the insect population. A representative of the USFS visited the damage area shortly after the May 18 eruption. His observations confirm the fears common among ichthyoloists. "In one of the streams, in Elk Creek," said Lyle Burmeister, a fisheries biologist for the USFS, "he found a fairly high concentration of nitrates and ammonia. There were not many caddis flies, nor many stone flies. There were very few left, and they were spread out—tremendously. And he also found the beginnings of a population of long green algae. Apparently it's coming in response of the concentrations of ammonia." Ammonia, in high concentrations, is toxic to certain fish.

What is the most serious problem facing our fisheries? "The ash, I think—from the fisheries standpoint—will be the biggest problem," says Burmeister. "We're hoping that, if we get a good runoff this fall, maybe it'll flush some of [the ash] out of the stream systems. But we may have more coming in than is pushed out. We expect to get a pretty good slug of it this fall with the runoff." The erosion of ash and other debris into surrounding stream systems is likely to be a serious and ongoing problem. So, too, are flash floods, which may come about easily and quickly as a result of vegetative devastation.

At a news conference held nearly a month after the big May 18 explosion, Burmeister was asked if it would be feasible to "stock" insects into the areas most heavily impacted. "The area is so large that I hesitate to even attempt anything like that," he said. "In the first place, we don't have a stock of insects to draw from. In the second place, I suspect that, if we get the heavy runoff and we do get more ash and sediment coming into the streams, then I would think the insects would have problems again this fall."

Asked what he considered the biggest tragedy for salmon and salmon fishermen, Deputy Director Haw answered, "It was a total loss of the '79 brood Chinook and coho salmon in the Toutle system. I'd say the loss of the Toutle as a sportfishing stream is a tremendous loss."

What about the future of the Toutle system? "The Toutle is partly at least going to have to recover on its own," said biologist Gilstrom, "although what we're going to try to do is to go in and help it out. It's going to have to sort of recreate its own channel and stabilize, probably over a period of years. The flow of water in the Toutle, at least for a period of time, will be less than it was. And [by] 'a period,' I'm talking 25 to 50 years. I frankly think that you're really not going to see the Toutle anything like its former self for 25 years, anyway."

"We're not writing off the Toutle as a salmon producer yet," said Haw. "We've got some problems up there, but we may be able to get those hatcheries back on line. We're going to make a good run at the disaster funds and the federal government. The Toutle Hatchery was a federally-funded hatchery. We ran it, but it was paid for from the lower Columbia River Fund. The structural damage there at this point isn't too bad. It's just that there's so much mud lying around, the river doesn't look too good."

Things, in fact, could have been worse. Indeed early "guesstimates" of salmon losses by Department of Fisheries officials included speculation that some additional 305,000 spring Chinook, being held at the Deer Springs Rearing Pond, were killed outright by the blast and debris when St. Helens erupted on May 18. Fortunately, such was not the case. Later observation indicated that most, if not all, fish were alive. Still, biologists are concerned at this writing that there may have been serious health hazards to the salmon; the fish were not fed for approximately two weeks. "There's some speculation that that period they went without being fed may have some ill effects on them regarding kidney disease," explained Fisheries' Hubert. "This subspecies is susceptible to kidney disease. Trauma induces it—stress. Of course, not being fed for two weeks might have done it."

Surprisingly, biologists found that the Green River—the Toutle tributary on which the hatchery is located—had bounced back quickly. Within two weeks of the big eruption and enormous fish loss, the Washington Fisheries Department had some reason for optimism. "The quality of the water in the Green River is okay," said Hubert. "There's some silt in it, but people have spotted fish swimming upstream from the hatchery. The tributaries to the Green River are [also] okay."

Asked about the possibility of siltation or ashfall causing problems for salmon which had already reached the Pacific, Fisheries' Haw said: "We're not aware of any problems." Haw also said the Kalama River, another Cowlitz tributary, looks "okay."

Biologists are cautiously optimistic that salmon and steelhead destined for their cradle streams—those most heavily impacted by the volcano—will divert into the Kalama. There were early, unsubstantiated reports of some spring Cowlitz-bred Chinook heading up that river.

Are there any benefits to come out of this eruptive destruction? "Benefits?" asked Hubert, puzzled. "Not so you could notice! We may learn possibly that these fish will divert to a stream, but there's no indication of that yet. It will be so long-range, the benefits of this thing, that it would take a real active imagination to look for benefits. This is just a *disaster* as far as we're concerned."

Haw allowed, "I don't know if there are any benefits. There may be some long-range benefits on water fertility but, hell, it's too early to say anything about that. They'd probably be overcome by the damage of the siltation and all that other business. It may work out all right for some of our descendants, but I don't think many of us will be able to reap the benefits."

Tim Hait, geologist with the U.S. Geological Survey in Denver, took a more optimistic view. "Just like the nuclear power plants have to have high-powered filters," he said, "then the fisheries may need high-powered screens upstream—or roofs over the breeding ponds. So there's going to be a lot of new technology, new protective measures that come out of it. We're going to learn to plan better for how to deal with the ash and how to deal with the plugged-up rivers. All kinds of new warning systems are going to come up. Pretty soon people will get the idea very clearly that they've got to start thinking about all these aspects. I think the benefits have to do with people getting a much clearer understanding of how unpredictable and how dangerous these kinds of volcanoes are. And that's immediate—that's an immediate benefit.

"I think there are definite benefits to come out of it. I mean, gosh, it's the silver lining to the cloud. Or what you see is the cloud, and then you notice that there *is* a silver lining to it. We're going to learn a lot about how to characterize volcanic hazards—out of what we're learning by being right in the middle of a volcanic eruptive period. "The benefits so far—the obvious benefits—have to do with our ability to describe these kinds of eruptions: the temperatures, the speeds at which they travel, the fallout of the ash, what happens to people who are too close. All these contribute toward being prepared. So that's a very definite and close-range benefit."

There's little doubt that the Toutle system will recover over time. In fact, it's possible to draw comparisons of the Toutle with the Puyallup River, which suffered severe mudflow problems associated with Mt. Rainier. "The Puyallup river has a similar history," explained the Game Department's John Gilstrom, "going way back, of course. About 300 to 500 years ago, the Puyallup went through a similar process. That would have been Mt. Rainier. And, of course, by the time the white man had come here, it had recovered. So that might be an indication of how long something like this could take."

Geologist Hait explained the process. "The Puyallup River has got a big mudflow in it. It's about 500 years old. It's called the 'electron' mudflow. No independent evidence has been found to suggest that the mudflow was caused by eruptive activity. It's just another one of the kinds of hazards that can come from the slopes of some of these big volcanoes."

What's the future of the salmon resource in Washington? "We're not in a state of despair," said Fisheries' Haw. "We don't like to see it. It's a serious thing, but it's by no means the end of the salmon resource. We expect that there's going to be a lot of good fishing. Fishing's going to tend to improve through other efforts. It's been a serious setback, but it's not the end of the world."

Of approximately 600 currently active volcanoes on earth today, Mt. St. Helens is by far the youngest. In fact, it is the youngest *mountain* in the U.S. But is it reckless, as well as young? Will it cause more problems for the fishery?

"If you like statistics," explained geologist Hait, "then just taking a look at Mt. St. Helens' history, the statistics are in favor of Mt. St. Helens' eruptive periods going on for more than just one burst—you know, going on for months or years."

Lassen Peak, the last volcano to erupt in the lower 48 states, experienced an extended eruptive phase which began in 1914 and did not end until 1921. In fact, Mt. Lassen erupted *at least 170 times* between May 30, 1914 and May 14, 1915—a period of less than a single year!

Is it possible that Mt. St. Helens will explode again like it did on May 18? "I guess it's an *extreme* possibility," said Hait. "We'e not looking for any major explosion like that. But it's still always a possibility."

What about so-called "earth tides" influencing Mt. St. Helens? "I guess we don't hold a whole lot of credence that these earth tides are going to cause specific mountains to erupt," Hait explained. "And you certainly can't use the earth tides as any way of *predicting* that specific volcanoes can erupt."

Will we at least be able to say that the disastrous eruption will provide new knowledge? "It'll force all of us to learn," said Hait. "We're all learning, day-to-day. It's a good learning exercise."

For salmon fishermen and fisheries managers, it's learning the hard way.

A.B.

PART ONE
PACIFIC SALMON

1
THE FISH

ALMON require little in the way of introduction. Fabled in modern angling literature and venerated in their natural habitat, they have attained a status accorded few sport species; in terms of both their warring ability and table value, salmon are regarded as a fish par excellence among even the most casual of anglers.

Through written accounts, salmon fishing may be traced to the time of Pliny the Elder in the first century A.D. As far as history discloses, the first sport salmon anglers were Romans who took notable delight in fishing the sylvan streams of distant provinces like Normandy and Galicia. These were the salmon of the Atlantic, and they were promptly and aptly named *the leapers*.[1] It was a name bred of both cursory observation and profound respect. And it was a respect of the highest order, coming as it had from the legions who were themselves known for their fighting capabilities. Subsequently, salmon won equal accolades at home, becoming an expensive and sought-after delicacy in the markets of Rome.

While we lack documented historical evidence, it seems reasonable to assume that salmon were being fished by the peasants of ancient European tribes long before the arrival of the descendants of Quirinus. It's likely that the French, British, or Spanish were among the earliest sport salmon anglers. In any event, salmon were so highly prized by the inhabitants of thirteenth-century England that they forced a supplement to the Magna Carta which precluded the government's tampering with brood stocks and fishing rights.[2] Like all things of value, the fish were not only the object of great

esteem but were also covetously protected in the early days of fisheries management: one Scottish monarch made the illegal taking of salmon a criminal offense punishable by death.[3]

In North America, salmon were an important food to the Indians long before the white man arrived. Moreover, they were a symbol representative of life itself to the primitive tribes of the Pacific Northwest. In solemn rites, the skeletal remains of salmon were offered to their cradle rivers to ensure the perpetuation of the species and the continuation of the resource. These were the Pacific salmon that were called *Chinook*, and the ancient name is still with us today.

British sailors fished the Canadian coast as early as 1824, and Lewis and Clark observed salmon during their Oregon exploration of 1804-06. Salmon brought about the establishment of a substantial commercial industry before the discovery and subsequent rush for gold and silver in Nevada and California. In fact, among the first ships to frequent the North Pacific coast were those seeking large cargoes of salmon—not precious minerals. By the mid-1840s, nearly a score of flourishing commercial canneries embellished the banks of the productive Columbia River alone.

But problems quickly beset both the resource and the industry. By 1890 or so, the rapid expansion of Northwest timber interests and the resultant damage to many river watersheds were beginning to wreak havoc with the salmon fishery. Later, the construction of dams and the vast commercial exploitation of the species brought about a noticeable reduction in the harvests. By the

19

mid-1900s, it was apparent that something would have to be done. At last interested sportsmen began to earnestly voice their concern and protests.

Much has been written about the lure of this great sport fish. Isaac Walton's early classic *The Compleat Angler*, first published in 1653, deified the salmon, and a considerable outpouring of literature followed. Roderick Haig-Brown, Lee Wulff, and a stable of other select writers worshipped the salmon spectrum in print—and in fact—nearly as wholly as had the ancient Indians of the Pacific Northwest. But Ernest Schwiebert perhaps best captures the appeal of the salmon as a game fish in his recent classic, *Salmon of the World*, where he terms the fish "the apogee" of sport fishing.[4]

But while the literature abounds, relatively little is known of the habits and behavior of salmon, an informational void which is compounded by their anadromous (sea-going, river-spawning) characteristics. Few species have received as much scientific attention and good press in the various sporting journals. Yet, while their habits are fairly well documented during their Act I and Act III fresh water lives, there's much still to be learned about their salt water existence. Moreover, even ichthyologists are in disagreement on matters as elementary as the salmon's evolutionary history: some believe the species is related to the cyprinoids (carplike fish), while others feel they more closely resemble the clupeoids (herringlike fish).

While their evolution remains a mystery, it is generally agreed that the species found their current distribution sometime during the Pleistocene (Ice Age). Although fossilized evidence is sorely lacking, remains of this period indicate that the salmon perhaps most closely resembles a smelt.[5]

Because salmon remain hidden from us—first beneath the gravel of their spawning redds (nests) and later during their extended ocean voyages—many of their habits remain enshrouded in arcanum. And yet numerous questions have been answered, problems resolved, myths dispelled. In salmon we have the opportunity to glimpse the Great Parallel: the complex, often delicate but always intricate means by which all living organisms are affected by their physical environment. In the natural order of things, the concept of an environmental idiopathy is without basis in logic, let alone fact. Man's intervention, whether benign or malevolent, will doubtless determine the scenario. For better or worse, the salmon species are a part of that scenario.

Of the North American salmon species, five are found along the Pacific coast, its rivers, streams, and estuaries: Chinook, coho, pinks, sockeye, and chums. They range from the Bering Sea on the north to approximately 100 miles below the Mexican-American border on the south, with the heaviest concentrations found between southeastern Alaska and California's Sacramento River.

All Pacific salmon species found along the West Coast have their origin in fresh water and—with the exception of landlocked sockeye (commonly called *kokanee*) which reside in inland lakes—all are anadromous. Beginning life in rivers, streams, and sometimes the gravelly areas of lakes, salmon depart their native freshwater haunts for sea, where they grow rapidly before reaching maturity and returning to their freshwater homes.

Salmon begin life as tiny *alevins*—newborn fish developed from eggs laid by the female and fertilized by the male. The alevins hatch in from two to four months (sometimes more), depending upon various factors. One of the controlling considerations is the water temperature where spawning has occurred. The alevins usually remain in the gravel for about a month, meanwhile sustained by nutrients in the yolk sac of the egg. This yolk sac remains connected to the stomach of the alevin during this stage of life and may, in fact, provide a diet for the newly hatched fish for as long as four months.

Salmon *fry* of about an inch in length emerge from the gravel when the yolk sac has been absorbed. This emergence normally occurs during the first spring of life. As fry, the small salmon feed voraciously on plankton (tiny animal and plant organisms) which is available in their fresh water environment and often on small insects. After spending various lengths of time in their natal streams (depending on species and race), the young fish migrate to sea as *smolts* and spend at least a year in salt water. All Pacific species remain in salt or brackish water until they reach maturity, which may come at from as little as fourteen months to as many as seven years, and possibly longer in rare instances. When maturity is attained, the spawning drive brings the fish back into the freshwater systems of their birth. It is a life cycle which is repeated again and again, among each species and each individual member of that species. It is indeed a homecoming—never ending and in cyclical fashion—of majestic proportion.

All Pacific salmon return to their parent streams to spawn, with the exception of an occasional fish whose navigational system apparently malfunctions. Passing from the salt or brackish water back into the turbulence of their rivers and streams, their spawning runs often include amazingly long journeys through a waterway environment which can be both hostile and exacting. Wending their way upstream, they may traverse a myriad of rapids, falls, and other obstructions—not to mention the lures and baits offered hopefully by anglers and a plethora of natural enemies, such as bear and other voracious predators—before reaching the same stretch of the stream in which they were born. In some cases, they must travel a staggering distance: salmon races re-entering the Yukon, for example, have been reported to swim upstream as far as two thousand miles![6] Such journeys occur after an ocean trek of several thousand additional miles.

Mature salmon return to the rivers and streams from late summer to early winter, although there are notable exceptions. The precise time varies between species and populations. During their upstream spawning migrations, salmon can move with incredible speed: they have been known to cover as many as twenty-five miles per day over extended periods; in sporadic bursts, they are capable of traveling over sixty miles in a single day—against the current.[7]

Spawning usually occurs high in the headwaters of rivers and streams, although pink and chum salmon regularly spawn near the salt or in brackish water. Upon reaching their spawning sites, the female digs a redd with her tail. Normally, the nests are dug in suitable gravel areas of the streambed; some sockeye salmon use the gravelly areas of inland lake bottoms.

Males play an important protective role during the nestbuilding stage, fighting off intruders and competitors while the female plies the gravel, and courting the hens as they work. When the nest is constructed, the female positions herself over it and oviposits. The male usually fertilizes the eggs as they are discharged. The female then positions herself so that, by using her tail, she can rapidly cover the eggs with gravel. Thus protecting the fertilized eggs by perhaps a foot or so of gravel, the female then moves on to the next suitable spot and begins the nest-building activity again. Sometimes as many as five or six redds are dug as receptacles for the eggs. With each redd cleared, the hen salmon deposits additional eggs, the male moves in to fertilize them, and the female again covers the eggs with a protective layer of gravel. As many as eleven thousand eggs may be laid by a single female.

Although there have been unsubstantiated reports of an occasional salmon surviving after spawning, all Pacific species die after the eggs have been deposited, fertilized, and covered. Their sex products exhausted and their life-giving, death-dealing runs completed, both male and female drift lifelessly downstream. Their progeny planted—if not assured—only the eggs now remain. The survival of the young depends first on the successful incubation of the eggs and later on a host of environmental factors.

While all but the infrequently lost or stray salmon display the homing instinct which urges them to return to the section of the river or stream in which life began, their methods of navigation remain a mystery. But because salmon apparently travel nearer the ocean surface at night than during the brighter daylight hours, some ichthyologists believe that they employ a type of solar and/or celestial navigation, much as some bird species.[8] Others emphasize the role of the olfactory sense in finding their way. By whatever means these fish find their cradle streams, their timing is sometimes no less amazing. Like the Capistrano swallows, some salmon runs arrive at a specific area in an almost clockwork fashion: Schwiebert, for example, speaks of Bristol Bay sockeye, which have been known to arrive on such a precise timetable that fifty million fish may reach the same area within a three-week period![9]

While each of the five Pacific species found along the West Coast is hatched in the freshwater gravel beds of rivers or streams (and sometimes lakes), the distance between spawning redds and salt water may vary considerably. Some fish spawn only ten miles from the sea, while others dig their nests hundreds of miles inland. Some salmon are known to travel five thousand miles or more during their ocean voyage while others remain within fifty miles of their parent stream. Geographic distribution often overlaps, with various species and races of those species occupying not only the same general distribution area but also the same streams within that area.

The size of individual salmon varies between species and between different populations of each species. In general, Chinook are the largest of the five major Pacific species found along the American-Canadian coast, followed by chums, coho, sockeye, and pinks. Chinooks often reach fifty pounds or more while mature pinks average about six pounds.

Salmon, like other anadromous fish, store up considerable body fat before migrating upstream. The extra energy is needed because fish stop feeding when they reenter fresh water. Thus, salmon taken in or near their parent streams are usually larger than are those taken during their migratory ocean routes or while feeding at sea. Moreover, adult salmon which are ready to enter the rivers are laden with eggs or milt.

Because salmon stop feeding when they reenter their spawning streams, taking them in fresh water is not a matter of offering a lure imitative of their natural feed. But biologists and sport anglers alike are in wide disagreement as to precisely what factors trigger ripe salmon to strike.

Some reason that their strikes are set off by the feeding of other fish in their vicinity—river trout, for example. Others believe that mature salmon strike instinctively, a vestige of their previous behavior when they resided in fresh water as young fish. Still another theory is that they strike out of simple curiosity—"because they don't have hands and fingers," as an acquaintance of this writer explained a number of years ago.

Perhaps salmon strike simply *out of habit* after feeding voraciously at sea for a year or more. At least such a theory seems more logical than to attribute their strikes to the pugnacious defense of their underwater territories or to be taken in by the old wives' tale that fish take food into their mouths, only to spit it out after relishing its juices. Still, the mystery persists, the arguments flourish.

One of the salmon's former mysteries has been solved—the ancient question concerning the ability of these fish to distinguish odors. Experiments have shown that salmon indeed have a highly developed olfactory sense and are able to distinguish scent in amazingly minute proportions. Schwiebert cites studies that show that salmon can distinguish chemical changes in water as minute as one part per billion.[10] Thus the likelihood that an angler dipping his hand in the river may frighten fish a block or more downstream. But not surprisingly, salmon appear to be alarmed only by certain scents which represent danger—odors associated with natural predators like bear and seal (and man), for example.

All Pacific species display silvery sides in their marine habitat. They also have white bellies and dark, sometimes spotted, backs. All have adipose fins consisting of fatty tissue and fins supported by soft rays. Ichthyologists are in general agreement that the soft-rayed species preceded those with spiny rays.

Salmon may be differentiated from trout by counting the anal fin rays. If the fish has from twelve to nineteen rays, it's a salmon; if the rays number eleven or less, it's a trout. Mouth coloration is another good way to distinguish salmon from trout. All Pacific species of salmon display some degree of dark pigmentation in their mouths, unlike trout, which lack oral pigmentation. Trout also have tails which lack the more sharply forked configurations of salmon.

Salmon also occur along the Asiatic coast. Pinks and chums are especially numerous along the northeast coast of Russia, while chums are cultured extensively throughout Japan. The Masu salmon, a sixth Pacific species, is also found along the Asiatic coast. But two of the Pacific species—the Chinook and coho—are most important to American and Canadian sport fishermen.

Chinook

The Chinook salmon is the giant of the Pacific species. Largest of its family, Chinook of one hundred pounds or more are sometimes taken by commercial fishermen. The largest Chinook on record at this writing was a fish weighing 126½ pounds; that brute was commercially trapped near Petersburg, Alaska.

Sport anglers have not fared quite as well: the world record Chinook taken on sport tackle weighed 93 pounds and was taken by Howard C. Rider from Kelp Bay, Alaska, in 1977.*

The species was more or less officially christened Chinook by Captain Robert Gray of the *Columbia* upon entering the river which now bears the name of

Bob Maschmedt, Seattle tackle manufacturers' representative and part owner of Rivers Inlet Resort, hefts a large *Tyee* which pushed the scales to nearly 65 pounds. *Author photo.*

* Record compiled by the International Game Fish Association (IGFA)

22

Fighting winter blackmouth, about to be boated near Sekiu, Washington. *Courtesy of Washington Department of Fisheries.*

his ship. The good captain found the Chinook Indians of the Pacific Northwest subsisting quite nicely upon the species and deemed the fish worthy of the tribal name. Even today a majority of Oregon and southwest Washington sport and commercial fishermen call the species by its proper name.

But various aliases are more commonly employed when the discussion moves to *Oncorhynchus tshawytscha*. In British Columbia, a Chinook weighing thirty pounds or more is called a *Tyee*, the legendary Indian name for the species, and many anglers refer to Chinook as *kings* or *king salmon*. Some Oregonians in particular call these fish *tules*, and they are also called *springs* or *springers* when mature. Alaskans refer to Chinook over fifty pounds as *soakers*. They are also called *sockdolagers* at times. The species, introduced into New Zealand a number of years ago, is also called *Quinnat*.

Sexually immature Chinook are frequently called *blackmouth*, regardless of size, although arguments continue among lay anglers, some of whom insist the term should be reserved only for fish of a certain size

range (usually under about fifteen pounds). Technically, however, a Chinook is a blackmouth only until it develops a mature reproductive capacity, and this definition precludes a determination on the basis of size alone. Conversely, any Chinook which displays signs of sexual maturity may be termed a king, although two-year-old Chinook which are sexually mature are commonly referred to as *jacks* or *jack salmon*. Blackmouth are frequently called *winter springs* in British Columbia, where they are available in numerous areas throughout the winter months. They are also called *winter-over* salmon in their more northerly distribution. Washingtonians often call these immature Chinook *winter blackmouth* because of their relative abundance, especially in that state's inland marine waters, during the cold-weather months.

Chinook salmon spawn earlier than other Pacific species and during two main periods: in June and July; and from July through year's end. True *spring* Chinook are those which reenter their native rivers during the spring months to spawn within the June-

23

July period, while *fall* Chinook are those which spawn during the second half of the year.

Most spring fish spawn in the headwaters of the larger, colder rivers, and in their tributaries. Conversely, fall Chinook tend to spawn in the main watersheds nearer the sea. Early spawners especially have dwindled in numbers in recent years because of various hydroelectric projects which have damaged numerous miles of prime spawning grounds and have virtually eliminated spring Chinook runs in many rivers.

King salmon prefer to make their spawning redds in these cool or cold river systems where gravel is about five or six inches in diameter. They often build their nests in the lower end of a pool where the water begins to move more rapidly. Frequently, they spawn just above—and sometimes in—stream riffles.

As spawning time nears, the ocean colors—silvery sides, white belly, a back of dark green with profuse black spots—gradually turn darker. While females are apt to turn nearly black, the males—especially the larger ones—take on a blotchy dark red color. Smaller males sometimes tend toward a yellowish shade. The teeth of the males become enlarged and almost canine in appearance; their jaws also become enlarged and often distorted. Like the other Pacific species, Chinook males typically develop the familiar, hooked snouts and steeply arched razor backs. Their adipose fins grow larger and their scales become more firmly embedded, even those of the females.

As with the other Pacific species, females use their tails to construct redds, into which they deposit their eggs. The males fertilize the eggs with milt, and the process may be repeated several times. Regardless of what time Chinook begin their upstream migrations, spawning invariably occurs during the fall. A single female may oviposit as many as eleven thousand eggs; the average is about half that many. The incubation period for Chinook eggs is from three to four months.

Spring Chinook usually spend a year or more in the river as fry before entering salt water, but fall fish normally head seaward the next spring, sometimes within three weeks after emerging from the gravel. Ichthyologists are able to distinguish between the *ocean* Chinook (those which migrate to sea during the year of their birth) and the *stream* Chinook (those which remain in the river until the following spring) by examining the patterns of their scales.

Female Chinook usually mature at four or five years of age. Males may reach maturity anytime between their second and seventh years of life.

Throughout the West, most mature Chinook are in their third, fourth, or fifth years of their ocean existence. Older fish are more prevalent in the waters of British Columbia and Alaska. Chinook over five years are rarely encountered in the waters of Washington, Oregon, or California. Researchers believe that Chinook that mature at a later age are those that have made more distant ocean migrations. Because of the varying lengths of time spent in salt water, sport fishermen find a mixture of both immature and maturing fish.

Chinook salmon may usually be distinguished by their fourteen to seventeen anal rays (since there is tremendous overlap in the anal ray counts of Pacific salmon, these numbers are not always useful) and the dark spots found on their backs, as well as on their dorsal, caudal, and adipose fins. Blackmouth is a term derivative of the invariable dark gumline found on all Chinook regardless of age, size, or degree of sexual maturity. Juvenile salmon are known as *grilse* throughout Canada.

Chinook occur from southern California to western Alaska and into the Bering Sea. They are also found along the northeast coast of Asia and in rivers running to the Okhotsk Sea and the Kamchatka Peninsula. They are most abundant from Monterey northward along the American and British Columbian coasts. Some of the West's most populous Chinook rivers are the Yukon, the Columbia, and the Sacramento, although sizeable runs also occur in many other large river systems and indeed in some astonishingly small tributaries.

In open water, Chinook are found spread over a broad area, often a considerable distance from shore. Some fisheries biologists believe that their ocean distribution is scattered because of the general uniformity of the Pacific's formless, sandy bottoms and its generally amorphous shoreline.

Most commonly, however, Chinook are closely associated with specific geographical distinctions, such as land projections or other shoreline features, particularly in areas where abrupt depth disparities occur, as in underwater shelves or reefs. The rougher, rockier underwater terrain of certain Alaskan, British Columbian, and Washington areas provide more irregularities in shoreline, current, and depth, and Chinook tend to congregate at these points. This is especially true in the myriad of Pacific bays and inlets, where fish are usually sought near distinctive land masses or promontories. Offshore fishing is frequently done at depths of two hundred feet or more, while inshore anglers often find Chinook in water of from twenty-five to sixty feet.

Chinook salmon are somewhat more predictable

than coho, and expert anglers apply this knowledge in order to achieve a greater degree of success. In addition to looking for distinct land masses or holes where Chinook are likely to concentrate, knowledgeable salmon fishermen are aware of the best times to find them. While peak fishing seasons vary by area, Chinook are notorious early feeders, and anglers stand a good chance of taking them near dawn. Likewise, many Chinook are taken during the last hour or so of daylight, and peak Chinook bite periods often occur on or near tide changes.

Chinook salmon are typical of the other Pacific species. When young, they have distinct black parr marks extending almost completely across the body from their backs to their lower sides. In fresh water, Chinook fry lack the more brightly colored markings of coho fry; coho have somewhat orange fins, edged in black and white. The black spotting on the backs of adult fish is more pronounced and the spots somewhat larger than on coho. The most reliable means of differentiating Chinook from coho is to check the mouth: in Chinook, the bases of the teeth, as well as the gums and lower jaw, are heavily pigmented and nearly black; in coho, there is little pigmentation, and mouths appear almost white, especially at the base of the teeth.

Fisheries biologist Lloyd Phinney takes time out from his normal duties to sample the fishing for Chinook jacks. *Courtesy of Washington Department of Fisheries.*

Some Chinook remain within a relatively close distance of the rivers in which they were bred, but others migrate long distances. Chinook from the Sacramento River travel southward along California's coastline in large numbers to Monterey Bay. Others from the same river roam as far north as Washington, and a smaller number may be found off Canada's Vancouver Island. The California Department of Fish and Game notes that, of the salmon taken in the vicinity of the Golden Gate, over ninety percent are fish from the Sacramento-San Joaquin River system.[11] The percentage drops in the more northerly waters of that state, but even in northern California, more than half the Chinook appearing in the commercial harvest are Sacramento fish.

Few salmon ascend any but their cradle streams, although occasional straying into the wrong tributary is somewhat more common. California's DFG found that salmon which were heading for particular tributaries will ascend others if their natal streams are inaccessible.[12]

Spring Chinook apparently time their river arrivals so that cool water will be available throughout the summer months, and runs tend to coincide with optimum snowmelt and runoff conditions. This assures the fish of ample water for upstream migration. Fall Chinook usually time their upstream runs to coincide with sufficient rain so that a suitable supply of cool water is available for their late fall-early winter spawning rites. Streams which are too warm or too dry are not prime Chinook waterways, although some streams which are too warm or dry during the early part of the year may host large runs of fall Chinook when conditions have become suitable.

Winter-run salmon are relatively scarce, although the Sacramento River system sees Chinook which normally begin to arrive at about the holiday season. These fish may be available until spawning, normally about May or June. A select list of other Western river systems hosts winter-run Chinook.

Kings frequently stop to feed at specific areas as they migrate toward their parent streams, and they are much easier to take when feeding than when simply making time. That area lying east of the continental shelf is a favorite feeding area for large Chinook and is highly productive.

Few fish have as high a percentage of edible flesh as the salmon, and few salmon are as large as a mature Chinook. Their table value has become legend since they were eaten by Lewis and Clark in 1806.

Coho

Coho are considered by most veteran salmon anglers to be the nonpareil member of the Pacific species. Pelagic denizens of the West, coho frequently roam relatively near the water's surface and display dazzling, acrobatic leaps when hooked, in contrast to the somewhat more sluggish Chinook.

Oncorhynchus kisutch are known by other names but are frequently called *silver salmon, silvers,* or *silversides*. In British Columbia, these fish are sometimes called *bluebacks*. The late summer and fall months offer excellent sport fishing opportunities for large, mature coho, often called *hooknose* or *hooknose salmon* because of the distorted snout which develops on sexually ripe fish. Mature two-year-olds, like Chinook, are called *jack salmon* or *jacks*.

Coho are nearly as wide-ranging as are Chinook. California fisheries biologists report fish showing as far south as approximately one hundred miles below the California-Mexico line. In their more northerly distribution, they appear in northwestern Alaska and the Bering Sea. The majority of coho, however, appear between Monterey and southeastern Alaska's Panhandle. Coho are also abundant along the northeast Asian coastline and in the Okhotsk Sea and the Kamchatka Peninsula.

Recent efforts by the California DFG to establish a coho sport fishery off that state's southern coast appear to hold some promise of extending the species' southerly range. Additionally, an interesting and significant coho fishery has developed in the Great Lakes in recent years.

Coho were introduced into the Great Lakes in order to combat an overpopulation of alewives. The

A tavern in Michigan claims to be the first site of the planting of coho salmon, shipped from Washington State to Lake Michigan a number of years ago. Coho proved to be just as acclaimed for their fighting ability in the Great Lakes as on the Pacific coast. *Courtesy of Washington Department of Fisheries.*

26

introduction of these fine sport fish not only brought about the desired reduction in the alewives population but also provided an excellent Midwest fishery. Great Lakes salmon anglers have since developed and refined successful techniques for taking these fish on flies and other effective terminal gear.

Coho are fall spawners, reaching maximum size immediately before beginning their upstream spawning migrations. In late autumn, they begin to build their redds, preferring medium-sized gravel. In contrast to Chinook, which typically spawn in the larger, glacial river systems, coho spawn in many of the West's smaller, unsullied coastal streams. They may be found at times, however, spawning in the same larger river systems as do Chinook.

Female coho lay about three thousand eggs, on average. They appear to prefer relatively slow, shallow water. The fertilized eggs incubate in the nests for between 100 and 115 days, depending on water temperature. At the end of the incubation period, young coho fry emerge from the gravel. Coho fry usually remain in the river or stream for about one year before migrating seaward, although fish may head for saltwater anytime between their first and third years of life.

Coho may mature at any time between three and five years, but most spawners are three or four years of age. Adult fish enter their native rivers between October and December, with November seeing the peak of spawning arrivals. They begin their freshwater spawning runs into British Columbia's famed Campbell River during September and start their entry into Washington-Oregon's mighty Columbia during the same month. But in some instances, fish do not migrate upstream until as late as February.

Coho typically average between four and eight pounds, with most fish weighing about five or six pounds at maturity. Silvers to over twenty pounds are sometimes boated, however, especially during the late summer and fall months. At this writing, the sport record is a thirty-one pounder which was taken by Mrs. Lee Hallberg in 1947 at Vancouver Island's Cowichan Bay.* But coho over about fifteen pounds are not that common. In fact, most sport fishermen who believe they have landed silvers

* Record compiled by the IGFA

Early fall silver is lead to the side of the boat. Fish struck a rapidly trolled streamer fly decked with beads. Note the first signs of hooking of the snout, the reason why mature coho are often called *hooknose. Author photo, courtesy of* Salt Water Sportsman.

of twenty or twenty-five pounds have actually caught Chinook which they are unable to correctly identify.

Coho fishing improves as the spring-fall season progresses. During the late spring and early summer months, coho average two to three pounds. By June, they are likely to weigh four to five pounds and, at this stage of their lives, they enjoy extremely rapid growth; biologists confirm that, from June through about September, coho normally more than double their weight. Their voracious and often indiscriminate feeding habits during late summer and fall account for some of the most outstanding sport fishing opportunities along the West Coast.

In their native rivers and streams, young coho display distinct parr marks extending almost completely from their backs to their bellies. These dark, oval-shaped spots are well defined even in very young fish. Lower fins are typically brightly colored in hues of orange, highlighted with black and white. The lower edge of the anal fin curves backward more noticeably than in the other Pacific species.

At sea, coho display small black spots on their backs, as well as on the upper lobes of their tail fins. Normally, these markings are smaller and less pronounced than those found on Chinook. The latter also typically displays spots on both the upper and lower tail fin lobes.

Ocean coloration is a metallic blue along the back, silvery sides and silvery white bellies. Saltwater coloration changes quickly after fish have entered fresh water, however. During their spawning migrations, coho appear dark reddish.

Coho may be differentiated from the other Pacific species by their nineteen to twenty-five gillrakers and their white gumlines, unlike Chinook, which always have dark, nearly black, pigmentation at the base of their teeth. Like Chinook, however, coho usually have fourteen to seventeen anal fin rays, but their tails are more sharply forked than those of Chinook. Another feature that is different is the relative size (diameter) of the caudal peduncle (the stalklike tail base located just forward of the tail): Chinook have narrow tail stems which provide "handles," while coho display wide stalks which are difficult for the angler to grip. Additionally, Chinook have a definite odor; fresh coho are essentially odorless.

Silvers do not usually migrate far from their cradle streams, although some Washington-reared fish appear as far north as British Columbia's central Pacific Coast and as far south as northern California. Similarly, Oregon coho sometimes range from northcentral California to British Columbia, while California fish are often taken as far north as Washington. Most Alaska silvers remain in the waters of that state, and recent efforts to rear fish which remain in Washington's Puget Sound have met with spectacular success. British Columbia, too, has resident coho, especially those which occur in the Strait of Georgia.

At sea, silvers are usually found farther offshore than are Chinook, which are most commonly associated with specific land features. In fishing for coho, it is a good idea to look for tide rips. These are tides opposing one another, causing considerable turbulence; they are easily spotted because floating debris tends to collect where such riptides occur. Unlike Chinook, coho are rarely associated with land masses or underwater geographical distinctions. Most commonly, they are found at depths of from thirty to forty feet below the surface.

Especially along the Pacific coast, coho are usually found much farther offshore than are Chinook. But while this is true throughout much of the summer feeding period, they are often taken nearer the shoreline as they begin to mill around their parent streams in preparation for their spawning runs.

Because coho spawn in the smaller coastal streams, they are affected by problems foreign to most other Pacific salmon species. For one thing, such streams can supply living space for only a limited number of fry during their year or more of early freshwater life. In many cases, more fry are hatched from a specific spawning run than the particular stream is able to support. At times large numbers of young coho are displaced downstream and wind up in the estuarial waters where a variety of adverse conditions (including the salinity of the water itself) bring about premature destruction.

Another problem faced by coho is that—again, because of the small scale of their spawning streams and tributaries—parent waters are susceptible to great variations in rearing capacities. Such rearing capacities may be adequate one year but not the next, thanks to climate considerations. Adequate stream flow volumes are critical to rearing success, with wet summers providing living space for a large number of fry, but dry summers spelling doom for many young coho. Abundant precipitation during the months preceding the spawning runs help to ensure a subsequent abundance of fish, but drought or near-drought conditions, such as those experienced during the summer of 1977, negatively affect the fishery two or three years later. The Canadian Fisheries and Marine Service notes that, although ocean conditions are very important to the survival of coho to the adult stage, the "first major condition" determining the ultimate abundance of

28

Jerry Ray, a sport fisherman as well as a commercial angler, unhooks a fat fall coho. *Author photo, courtesy of Salt Water Sportsman.*

fish is the climate prevailing during the year in which coho reside in their cradle streams before migrating to sea.[13]

Fisheries biologists Frank Haw and Ray Buckley, co-authors of *Salt Water Fishing in Washington*, point out still another of the hazards to our coho fisheries: "Since the coho fishing at any one time is dependent on a single age group of fish, a dry summer can damage coho fishing for an entire season."[14] The biologists note that we depend upon one year class, each season, for our harvest. During 1979, for example, the sport catch will come from coho spawned in 1976. With Chinook, however, other year classes can provide a "buffer," since we harvest two-, three-, four- and even some five-year-old Chinook each season.

Other biologists argue that coho have perhaps the best chance for survival in our ever-changing, progressive culture. The species appears to be more adaptable than other Pacific salmon. But most ichthyologists agree that the greatest hazard to our coho runs is the long period in which these fish must reside in their parent streams before heading for the sea. Excessive water flow and temperature variations, it appears, are more dangerous to young coho than even their ten mile runs through the hordes of freshwater trout anglers.

Whatever the outcome of our coho fisheries, it is clear that the future rests heavily upon our commitment to artificial hatchery production in order to supplement natural brood stocks. Of course, sound fisheries management, too, will play a decisive role. Washington State has been especially cognizant of such factors and has initiated comprehensive hatchery and experimental programs in recent years. The enormous success of such enhancement efforts is already apparent in both that state's offshore and inland marine waters. Other state—and federal—agencies have also begun to expand coho enhancement programs.

Pink Salmon

Smallest of the North American salmon species which occur in the Pacific, pink salmon are found from northern California to the Arctic, and even along the North Korean coast. They are most abundant, however, throughout Alaska (especially in the Colville watershed) and northern British Columbia but appear in numbers as far south as Washington's Puget Sound.

In their more northerly range, pinks may reach maturity in both odd- and even-numbered years, depending upon the particular stream. Below British Columbia's Fraser River, however, these fish mature during only odd-numbered years (1977, 1979, 1981, etc.). This is because pinks invariably mature during their second year; there is no overlapping of generations. In fact, the Washington State Department of Fisheries has attempted to introduce even-numbered runs into that state, but without sufficient success. Pink runs have been generally disappointing in recent years (especially in Washington), and sport and commercial anglers alike have felt the dismal shortage. Attempts are currently under way to restore the runs, but certain fishing restrictions remain in effect at this writing.

Oncorhynchus gorbuscha has lighter colored flesh than most other Pacific species, hence the name. Often called *humpbacks* or *humpies* in reference to the large, pronounced humps displayed by the males as they reach spawning maturity, pinks are late summer or early fall spawning fish. Their spawning rites typically occur between July and October.

Pinks typically spawn in rivers and streams with suitable gravel stretches. Spawning usually occurs close to salt water (and sometimes in brackish water), but there are notable exceptions. In British Columbia's Skeena River system, for example, pinks are known to make upstream migrations of about three hundred miles into the Bear River.

Females deposit about two thousand eggs into the redds. The eggs are then fertilized by milt from the males and covered with gravel. The young fish emerge from the gravel in from 110 to about 130 days and migrate directly to sea — at times before the yolk sac has been completely absorbed. Like the other Pacific species, the ocean voyages of pinks may be extensive, encompassing several thousand miles.

As young fish, pinks feed extensively on plankton, but their ocean diet consists primarily of baitfish, squid, and small crustaceans. In salt water, sport anglers frequently hook pinks on baitfish and squid-type lures, but even fly fishermen using patterns designed to imitate their staple diet have begun taking pinks with some regularity. Salmon roe, spinners, and spoons are highly effective, especially when fished near the mouths of pink salmon rivers and streams. At times, pinks will readily take hooks baited only with a length of colored yarn, much as will steelhead.

Pinks are especially important to commercial fishermen. In British Columbia, they are the most numerous of all Pacific salmon species and comprise the bulk of the commercial catch. But they have also become increasingly important to sport fishermen as more effective techniques for taking them have been devised and refined.

Pinks found in Alaska and northern British Columbia typically average about three pounds, although five-pounders are not uncommon. Ten-pound pinks are rare, and their maximum weight is about fifteen pounds. Large fish are more prevalent during years in which the total number is relatively low. That is, their size appears to be inversely related to their abundance. Still, pink salmon occurring in Washington's Puget Sound and British Columbia's Fraser River are clearly larger than those found in more northerly waters, averaging close to six pounds.

At sea, pinks display bluish green backs and silvery sides. Large, dark spots appear in generous numbers on their backs, sides, and both lobes of the

Pink ("humpy") salmon in spawning condition: female, top; male, bottom. *Courtesy of Washington Department of Fisheries.*

30

caudal fin. They have scales which are smaller than those of the other Pacific species, and they may usually be distinguished by their thirteen to sixteen anal rays. The first gill has between twenty-four and thirty-five rakers.

Spawning colors include dark brown, almost olive, backs, fading to nearly white underbellies. Males develop the prominent humped back, and their jaws become elongated. The nose hooks sharply downward at its tip.

Pink salmon fry may be distinguished from other salmon fry by their noticeable lack of parr marks. Although they attain a relatively modest size in relation to other Pacific salmon species, pinks grow most rapidly, reaching an average length of about two feet between the time they migrate seaward as fry and return as adults. Their marine life is limited to a period of approximately fourteen to eighteen months.

Pinks are rarely taken by sport fishermen while at their feeding grounds. Instead, most fish are caught during their spawning migrations from the Pacific to their parent streams. Like Chinook and coho, these salmon make excellent eating, although many anglers prefer to smoke their somewhat softer, lighter flesh, especially if fish have begun to take on their spawning colors.

Aside from the Alaskan and British Columbian sport fisheries, Washington is the most important pink salmon state. There the odd-numbered years provide an important sport and commercial fishery during years of relative abundance, particularly along that state's Juan de Fuca Strait and in Puget Sound. In fact, some pinks spend their entire lives within the relatively limited boundaries of Puget Sound. As may be expected, these resident fish are usually significantly smaller than their ocean-going counterparts.

Sockeye

Sockeye salmon (*Oncorhynchus nerka*) are referred to by various names throughout their distribution pattern. They are frequently called *red salmon* in Alaska and *bluebacks* in their more southerly range. In their landlocked form, they are usually called *kokanee, silver trout, silvers, bluebacks, little reds,* or *yanks.*

Sockeye of the ocean-going variety appear to travel rapidly to their native streams from their North Pacific feeding grounds. They are most important to commercial fishermen and to Alaskan and British Columbian sport anglers.

Sockeye spawn only in streams which have inland lakes at their headwaters. Because of their lake system spawning habits, their distribution is limited, especially below British Columbia. While the species is found from the Columbia River to Alaska, its range extends to the North Pacific rim and to Russia's Kamchatka Peninsula.

Among the largest runs of sockeye are those of British Columbia's Shuswap Lake and of certain Alaskan watersheds. The largest substantial sockeye runs below the Canadian-American border occur in the Columbia, Skagit, Quinault, and Ozette Rivers, as well as in Seattle's Lake Washington system.

Sockeye average about two feet in length and five pounds at maturity. Maximum weight is about fifteen pounds. Size of individual fish may differ greatly from area to area. Their ocean colors include bluish green backs and silvery sides. Their scales are small and cycloid; their gill rakers are long, thin, and rather delicate.

Spawning brings about the typical color changes found in all Pacific species, namely a noticeable darkening of the body. But in sockeye, spawning colors are apt to be from brick red to a very bright red. Their heads remain bluish green, however. Males develop a prominent hump on their backs, strong teeth, and a pronounced hooking of the upper jaw. Intestinal tracts become atrophied, and feeding ceases.

Sockeye enter their native streams during June or July to spawn during the last three months of the calendar year. They spawn in the lake-river systems and sometimes in the gravel of the lakes themselves. Females excavate the redds and deposit as many as four thousand eggs, although three thousand to thirty-five hundred is about average. Eggs are fertilized by one or more males which leave the spawning grounds before the females, which generally guard the nests until death.

The incubation period for sockeye eggs is from three to four months, and mortality is extremely high: some estimates indicate that as few as two percent of the young live to reach the Pacific, and some ichthyologists say that only one fingerling may result from one hundred eggs.

The fertilized eggs hatch during the winter months, with alevins developing into the fry stage by about mid-year. Young fish then enter the lakes and spend a year or more there before heading seaward as smolts of from three to six inches in length. In the North Pacific, they range widely, feeding and growing quite rapidly.

Both young and adult sockeye feed heavily upon plankton. In their lake existence, they feed exclusively on freshwater plankton. Until recently, anglers assumed that sockeye would not strike a bait-

Clarence Hasenwinkle of Seattle displays a fine sockeye taken during a rare sport fishery in Lake Washington. *Photograph by Paul Vauchelet.*

fish or artificial lure. But British Columbian trollers have recently dispelled this myth and, as a result, sockeye are gaining in popularity as a sport salmon species throughout the Pacific Northwest.

In Alaska and British Columbia, sockeye provide an important sport fishery in numerous lakes and streams, where they are tricked by a variety of artificial lures. Even fly fishermen have begun taking sockeye on fly patterns intended for trout. The males are especially bellicose and protective during their spawning rites and are thus especially susceptible to properly presented lures. But most fish are taken in the salt or brackish waters near their native watersheds.

Canadian commercial trollers now harvest large numbers of sockeye off Vancouver Island, using flashers and squid-type lures. South of the Canadian border, however, relatively few sockeye are taken by sport fishermen, with the exception of those which are landlocked.

After spending one year or more in the lakes, sockeye emigrate to sea. There they feed for one or more years before returning to their cradle streams to spawn. Fish usually mature at three to five years of age. In their more northerly latitudes, they may reach maturity at as many as six years and weigh up to seven or eight pounds. British Columbia sockeye generally reach maturity at four or five years, but runs usually include some sexually precocious three-year-old jacks.

Landlocked sockeye—frequently called *redfish* or *kickaninny* throughout Canada—display a life cycle which is very similar to that of their anadromous brothers, except that their entire lives are spent within the lake systems. Thus their growth is restricted by their freshwater environment and limited lake feed, and landlocked sockeye rarely exceed about twenty inches or three pounds in weight.

While the sea-going sockeye are most important to sport fishermen of Alaska and British Columbia, a relatively new and important fishery has developed in Lake Washington, near Seattle. It is indeed a unique fishery in that sockeye are not native to the lake and its tributary Cedar River but were planted during the 1930s.

Until the sixties, sockeye returns were minimal. But quite suddenly, their numbers increased

Metropolitan fishing at its best! Sockeye fisherman plays his catch on Seattle's Lake Washington. *Courtesy of Washington Department of Fisheries.*

dramatically. Although small sockeye returns and ongoing legal battles kept the Lake Washington sockeye season closed to sport angling during 1975 and 1976, an unexpected bumper crop during the summer of 1977 resulted in a resumption of sport angling. This on-again, off-again fishery is extremely popular with local anglers, and it is hoped that the Cedar River sockeye runs will be sufficient in future years to withstand an annual sport fishery.

Chum Salmon

Chum salmon, frequently called *dog salmon, fall salmon, qualla, keta* or *calico salmon,* like sockeye, travel rapidly to their parent streams from their North Pacific feeding grounds. Most numerous in Alaska, their numbers have declined greatly in Washington, Oregon, and British Columbia in recent years.

The chum's North American range extends from the Sacramento River to the Arctic and as far east as the Mackenzie River. Chum are also found off the Asian coast, from South Korea to the Arctic and as far west as the Lena River. In practical terms, however, these fish are rarely encountered south of the Columbia River. Besides certain Alaskan rivers, the most notable chum river is the Yukon.

Chum salmon flesh is pale in color — lighter even than that of pink salmon. They make excellent eating, although many anglers recommend that they be smoked.

Chum average about ten pounds at maturity, although twenty pounders are not uncommon. Maximum weight is about twenty-five pounds. A new sport record of 27 pounds, 3 ounces was established at Raymond Cove, Alaska, during 1977.* Their ocean colors include metallic blue backs with occasional black spotting and silvery sides and bellies. Black edging occurs on the tips of the anal, caudal, and pectoral fins. These tinges are particularly noticeable in the males. Teeth are strongly developed and resemble canine fangs in adult males.

* Record compiled by IGFA

33

During spawning, chum become dark with irregular blotching of red and yellowish green on the body, giving them their *calico* appearance. The tips of the anal and pelvic fins turn pale, almost white, and the males develop the familiar hooked snout. Chum usually have thirteen to fourteen anal fin rays and nineteen to twenty-six gillrakers.

Chum are essentially late fall spawners, although they may spawn as early as late summer in their more northerly range. Being essentially late fall spawners, however, chum are extremely sensitive to wide fluctuations in water volume and temperature; thus, their survival rate is relatively low.

Chum salmon spawn near the sea and, at times, in brackish lagoons or in tide flats near freshwater streams. The female oviposits about three thousand eggs. After the eggs have hatched, chum fry of about an inch or two in length emerge from the river gravel and immediately emigrate to sea.

In the ocean, chum feed heavily on plankton, small crustaceans, baitfish, and crabs, and they will readily take a properly presented lure. They grow rapidly in their marine environment and appear to travel northward during the spring and summer months and southward during fall and winter. Canadian fisheries biologists report that chum which originate in British Columbia spend most, if not all, of their ocean lives in the Gulf of Alaska.

Chum mature at from three to five years. Numerous stocks are native to rivers and streams which empty directly into open salt water, but other chum stocks spawn in streams which are more protected.

While their numbers have dwindled throughout their southerly range in recent years, chum are occasionally boated by sport fishermen at various Pacific points, as well as in Washington's Puget Sound, along the Strait of Juan de Fuca, Johnstone Strait in British Columbia, and on the eastern coast of Vancouver Island. They appear in limited numbers in the Washington State sport catch but are taken infrequently by Oregon fishermen.

Notes

1. Ernest Schwiebert, *Salmon of the World* (New York: Winchester, 1970), p. 10.
2. Ibid.
3. Ibid., p. 11.
4. Ibid., p. 9.
5. Ibid., p. 19.
6. Ibid., p. 33.
7. Ibid., p. 26.
8. Ibid., pp. 26-27.
9. Ibid., p. 26.
10. Ibid., p. 28.
11. California Department of Fish and Game, *Salmon & Steelhead Fishing Map: Description of the Fishery and What Is Necessary to Maintain It* (Sacramento: California Office of State Printing, 1969), p. 5.
12. Ibid.
13. Canadian Fisheries and Marine Service, *Fisheries Fact Sheet: Coho Salmon* (n.p., n.d.), p. 1.
14. Frank Haw and Ray Buckley, *Salt Water Fishing in Washington* (Seattle: Stan Jones, 1973), p. 15.

PART TWO
SALTWATER SALMON FISHING

2

THE EQUIPMENT

SALTWATER salmon fishermen have a wide range of tackle, lures, and ancillary equipment from which to choose. Specific selection depends on a number of factors, including the particular species being sought, the anticipated size of the quarry, the particular angling technique to be employed, and some study of the area to be fished and the tackle which normally produces the best results in that locale. Additionally, equipment selection ultimately depends on individual angling preference, sometimes tempered by past personal experience or the advertising and promotional efforts of tackle and ancillary equipment manufacturers who often aggressively hawk their wares.

Modern fishing tackle has undergone sophisticated changes in recent years, and salmon gear is no exception. From split bamboo rods and old-fashioned, direct-drive reels (often appropriately called *knuckle dusters* or *knuckle busters*) has evolved a whole new spectrum of efficient, often fanciful and expensive, equipment. Fiberglass, graphite, carbaloy, plastics, and other materials have combined with technological ingenuity to make today's tackle the best ever devised for the taking of sport-caught fish, the various Pacific salmon species among them. Our advances in equipment, however, may be at the expense of the very quarry we continue to seek: fish-and/or depth-finders, for example, now give us the deadliest weaponry imaginable for pursuing the hunt, especially when teamed with other highly sophisticated gadgetry like metered downriggers, rotating flashers, and the like.

But even the finest, most advanced tackle will not assure us of piscatorial success. Only knowledge, experience, and the application of equally sophisticated angling techniques will put more fish in the cooler. A combination of *both* the proper equipment and its correct use, however, will give us the most desirable odds on the fishing grounds.

Frank Woolner, the erudite professor of marine angling and editor of *Salt Water Sportsman* magazine, wisely notes in his book, *Modern Saltwater Sport Fishing*: "Only a great fisherman has the right to call a rod a 'pole,' and a fishing line a 'string.' "[1] While Woolner has earned the right to call these tackle items anything he wishes, he declines to do so. His admonition is duly noted, and I, too, will stick to "rod" and "line." But his proclamation is founded on pragmatic reason as well as wit and humility; modern tackle has evolved to such an advanced state that the old nomenclature—let alone the traditional methods of employing ancient equipment—is now ill-suited to the recreasport of angling.

Newcomers to the sport of saltwater salmon fishing are often surprised at the range of light tackle which may be used effectively to hook and land these fish. Even the largest Chinook are taken on relatively light action rods and compatible gear, and silvers are taken frequently on light spinning or fly tackle, while pinks are sometimes fished with freshwater trout rigs. Novitiates to the sport may net any of the Pacific species on such tackle, provided they assimilate a modicum of information and exercise a bit of common sense.

But while light tackle enthusiasts abound

order. Fish-finders, hand-crank downriggers, expensive fiber-glass rods, and shiny reels may be the answer for angling royalty, but items of this nature are bound to break all but the wealthiest of beginners before they have a chance to assess the merits of such gear. In fact, only the relatively inexpensive basics—good quality glass rod, twenty dollar reel, a couple hundred yards of nylon line, as well as a few leaders, hooks, and sinkers—are necessary. After all, an angler so equipped is not only far better decked out than were his fishing forefathers, but he is also in possession of all the elements required to take salmon, both consistently and in a true sporting fashion. Later, after considerable experience and when his tastes and preferences have become defined, there is nothing save the pocketbook to restrain him from sampling the gamut of available tackle.

Regardless of the items chosen, special care is required of all gear because of the devastatingly corrosive effect of salt water. Boats, motors, tackle, and other items should be rinsed thoroughly with fresh water after exposure to the brine and then wiped dry to further minimize rust and allowed to air-dry individually, rather than being grouped or heaped together. Entire volumes concerning the proper care of fishing tackle and related gear have been written, and the saltwater angler in particular would do well to heed their advice.

Pacific salmon fisherman uses relatively light tackle to do battle with an ocean salmon. *Author photo, courtesy of Salt Water Sportsman.*

throughout the Pacific coast and its inland waters, heavy tackle fishermen are increasing in numbers. Spurred on by the consistently high success demonstrated by commercial trollers (especially in their use of rotating flasher equipment), sport fishermen are beginning to realize that even the heaviest salmon gear has merit. Whether with downriggers and as much as eight pounds of lead or with the lightest of fly tackle, knowledgeable anglers find that each combination, properly fished, is both effective and pleasurable.

Saltwater salmon fishing is not necessarily a sport for weightlifters. Indeed finesse plays a considerable role, even when the heaviest of sport gear is used. This is true not only in playing the fish, but in enticing it to strike in the first place. Like fishing for other species, deftness is the watchword, and there is no tackle which is too heavy or light. Instead the experience of hooking and playing the various members of the Pacific species—especially Chinook and coho—should serve as the best guide when it comes to tackle selection.

But for those who are new to the sport and lack the experience required to make well-informed judgments at the fishing tackle counter, I would suggest that a certain degree of restraint may be in

Rods

Saltwater salmon rods run the gamut from lightweight fly casting models to short, relatively stiff broomsticks or clubs. Each has its place, and the main determining factor in selecting the proper rod is what kind of terminal gear it will accompany.

Recommended for the heaviest terminal gear are rods of approximately seven feet in length. These should possess enough spine to cope with sinkers of up to about thirty-two ounces, about the maximum amount of weight used with rotating flasher gear unless downriggers are used. Yet the rod tip must be sensitive enough to transmit the feel of the terminal gear and the regular, metronomic dipping movement produced by trolled flashers.

Heavyweight salmon rods may consist of virtually any of the popular materials used in modern saltwater sport fishing, but fiberglass, graphite, and wood are most popular. For today's aficionados, it is difficult—if not impossible—to beat fiberglass: modern glass rods, whether solid or tubular, are nearly immune to the killer effects of salt water, and

Private and charter or party boats alike ply the Pacific coast in search of salmon. Note sturdy rod and reel used to troll a single baitfish. *Author photo, courtesy of* Salt Water Sportsman.

they offer the angler the utmost in balance and action. While it is true that fiberglass will fatigue in time, modern glass rods are produced in large quantities and are relatively inexpensive when it comes time for replacement.

The heavyweight trolling rods, like their light-weight counterparts, may be solid or tubular. Many anglers prefer solid glass rods when considerable weight is to be trolled. They may come in either one piece, without connective ferrules, or in various break-down lengths. Most commercially produced trolling rods intended for the heaviest of salmon gear are two-piece models. While some anglers argue that one-piece rods offer the greatest action in trolling and playing a fish, the two-piece rods are both more versatile and convenient to transport to and from the fishing grounds. One might argue further that the single connective ferrule of a two-piece trolling rod does not pose action or balance problems which might be detected by most anglers. When long treks are necessary, the one-piece rods are a liability at best; air flights from one area to another, for example, make transportation of seven-foot rods nerve-wracking, if not impossible. For this reason, the two-piece rods both dominate the market and provide the best answer for anglers who do

not have suitable rod racks for vehicle storage.

Rod guides should be of the highest quality, and these should be maintained regularly to ensure that corrosion, nicks, and the like do not interfere with the ease of line movement or, worse yet, cause unnecessary blemishes in the line. The latter may result in line breakage at the most inopportune moment—when playing a fish. Rod guides are available in various metals. The best are those of carbaloy or those which are lined with ceramic. These do not have the tendency to become grooved, as do the cheaper, poorer chrome-plated models. Because guides are relatively inexpensive, it pays to buy and use the finest available. High quality rod guides which are properly maintained will pay dividends on the fishing grounds.

When selecting a rod intended for trolling heavy terminal gear, look for those displaying sturdy rod butts. Likewise, metal reel seats are mandatory, and these should be designed to handle moderately large saltwater reels. Rods of this type are frequently used to troll offshore and may be found as standard equipment aboard many charter and party boats offering seasonal salmon trips from California to Alaska. They are good, functional rods, expressly intended for trolling heavy terminal tackle combinations, sometimes including metal line.

Standard trolling rods of about eight to nine feet are used with somewhat lighter terminal gear. Essentially, these are simply elongated—and lighter —versions of rods used for trolling rotating flashers and other heavy terminal tackle. Light-tackle trolling rods should have good quality rod guides, metal reel seats, and sufficiently long butt ends, but their weight may be considerably lighter and the tip action less stiff. These rods are normally reserved for trolling, say, five to eight ounces of weight. The most popular are tubular fiberglass models with a single joint, although fishermen who can manipulate one-piece rods to and from their boats usually prefer rods without the usual connective ferrule.

Rods of still lighter weight and with even more sensitive tips are recommended for mooching techniques, in which lightweight sinkers of from one-half of an ounce to about four or five ounces are used. These rods range from approximately eight to ten feet in length—infrequently longer; most mooching purists prefer the longer versions. They have metal reel seats designed to handle the smaller saltwater reels. Long butt ends are essential, and fiberglass is again the most popular material. In mooching, the rod tip must display a very sensitive, soft action which permits the angler to readily discern the sometimes gentle bites produced by slow-feeding salmon.

Long, light-action rods are favored by small-boat moochers. *Author photo, courtesy of* Salt Water Sportman.

Light-action spinning rods are used also, although not as frequently as trolling or mooching models. Because most saltwater salmon fishing is done by boat, casting is rarely a consideration. Surf and jetty fishermen, however, often use rods designed for casting. The spinning models should be about six to seven feet in length, have relatively light-action tips, and should be capable of handling medium-sized fresh or saltwater spinning reels. Usually, sinkers of three ounces or less are used.

Casting distance should be the major consideration in selecting the proper spinning rod and other gear, since distance may be crucial at times when salmon are foraging on or near the water's surface. At such times, a properly placed lure will greatly increase the angler's chance of connecting.

For jetty fishing, I prefer a standard steelheading rod. These are designed to permit distance casting yet provide the ultimate in balance and action. Their tips are light-action and quite sensitive, and they may be used with either spinning or baitcasting reels.

Fly rods are seldom used by Pacific salmon fishermen in salt water, although they are employed extensively throughout the pools and riffles of freshwater rivers and streams. Since relatively little fly casting is done for salmon while the fish are in salt or brackish water, angler preference is the overriding factor in selecting the proper rod. Most Pacific salmon "fly fishing" is conducted with streamer flies trolled rapidly behind the boat, a technique directed almost exclusively at coho—at least, when flies are trolled on or near the surface. Since silvers seldom exceed about fifteen pounds, the lighter fly rods may be used. In fact, many fishermen who troll on the surface for coho use fresh water fly casting models intended for trout and other small inland fish.

One of the important considerations in selecting a rod for any technique or terminal combination is length: leader and terminal rig length should never exceed the length of the rod (with a certain, unique exception described later in these pages), since a rod of insufficient length will result in considerable difficulty in bringing a fish to net or gaff. It is the angler who chooses unwisely to match an eight-foot rod to a terminal rig-leader combination of twelve or fifteen feet who gives rise to the oft-repeated cliche: "He should have brought a stepladder!" Such an ill-suited tackle combination will preclude the angler from being able to net or gaff a salmon which has been tired and is ready to be boated without laying aside his rod. This is especially important when fishing alone, without the aid of an angling companion who is both charitable and adept at applying the net's twine at the proper moment.

Reels

Like rods, saltwater salmon reels vary considerably in quality, type, price, and use but are

Elling Simonsen (left), Bremerton *Sun* Outdoor Editor, and Ray Buckley, fisheries biologist and author, used flyrods and flycasting reels to come up with these saltwater salmon. *Courtesy of Washington Department of Fisheries.*

40

Lightweight spinning tackle is used extensively by Pacific salmon anglers but is generally a poor choice for saltwater action. *Author photo, courtesy of* Salt Water Sportsman.

chosen primarily to accompany the rod and terminal gear as well as angling technique to be employed. In general, anglers are well advised to stay away from the freshwater models.

Reels may be of the single-action, direct-drive type or of the multiplying, revolving spool variety. Spinning models — whether open- or closed-faced — are used chiefly with lightweight tackle but are poor choices for most saltwater salmon angling techniques because they have too many areas open to the corrosive effects of salt or brackish water.

Single-action, direct-drive reels work on a one-to-one gear ratio and usually lack the adjustable drag feature found on most salt water salmon models. On the Pacific and its adjacent inland marine waters, these direct-drive reels are less popular now than they were during an earlier era but are still consider-ed by some die-hards to be the most efficient reels ever devised for taking salmon from the brine — especially from a boat, where casting is usually

unnecessary. There is little room for angler error with direct-drive reels, since applying too much pressure or cranking in line at just the wrong moment may easily result in broken leaders and lost fish. Knuckles must also be quickly removed from the crank handles when fish decide to run or they are likely to be dusted or busted. The newer models sometimes offer drag features, however, eliminating this problem. Novice salmon anglers are advised to opt for reels with some sort of drag built in.

Most popular for all salmon trolling and mooch-ing techniques are the revolving spool reels with multiplying capabilities. Of those now on the market, I prefer the level-wind, star-drag type. The level-wind feature suffices to keep the line evenly distributed across the spool, and star drags are easily and quickly adjusted. Good star-drag, multiplying reels can be purchased for between twenty and thirty-five dollars, depending on line choice and spool capacity. While more expensive reels are avail-able, these basic salmon trolling/mooching reels are more than adequate.

41

Most charter or party fishing for Pacific salmon calls for star-drag, multiplying reels. *Author photo.*

Line length and diameter are primary considerations in the selection of any saltwater salmon reel; thus, spool capacity is an important factor. For deep trolling with heavy terminal gear, two hundred yards or more of heavy metal line may be required, as is often the case when trolling for Chinook with rotating flashers and heavy weights or downriggers. Moochers using only one hundred or one hundred fifty yards of relatively lightweight monofilament nylon line may select a small saltwater reel model which is incapable of handling more—or heavier—line. Sometimes such mooching techniques call for line as light as eight or ten pounds breaking strength. It is obvious that there is considerable latitude within which to work: the deep troller dragging perhaps thirty-two ounces of lead weight and large, rotating flasher gear will be unable to function properly with anything less than a reel and spool of adequate capacity, while the salmon

moocher using only one hundred yards of ten-pound-test line and a two-ounce sinker will be encumbered by an oversized model.

Regardless of reel choice, a high-quality drag feature is essential. Drags which are less than smooth are useless and may, in fact, be detrimental. In terms of both enjoyment and problem-free angling, only the finest reel drags should be considered.

If fly reels are to be used, they should be intended for salt water use and should be capable of handling at least 150 yards of line or line with backing. Since actual casting is rarely done when salmon are in salt water, anglers may be well-advised to opt for the multiplying, level-wind, star-drag reels.

Line

Fishing line used for taking salmon from salt or brackish water should be matched to the technique and terminal tackle, and virtually the only latitude

42

for individual preference exists within a rather limited range of line materials and breaking strengths.

Fishing lines have come a long way. From ancient lines fashioned from horsehair, linen, silk, and other natural fibers have evolved today's lines—much more efficient and easy to handle than those of our grandfathers. The various metal lines concocted by alchemists and their modern counterparts, the synthetics developed by scientists since World War II, now offer the saltwater salmon fisherman a wide range of possibilities.

In general, metal line is by far the best choice for deep trolling with heavy terminal gear, such as sinkers of up to thirty-two ounces, heavy sinker-release device rigs, dodgers, and flashers. Usually, the synthetic lines lack the efficiency of metal in such instances, although they are too often used to accomodate such gear.

Synthetic lines make it difficult for anglers to reach the deeper water strata, because of their relatively light weight. Additionally, most synthetics still display an inherent elasticity (although this has been reduced in recent years) which necessarily results in some distortion of the terminal gear. This is especially true when trolling dodgers or flashers which must move in a certain, specific fashion. Conversely, metal line possesses very little elasticity.

Metal lines are available in three basic forms: single-strand, braided, and lead-core. Of the three, perhaps the best choice for salt water salmon trolling is the first—single-strand metal, usually stainless steel.

The primary drawbacks of single-strand metal line are that it is difficult to handle and, without proper care, may result in kinks. Newcomers to metal line often learn the hard way that it is particularly susceptible to backlash and tangles, and

Nylon monofilament of sufficient breaking strength is standard equipment aboard most charter or party boats. Here a youngster uses mono to take a scrappy coho. *Author photo.*

43

special care must be applied when winding it onto the reel spool. Likewise, special care must be exercised to assure that kinks are avoided at all times; if kinks do occur, they may easily result in ultimate line separation.

Presently on the market are several types of synthetic fishing line which may be used by saltwater salmon fishermen. Deep and/or heavy trollers sometimes opt for braided Dacron over the heavier metal lines, although considerably more weight may be required to take the lighter line to the desired depth. Similarly, braided nylon lines are sometimes used but appear to be decreasing in popularity.

For light tackle trollers, moochers, surf, and jetty fishermen intent on taking Pacific salmon from the brine or estuarine waters, single-strand nylon line is perhaps the best all-around choice. Nylon filament line is particularly well-suited to accompanying salmon tackle which does not require more than, say, six or eight ounces of weight, and it is used almost exclusively these days in conjunction with modern downriggers when trolling deep for Chinook.

Mooching lines are lightweight monofilament nylon of from about eight to twenty-five pound test. In mooching, only a single baitfish and relatively light sinker are required. Typically, these sinkers weigh from about one-half an ounce to about five ounces. With mooching techniques, the selection of line breaking strength depends mainly upon the approximate size of the anticipated quarry and the skill and experience of the individual salmon angler. For coho, the majority of which weigh fifteen pounds or less, nylon mono of about ten pounds breaking strength is usually adequate. Large, mature Chinook in the thirty- to fifty-pound range, in fact, seldom require anything heavier than twenty-pound test, especially in the hands of a skilled, experienced fisherman (or one, at least, who is not intent upon horsing the fish to the boat). The smaller Pacific salmon—sockeye, pinks, and immature Chinook (blackmouth)—rarely require more than six- or eight-pound test mono.

Since breaking strength should be suited to experience and ability, inexperienced moochers or anglers trolling light terminal tackle should opt for somewhat heavier line than do their veteran counterparts. An excellent all-around line choice for beginner and experienced hand alike is twenty-pound test monofilament. Good quality mono of this breaking strength will easily permit the angler to handle all but the largest of kings. Twenty-pound mono, in fact, is sufficient for playing Chinook of giant proportions; I use line of this breaking strength, for example, when fishing the legendary

Tyee salmon of British Columbia's Rivers Inlet, where forty-plus pounders are common and seventy-pound Chinook are not unheard of. Indeed the angler who finds himself in the enviable position of having hooked a fish of such large proportion is able to make compensations for the relatively light breaking strength of the line. The rod itself should do much of the work of tiring the fish; additionally, reel drag adjustments may be made. Moreover, the application of simple old-fashioned *patience* should preclude the line's parting. If the truth be known, fifty-pound Chinook may be taken with ease on as little as ten-pound test mono—and, yes, even lighter! It all depends on the angler's skill and patience: the restraint required to fight the natural tendency to get the fish into the boat as quickly as possible. More lines and leaders are parted because of this hurry-up attitude than for any other reason.

Too, many of the line manufacturers are prone to understate the breaking strengths of their merchandise. Ten-pound test line is just as likely to hold to fifteen pounds as to part at ten. This tendency to understate the breaking strength of their products is probably the result of anglers' attempts to find "stronger" lines of a specific breaking strength. This, of course, is a contradiction in terms. Underrating breaking strength is tantamount to marketing a sixteen-foot boat which measures an actual twenty feet in length. You may be getting your money's worth, but you'll certainly have the longest sixteen-footer on the block!

Spinning and bait-casting reels should be loaded with nylon monofilament in virtually all instances. Mono has superior strength for its diameter and is an ideal choice when casting is necessary. Fly line choice depends on the specific rod and reel (as well as terminal rig) used for casting, and manufacturers' recommendations are usually the best guide to ensuring that the complete outfit is ideally matched if fly casting techniques are to be attempted. When flies are simply trolled on or near the surface, reels are frequently loaded with mono of sufficient test strength to handle coho, and fly lines *per se* are not required, although they may be used.

Mono, like the heavier metal line, has a couple of drawbacks. The first is that it has a built-in memory: an inherent elasticity which permits the line to stretch but which, in time, causes it to return to its former state. In rare instances, this memory factor can cause reel spools to shatter because of the tremendous pressure exerted by the line as it contracts. Most modern reel spools have been beefed up to handle this contraction, and many—like the multiplying, level-wind, star-drag models previously recommended—are now made of heavy (sometimes solid) metal which is impervious to mono memory.

A second drawback of nylon monofilament line is that special care must be taken to see that there are no nicks, cuts, abrasions, or other abnormalities which may result in line breakage. Being essentially a soft material, mono is particularly susceptible to cuts and the like. Rocks and other underwater obstructions may damage line at any time, and even a gentle scraping against boat or dock may cause blemishes. For this reason, many salmon fishermen periodically check their lines when reeling in their terminal tackle. Still others routinely cut a few feet of line—that which has been exposed to wear and tear—from the terminal end before fastening leaders and other hardware at the beginning of each fishing day. Salmon line—the link between man and fish—should be without flaw at all times.

Leaders

Salmon leaders, like salmon line, should be selected on the basis of the terminal tackle which is to be used, rod length, the estimated size of the fish being sought, and individual experience and preference. While metal leaders are sometimes used, they are usually regarded as unnecessary unless dogfish and other leader-damaging species are abundant. In fact, forty- to fifty-pound test monofilament nylon leader is sufficient for even the heaviest terminal gear; the single exception is perhaps in rotating flasher trolling, where single-strand metal lines, and sometimes leaders, are recommended.

Some salmon fishermen may make a good argument for the use of single-strand metal or wire leaders when the quarry are large, mature Pacific salmon species, such as coho taken off Washington State's Cape Flattery during late summer and fall or giant Chinook, such as those frequently encountered at British Columbia's Campbell River or Rivers Inlet. Adult males of certain species develop enlarged, canine-type teeth at maturity, and such sharply pointed teeth can wreak havoc with standard nylon leaders.

I remember fishing for brute-sized Tyee salmon at Rivers Inlet a few years ago. Al Cooper, my fishing partner for the day, and I had decided to return to the water following a hearty lunch enjoyed after a full morning of no-action trolling. The locals, experienced Owikeno Indians and the owners and employees of the resort at which we were staying, warned us that we would be wasting our time. "Everybody knows that there's no such thing as a 'tide bite' here," they said. "You might as well wait till evening; mornings and evenings are the only time anybody catches fish here."

Al and I decided to try our luck anyway. We wanted to fish the early afternoon low slack tide. Within a few minutes' run, we were at the spot we had decided to fish. It was an area where sporadic salmon strikes had been reported the previous day. We lowered our herring baits into the water and, within minutes, I encountered a sudden, titanic strike. I paused an instant until I could feel the strong, steady tug of the Tyee, then I firmly set my hooks. The fish lingered on the line momentarily and was gone. When I reeled in my line, both hooks were gone; the frayed end of my leader told the tale: as I had set the hooks, the leader—a light mooching length—had apparently been parted by the jagged teeth of the Chinook. I managed to connect on a thirty-eight pounder on the next pass through the same small bay and, after three or four hours' time, Al had put a pair of forty-five pounders in the boat (one of them foul-hooked near the tail and which took us over an hour and a half to land). When we returned to camp, we were naturally pleased—for a couple of reasons. First, we had taken three large Tyees; second, we were beginning to find a host of converts to our tide bite theory. Despite our success, however, I spent seemingly endless hours agonizing over my first strike. With luck—and in my opinion, a good *wire* leader—we would have had a fourth lunker for the cooler.

That wire leaders have their place in Pacific salmon fishing cannot be disputed. Many anglers have had their nylon leaders cut while applying the pressure to teethy salmon—especially if leaders are dragged across the teeth at a right angle. But such instances are relatively rare, and each enthusiast of the sport is entitled to his preference. Despite my own experience, I still prefer the softer, more pliable nylon to wire when it comes to leaders. I find the synthetic leader material much easier to work with when threading hooks through herring, which often have soft flesh. At such times, nylon may be used without damaging baitfish; wire leaders are prone to result in herring which appear sloppy, the last thing desired by a serious salmon fisherman.

Regardless of leader material, leader lengths, as previously noted, should not exceed the length of the rod. They should be of the same breaking strength as the line—or of a lighter breaking strength—so that any breakage which may occur will result in the separation of the leader, and not of the line itself. Should the *line* part, all terminal tackle will be lost; if the *leader* parts instead, only the leader, hooks, and baitfish will disappear.

As with salmon line, leaders should be inspected

carefully and frequently for cuts, nicks, and abrasions. Those which are damaged—even minutely—should be changed promptly. With nylon leaders, it is often difficult to actually see such blemishes, and the best way to detect their presence or to ensure their absence is to run the leader between thumb and forefinger. Many fishermen make it a practice to change leaders each time a fish is hooked, as even small nicks caused by the small but sharp teeth of salmon are prone to cause the leader to part when the next fish is hooked.

Light trolling techniques call for relatively lightweight leaders of between six- and twenty-pound test. Mooching lines of twenty-pound test are best accompanied by leaders of, say, fifteen or seventeen pounds breaking strength. Given standard rod length dimensions, most mooching and trolling leaders should measure from six to nine feet in length.

Spinning tackle calls for somewhat shorter leaders, and these are usually single-strand nylon of the type used for mooching and trolling, but in considerably lighter breaking strengths. For casting flies, tapered leaders specially matched to the rod and line are used. Fly tackle enthusiasts who take salmon while trolling streamers on or near the surface often tie a simple length of nontapered mono behind the swivel or simply tie the fly directly onto the salmon line.

If tapered, shooting fly lines are used in casting for salmon (a relatively new technique finding increasing popularity, especially in Washington State's southern Puget Sound) an adequate length of backing material should be loaded onto the reel spool. Backing is just as important as the line itself and should be carefully chosen.

Perhaps the best choice for saltwater backing is braided Dacron line. Strong and small in diameter, Dacron backing of fifteen to twenty pounds breaking strength will serve the purpose in almost all instances. While a small swivel connector may be used to cement fly line to backing, carefully tied knots are probably best for this purpose. A spliced loop, executed perfectly and leaving a smooth connection, will suffice. As with most marine angling, the more line the better, and this same advice holds for backing as well.

Snaps and Swivels

Salmon fishermen use an almost endless variety of different snaps, swivels, and other connecting hardware. These are designed to keep the line and leaders from tangling and to provide an efficient means for quickly and easily changing leaders and other terminal gear.

Except when using spoons, spinners or other artificial lures which have built-in swivels, all terminal salmon rigs should include a swivel of some sort. Most commonly used are the snap-swivel combinations which act somewhat like a safety pin in that they not only allow rapid changing of leaders or other terminal rigs but also offer the advantage of preventing twisted and tangled lines. Snap-swivels include a series of small, round beads (or a single revolving ball) which rotate on a thin metal shaft. The line is attached to the eye at the end of the bead series, and the artificial lure or leader tied with a loop is slipped into the snap and held in place.

Another choice is the *barrel* or single ball bearing swivel which is similar to the snap-swivel but does not have a snap attached. While these are effective for preventing the tangling of line and terminal gear, they require that the angler tie the leader or other terminal tackle line rig directly to one of the swivel eyes. Thus, barrel-type swivels do not facilitate the rapid changing of terminal gear, as do the snap-swivel devices.

A third type of swivel is often used by salt water salmon fishermen. Three-way swivels are important

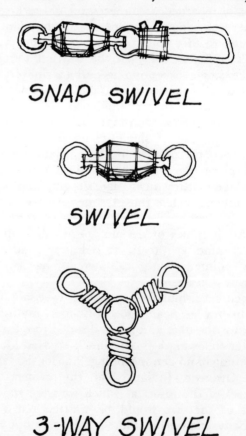

SNAP SWIVEL

SWIVEL

3-WAY SWIVEL

to trollers, particularly those dragging heavy terminal gear. With a three-way swivel, the line is tied to one eye, the leader to another, and the third eye holds a short length of line to which is attached a lead sinker. These swivels are used frequently with flasher or dodger gear.

Most salmon swivels and connectors come in various sizes and should be chosen to suit the terminal tackle. Heavy flasher rigs, for example, require relatively large and strong three-way swivels, while light mooching gear calls for smaller snap-swivels. In general, the larger and stronger swivels and connectors should be employed when the anticipated size of the quarry is substantial, as with mature Chinook which may run to forty pounds or more. The smaller, lighter swivels and connectors should be used when anglers seek pinks, sockeye, small- to medium-sized coho, or immature Chinook.

Brass or stainless steel swivels and connectors are generally recommended for use in salt water, although some anglers prefer the duller blued or bronzed finishes, reasoning that, since these reflect less light, they are less likely to spook wary salmon. The selection of swivels and connectors thus depends to a large extent upon individual beliefs and preferences.

For salt water trolling, mooching, casting, or spinning techniques, separate swivels are not usually required. Crescent-shaped sinkers with built-in swivel bead series are frequently used; these eliminate the need for additional connectors. Similarly, most diving plane sinkers include attached swivel features.

Sinkers and Diving Planes

Because only coho consistently roam and feed near the water's surface, anglers must usually use some weight in order to get the baitfish or lure to the desired depth. Virtually the only exception is in employing streamer flies which are presented either through casting or trolled on or near the surface. Thus, by far the greatest number of Pacific salmon angling situations call for the use of some sort of weight.

There are many kinds of lead weights and sinkers which may be used for saltwater salmon angling. Most common are round lead balls, crescent-shaped sinkers, sliding, and slip sinkers. Alternatives to using such terminal line sinkers are to employ one of the diving plane sinkers or to use a downrigger device.

Heavy or deep trolling techniques are usually accompanied by round or oval-shaped lead sinkers

A La Push, Washington, charter skipper uses a "cannon-ball"—a heavy weight fished in simple downrigger fashion—in conjunction with a sinker-release device. The combination is very effective. *Author photo, courtesy of Salt Water Sportsman.*

which may weigh as much as thirty-two ounces when used with rotating flashers. Downriggers employ the use of large, round or semi-round balls weighing eight pounds or more. Similarly, sinker-release devices are frequently used. These are designed to permit the heavy lead weight to fall free of the line when a salmon is hooked.

For light trolling or mooching, kidney or crescent-shaped sinkers are most popular. These banana-shaped sinkers usually have bead swivels attached to them, precluding the need for additional connecting gear. Most popular are sinkers of from one-half an ounce to about eight ounces in weight.

Kidney-shaped sinkers, sometimes called *slip* sinkers, are also used, although not as extensively as the crescent-shaped type. In general, kidney sinkers are reserved for light to medium trolling techniques. Like the other sinkers, slip sinkers are available in various weights, but trollers usually favor weights of from about six to ten ounces.

Kidney sinkers are designed so that they may be

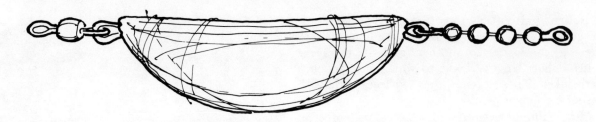

CRESCENT SINKER

quickly and easily adjusted along the length of the line. Their design includes a wire bar at the top, bent at an angle which permits the line to be threaded conveniently through the space between wire and lead. They also display round wire clamps into which the line is inserted. These clamps hold the sinker in place.

Sliding sinkers (often called *slip weights* but not to be confused with the kidney-shaped sinker described above) are gaining in popularity among salt water salmon anglers, especially light trollers and moochers. Unlike the standard banana- or crescent-shaped sinker, the sliding sinker has no attached swivel. Thus, anglers using this type of weight should tie a swivel between the line and leader to help prevent tangling and twisting.

The sliding sinker is shaped much like the crescent- or banana-shaped weight but has a hollow core through which the line is threaded. It is designed to minimize the drag of the weight—to both angler and fish. The fisherman is aware of the increased sensitivity possible with this type of sinker when a strike occurs; moreover, the salmon is not suspect of any unnatural tug from the weight, since the baitfish or lure slips freely through the sinker when mouthed by the fish. In addition to providing a better means of light tackle sport, sliding sinkers are generally regarded among expert salmon fishermen as more effective than the standard, non-sliding type.

Sliding sinkers have the further advantage of minimizing the possibility of the line or leader snapping while a fish is played. Instead of being able to apply undue stress on the line by jerking the sinker in sudden directional changes, a salmon which is hooked on tackle rigged with a sliding sinker will be able only to pull line *through* the weight and not work the weight against the line to its own advantage—and to the detriment of the angler.

Fishermen opting to use sliding sinkers instead of any of the stationary models should note that they may wear against the knot separating the line from the leader or, more correctly, the knot to which a swivel should be attached. For this reason, it is a good idea to protect the line-swivel knot in some fashion; a good way to do this is to thread a short length of surgical tubing over the knot. In this manner, the sliding sinker will bump against the tubing itself and not weaken the knot.

Diving plane sinkers are stabilizing devices designed to allow the angler to reach and maintain the proper trolling or mooching depth without the use of standard lead sinkers. They also offer the advantage of permitting the fisherman to play his catch unhindered by excessive water drag, since these devices trip when strikes occur. Nevertheless, even after a diving plane has been tripped, it is likely to offer considerable drag through the water as the hooked fish makes long runs against the line; their flat metal or plastic surface areas make such drag almost inevitable. Compared to a standard mooching sinker of, say, four or five ounces in weight, the drag exerted by the diving plane sinker is likely to be only slightly greater.

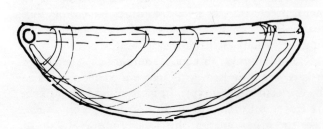

SLIDING SINKER

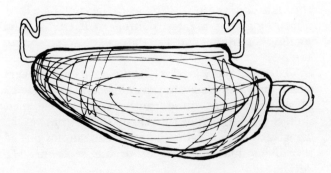

SLIP SINKER

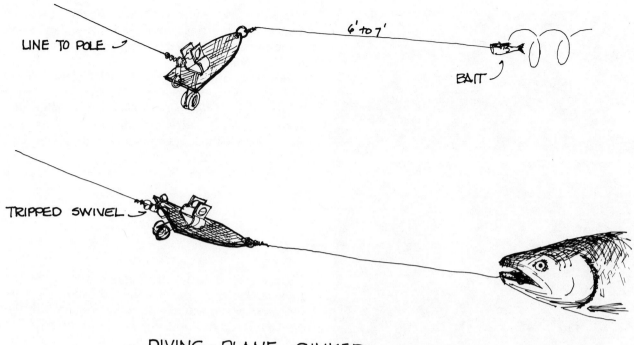

LINE TO POLE

6' to 7'

BAIT

TRIPPED SWIVEL

DIVING - PLANE SINKER

The chief objection to the use of diving planes is that they cause a strong, steady pressure against the line and rod tip while being trolled (or even drift-mooched) and until they are tripped. A rod holder, while not a necessity, is certainly a convenience when trolling a diving plane, and rod tips must be stiff enough to compensate for the added drag. Most experienced moochers favor the crescent or sliding sinkers over diving planes for this reason.

Diving planes come in various sizes, the selection of which depends on terminal tackle and the desired depth. The larger the plane, the greater will be the bite into the water and the greater will be the depth achieved. They are usually constructed of plastic or other synthetic materials and often weighted with lead on their undersides to give them horizontal stability.

Diving planes are used with a simple baitfish or artificial lure hookup but are seldom used with dodgers or rotating flashers because they have a tendency to minimize the action of the rod tip, thus making it difficult for the angler to determine if the terminal gear is working properly at all times. Additionally, the use of diving planes with such terminal gear greatly increases the water-drag of an already sufficiently heavy tackle combination.

The above notwithstanding, diving planes have become quite popular with some private sport fishermen and certain charter and party boat skippers in recent years. Despite their relatively expensive price tags, some believe that their bright pink, green, and other colors attract salmon toward the lure by arousing the interest and curiosity of nearby fish.

Flashers and Dodgers

Flashers and dodgers perform similar functions but are dissimilar in their movements through the water. Used primarily in deep or heavy tackle trolling, these devices are designed to provide an effective means of attracting the attention of passing salmon and to impart a certain action to the trailing baitfish or artificial lure.

Flashers are designed to loop or *rotate* when trolled at the proper speed, while salmon dodgers simply dart or *dodge* from side to side. While the latter also rotate if trolled too rapidly, they should display only a side-to-side—and not looping—motion.

Both devices are used with artificial spoons, plugs, and spinners but are more commonly employed in conjunction with rigged baitfish, salmon streamer flies, or rubber or plastic squid-type lures. In general, unless followed by an artifical lure which has some swimming action of its own, the trailing bait or lure should not display an independent motion but should instead follow the specific action created by the dodger or flasher. For this reason, baitfish trolled behind these devices are normally rigged rigidly and straight.

Salmon dodger (right) and flasher. Both make the bait or lure "swim" in a specific, desirable manner which is often irresistable to salmon. *Author photo.*

preference, and some fishermen believe that the metallic finishes attract more fish because they reflect the most light, while others swear by the duller or more subdued colors.

Both flashers and dodgers are oblong metal plates which display their specific actions because of their various bends and/or curves. Each is invariably constructed of metal and is available in different sizes. Anglers seem to use a wider range of dodger sizes; most popular are lengths of from about four to ten inches. Rotating flashers are frequently a foot or more in length.

Dodgers come in a variety of colors and finishes. Most popular are variations of chrome or brass finishes. Solid white—and in some cases, the brighter fluorescent red tones—are also frequently used in trolling. Sometimes the metal is hammered to vary the normal smooth finish; some dodgers display a combination of one or more colors or finishes.

Flashers, too, come in a variety of sizes and colors. The most popular are those of solid stainless steel which display a chromed finish. White is perhaps the second most popular finish.

Dodger and flasher finishes are a matter of personal

Hooks

Hooks are an extremely important part of any salmon tackle combination. Since they are the only tackle item which actually comes in contact with the fish, they should be of the finest quality and should be kept sharp at all times.

As with other salmon tackle items, hooks should be matched to the size of the baitfish and the approximate size of the quarry. In general, smaller hooks are required for relatively small baitfish such as candlefish, plug-cut herring, and herring strips, while somewhat larger hooks are reserved for relatively large baitfish and bigger game.

Many anglers arm themselves with expensive and profuse tackle items but fail to give considerable thought to hook choice. If a hook should fail to do its job, that of picking up and holding a potential catch, no array of lavish equipment will help. Because salmon hooks are of primary importance, they should be chosen wisely and with some knowledge of their characteristics.

In general, many of the smaller salt water hooks are made of metals which are *bent*. In contrast, the

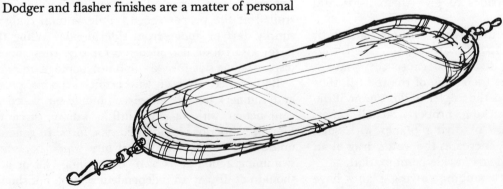

SALMON DODGER

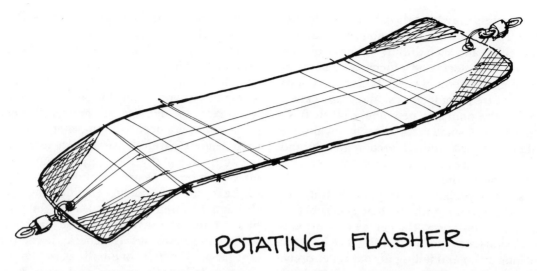

ROTATING FLASHER

larger hooks are often *forged*. Regardless of the process, salmon fishermen should select the finest (usually most expensive) hooks available for the task.

Only hooks intended specifically for use in salt water should be considered. Generally speaking, hooks designed for fresh-water use will not stand up to the corrosive effects of the sea. After using them once, anglers normally have to discard such rusty, ruined hooks. Hooks which are blued or bronzed typically turn rusty in short order, although there remain certain anglers who prefer to use hooks of these varieties, claiming that since they do not reflect the light as readily as do shiny stainless hooks, they are less apt to discourage hungry fish from striking. While there may be some validity to the notion, most veteran salmon anglers—trollers, moochers, party and charter boat operators, as well as commercial trollers—seem to prefer the standard stainless or other noncorrosive hooks and have demonstrated excellent results with them.

Stainless steel hooks are gaining in popularity among the West's sport salmon fishermen, although hooks which are plated with such materials as tin, cadmium, or nickel are also used. While the stainless hooks are both popular and effective, those fashioned of high-quality carbon steel are also to be sought by serious salmon fishermen.

Salmon hooks range from size 2/0 to 6/0, although both smaller and larger hooks are used infrequently. Given baitfish of the proper size, 2/0 hooks are normally sufficient for small coho, immature winter blackmouth, and pink salmon, for example, while 2/0 or 3/0 hooks are recommended for mature fall silvers, sockeye, chum, and medium-sized Chinook. Adult Chinook in the thirty- to forty-pound class are taken easily on strong, high quality hooks sized 3/0 or 4/0, while 5/0 or 6/0 hooks are suggested for extremely large kings, such as those sometimes encountered in the famed Tyee waters of Rivers Inlet, British Columbia, and other large-salmon areas.

Salmon hooks should be kept needle sharp at all

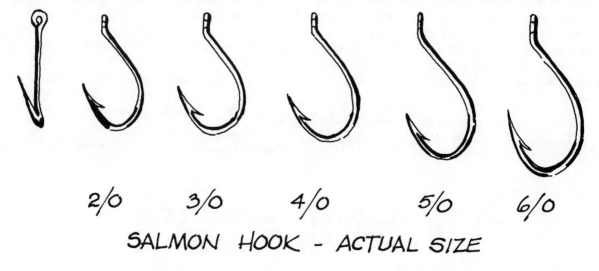

2/0   3/0   4/0   5/0   6/0

SALMON HOOK - ACTUAL SIZE

times. Hook points may be dulled by rocks, debris, and even by the somewhat bony mouths of salmon and other species, and such dulling of hook points is certain to result in decreased efficiency. The most successful salmon fishermen check their hook points for sharpness at frequent intervals, and many expert fishermen file the points of new hooks taken fresh from the package. A small metal file is an invaluable aid to salmon anglers and, if used regularly and properly, will ensure that hook points are sufficiently sharp at all times.

Sharpness is especially critical in fishing for Chinook, which often mouth the bait gently before taking it. In such instances, the degree of sharpness of the hook points may mean the difference between solidly hooking a fish and failing to connect entirely. And while an angler will never know if dull hook points are to be blamed when a strike is missed, the truly good salmon fisherman is able to greatly enhance his chances of success by regularly sharpening his hook points.

Salmon hooks are fished singly or in pairs. Most anglers prefer the double-hook rig, reasoning that two hooks increase the odds for success. If two hooks are tied in tandem, the trailing hook is normally one size smaller than the leading hook. This is so that the trailing hook may be better concealed in the aft portion of tapered baitfish.

Tandem hooks may be tied solidly to the same leader, or they may be tied so that the leading hook will slide along the leader. The adjustable or slip hook rigs are preferred by some fishermen because the distance between hooks may be modified to suit each individual baitfish. Adjustable hooks are also easier to work with.

Most expert salmon anglers prefer the solid tie hook/leader setup, however. They argue that sliding hooks may actually be counterproductive. That is, that they may accidentally twist and work against one another after a fish is hooked, thereby enabling the salmon to throw the hooks more easily.

Hooks may be purchased separately or already tied to leaders. While the pretied variety is adequate if of the finest quality (remember, both hooks *and* leaders must be of the finest quality available), most serious salmon fishermen prefer to tie their own leaders. And fishermen may save considerable expense by tying their own rigs, especially when dogfish, hake, or other unwanted species are present. These fish are notorious for taking salmon baits and are likely to damage numerous leaders in the process. Experienced salmon fishermen wisely check their leaders carefully after each such undesirable hookup, and many routinely change their leaders after such hookups are encountered. When dogfish or hake are abundant, salmon anglers may go through a dozen or more leaders in less than an hour. Thus, the savings can add up for fishermen who tie their own rigs. In general, home-tied leaders cost approximately one-half as much as do the commercially prepared, pretied leaders.

Whether pretied or home-tied hook/leader combinations are used, it is a good idea to have a wide assortment on hand at all times. Hooks of varying sizes should be available, already tied to leaders, to facilitate baitfish hookups. There is nothing quite so frustrating as to have to cease fishing temporarily in order to tie hooks to a leader—especially if there is a "hot bite" occurring simultaneously. Many a fish has been missed because of poor advance planning, and many an angler has learned the hard way to have an adequate supply of tied leaders on hand during his next outing.

Ancillary Equipment

With the exceptions of jetty or surf fishing (the former growing in popularity in recent years, the latter occurring only in rare instances) and fishing in or around the estuarial mouths of rivers and streams, virtually all fishing for salmon in salt water requires the use of a boat. Fishing from a privately owned craft offers the greatest freedom of movement. It also permits the angler the widest range of tackle and techniques.

Private boats used for saltwater salmon fishing

SLIDING HOOK FOR VARIOUS SIZE HERRING

range from small, freshwater models of fiberglass, aluminum, or wood to large, sleek pleasure cruisers capable of extended and wide-ranging trips. Such craft are hardly suited to the pocketbooks of most Pacific salmon enthusiasts but are favored by the wealthier angling/vacationing elite which frequent such popular areas as Washington's and Canada's San Juan Islands and other scenic areas.

But even the less affluent aficionados of angling for Pacific salmon species in salt water may do so from their own craft. The important consideration is that the boat be suited to the water to be fished.

In general, boats under about fourteen feet in length and without sufficient depth and beam to handle the normal ocean swells and sometimes rough wind-chops occurring even on the Pacific's inland marine waters should be ruled out. Even in the seemingly calm bays and harbors of the Pacific, waters are not always in line with the name of this great ocean. Sea-going vessels are *generally* those of about sixteen feet or longer, broad of beam and capable of coping with relatively rough water conditions, should they arise.

Despite the fact that numerous saltwater salmon anglers may be seen mooching or trolling from small canoes, inflatable rubber rafts, kayaks, and the like, such craft are perhaps better reserved for plying the inland lakes and calm, protected ponds in search of cutthroat trout. Even with the proper boats, numerous anglers lose their lives each year, usually while attempting to cross hazardous water during poor weather. Ocean fishing should be undertaken only by experienced boatmen who are familiar with

Small boat fishing is popular throughout the inland marine waters of the West, but is to be taken seriously by ocean-bound fishermen. These anglers, biologists for the Washington Department of Fisheries, are running up-wind for another mooching "drift" through productive king salmon feeding grounds. *Author photo.*

the water and whose judgment is sound at all times. The cardinal principle governing boat selection and use is *safety*; even where the admirable sport of angling is concerned, all else is secondary.

The same advice holds true for rental skiffs. While these are available at numerous Pacific ports, extreme caution should be coupled with solid experience. Some excellent skiff fishing may be found at various points where rentals are available. But anglers, even those who are sensible in matters other than those piscatorial, are often tempted into unwise decisions during questionable weather and water conditions. This is frequently the case in areas such as Washington's La Push and Neah Bay, for example, the harbors of which are well protected. But while no ocean bars exist here, conditions may be too dangerous for fishing at times.

In such instances, an excellent alternative is to opt for one of the charter or party boats which are available at most major salmon ports north of Monterey. In addition to offering a safe, worry-free means of ocean fishing, these craft are skippered by operators who are not only licensed but also familiar with the particular area, the tackle, and techniques. Moreover, they are likely to know the best times, places, and ways of taking salmon, and they will do virtually everything necessary to aid their angling patrons. Often this includes rigging and baiting tackle, netting, cleaning, and even filleting the fish. Thus, they provide perhaps the best means for achieving success, especially for novice fishermen.

But not all charter or party boat customers are new to the sport of salmon fishing. Many experienced anglers prefer fishing from such craft to running their own or rental boats. The chief disadvantage of fishing from a charter or party boat is that the individual angler has virtually no control: he may not determine the time of departure or return (unless otherwise prescribed by the boat operator), nor may he have much freedom in the choice of tackle and technique. Though he will be a paying customer, he is bound by common courtesy to abide by the wishes of both the skipper and his fellow fishermen, and only the most impolite of anglers impose their individual preferences on the majority. Charter and party boat fishing is not for the do-it-yourself angling fraternity.

Nor does a trip aboard a salmon charter or party boat ensure safety at all times. In candor, an occasional boat does run into trouble. Lives may be lost. I can think of a small number of such unfortunate occurrences which have taken place in my own bailiwick during the past few years. Still, such accidents are few and far between, if only because most charter skippers combine solid experience,

One of Washington-Oregon's most renowned charter boats, *Hobo* is among the new breed of offshore fishing craft—fast, comfortable, and extremely efficient. *Photograph courtesy of Hobo Charters, Inc., Ilwaco.*

Charter or party boat fishing isn't always hectic. There's often plenty of time to catnap while "the bite is off." *Author photo.*

(sometimes) formal training, and common sense. In most instances in which charter or party boat drownings or other serious accidents occur, bad weather is a primary contributing factor. A few boat operators continue to make trips during questionable weather because of economic pressures. But the majority, forever fearful of the consequences, opt for the safest alternative: when in doubt, don't fish! For any but the most reckless, the best idea is to pass up a salmon run if weather conditions appear to be hazardous. The best salmon trip is always the *next* one, and the next one may offer an additional margin of safety as well.

In addition to tackle and boats, salmon fishermen should be equipped with a number of other items. Sunglasses are recommended for all but the cloudiest of days, and polarized lenses are issued as standard equipment to field agents of numerous fisheries agencies throughout the country. Besides reducing glare, good sunglasses aid in the viewing of underwater objects and are particularly helpful when baitfish are being sought or when sharp rocks or other underwater obstructions are a hazard to boating safety.

Hats or caps are also recommended. They provide shade from the rays of the sun during a long day on the water and, if water-proofed, they will keep the rain from one's face. Foul weather gear, including both jackets and pants, are a virtual necessity during wet periods, and anglers are well-advised to purchase the best raingear available. This is especially true when fishing the waters of the Pacific Northwest, although sudden squalls and rain showers are encountered occasionally even in the more southerly latitudes. Good rain gear—including hats or hoods—can make the difference between a comfortable and enjoyable day on the water and a downright miserable one.

Boots are often necessary, and these should be treated to withstand water. Rubber boots are favored by most anglers. Even the sunniest of days does not preclude encountering water on the deck of a boat, and wet feet make for poor fishing companions. When boats must be launched from a trailer directly into the water, hip boots are most welcome.

Proper clothing is that which is suited to the particular locale and then-current weather. In general, it is better to have too much clothing than too little; excessive clothing may be removed quickly and easily as the weather warms. Wool stockings, insulated underwear and gloves, jackets, raingear, or other items of clothing, may provide welcomed relief from the cool morning and evening hours sometimes encountered during even warm weather trends.

Tackle boxes are necessary and come in a wide range of sizes and styles. Most salmon techniques require relatively little terminal tackle, and small- to medium-sized tackle boxes are usually adequate. On short-range fishing trips, it is seldom necessary to take the warehouse approach. Moreover, it is surprising how much terminal tackle may be fitted into a relatively small tackle box. The proper tackle box is the one which will hold only the terminal gear necessary for the specific angling technique or techniques to be employed.

At times, two tackle boxes are better than one. I routinely use two boxes, one large and one small. The larger box holds all gear which may possibly be required on a specific salmon trip; the small one holds only those items which I deem absolutely necessary for the task at hand. I make a habit of taking both aboard the boat. Although I rarely have to open the larger box, it is there in the event that I require additional hooks, leaders, sinkers, or other fishing items. Because the larger of the two boxes is a model designed to keep water from the inside while latched, I rarely have to clean or dry it or its contents.

While I strongly recommend traveling light when it comes to fishing Pacific salmon in salt water, it is

Good rain gear may not be absolutely essential for tricking fish, but it helps bring smiles of dry comfort. *Author photo, courtesy of* Salt Water Sportsman.

Sturdy rod holders are standard equipment aboard the Pacific coast's hundreds of charter craft. They're especially welcome when heavy tackle—such as this flasher combination—is used. *Author photo, courtesy of* Salt Water Sportsman.

Large, long-handled nets are required for taking Pacific salmon. *Author photo*.

far better to be overequipped than underequipped. It is a good idea to have a representative sampling of all fishing items which may be required under normal circumstances. The key word is *normal*; this does not mean that anglers should bring every piece of tackle from home. In most instances, however, an extra rod and reel should be brought aboard the boat: rods are apt to become broken and reels may follow suit. It is frustrating indeed to watch your fishing partner land fish after fish when your own

tackle is out of commission. To do so is only slightly less disconcerting than having to mooch in calm water with sinkers weighing twenty ounces apiece!

Rod holders are convenient for some salmon fishing techniques but are absolutely mandatory when fishing with the heavier terminal tackle. These should be strong and of good quality, capable of firmly holding a stout rod trolling a flasher and up to thirty-two ounces of weight. To hand-hold such a tackle combination for several hours is uncomfortable at best.

Rod holders should have a quick-release feature which allows the angler to take his rod in hand at a moment's notice. Especially with Chinook, which may mouth the bait gently before inhaling it deeply, quick-release rod holders give the fishermen the opportunity to rapidly feed out line to an interested salmon and to feel the sometimes sensitive and slight nibbling tug at the business end.

While some anglers prefer gaff hooks, nets are by far more popular among salt water salmon anglers. These nets are typically made of aluminum, have large frames and relatively long handles, and sufficient netting capacity to hold salmon of over fifty pounds. Smaller nets should be avoided; they are frequently incapable of handling salmon which may turn out to be larger than anticipated.

The properly equipped saltwater salmon angler will not only take more fish but will find considerably more comfort and enjoyment on the water than will his ill-equipped comrades.

Notes

1. Frank Woolner, *Modern Saltwater Sport Fishing* (New York: Crown, 1972), p. 13.

3
BAITS AND LURES

DESPITE the many advances in recent years in the development and production of artificial lures, baitfish remain the most popular sportfishing means of taking salmon from salt water. While candlefish and other baits are sometimes used, Pacific herring—in various forms and hookups—are the mainstay of the salmon-for-fun angling masses.

Pacific herring (*Clupea pallasii*) belong to that group of schooling fish which also includes sardines and the American shad. Salt water spawners, herring are abundant throughout the Pacific Northwest, and their range coincides to a large extent with that of the various Pacific salmon species. Unlike salmon, which invariably display adipose fins, herring lack such adornments; they are, however, soft-rayed fish (as are salmon) which display only a single dorsal fin. They typically measure five to eight inches but may run a foot or more in length.

Herring baits may be rigged whole, cut into "plugs" or "spinners." At times, whole herring are more effective for tricking salmon than are any of the cut types, and they are often trolled or mooched when baits are exceptionally small and of an inadequate size for cutting. When baitfish have rather soft flesh, anglers fare better fishing them whole than attempting to cut them.

While larger herring are sometimes trolled or mooched when the quarry are exceptionally large Chinook, the most effective whole herring baits run between about five and seven inches in length. Usually, veteran salmon fishermen prefer fresh-killed baits, although frozen herring of good quality may also be fished whole.

There are several ways in which whole herring may be rigged. While each method has its own champions, all are effective at certain times and in certain places. Relatively little experience in hooking herring baits is required; even novice anglers may learn the various rigging methods after a few attempts.

One effective means of hooking a whole herring with tandem hooks is to insert the trailing hook through the fish's lower jaw, letting it exit through the top of the nose. The leader is pulled through until the leading hook nears the point of entry at the lower jaw. The second hook is then threaded through the same channel as the first. The trailing hook is next run through the eye sockets, but so that there is no damage to the eyeball, exiting on either right or left side, and the leading hook follows suit. The trailing hook is embedded on the side of the baitfish which is opposite the exit point from the eye socket. The hook should be embedded between the dorsal fin and tail, about halfway down the fish's side. The leading hook is seated on the side opposite the trailing hook. The recommended placement point for the leading hook is about one-third of the way down the side of the baitfish.

Whole herring may also be rigged so that both hooks are embedded in the same side of the fish. In this method, both the trailing and leading hooks are run from the lower jaw through the nose and from one eye socket through to the other, exactly as described for the baitfish hookup above. Instead of placing the trailing hook in the side opposite the eye socket exit point however, the trailing hook is embedded between the dorsal fin and tail on the *same* side as the eye socket exit point. The leading

A herring turned the trick for this happy salmon angler.
Author photo.

hook is seated mid-way between the head and dorsal fin on the same side as the trailing hook, again about one-third of the way down the side of the fish.

A third popular means of fishing herring whole revolves around the use of only a single—and not tandem—hookup. In this method, the single hook is run from the lower jaw through the nose, then passed from one eye socket through the other, just as in previous examples. The single hook is embedded at a point about halfway down the side of the baitfish, roughly parallel to the dorsal fin.

Double (tandem) hooks may be used to rig whole

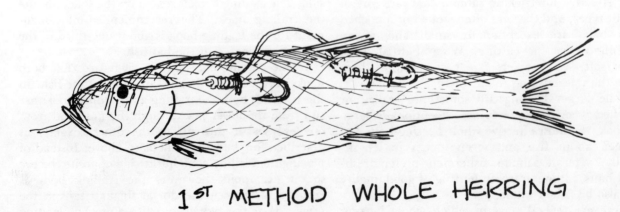

1ST METHOD   WHOLE HERRING

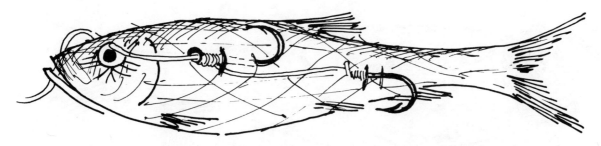

2ND METHOD WHOLE HERRING

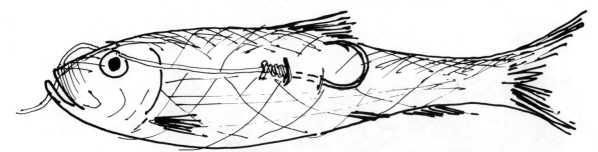

3RD METHOD WHOLE HERRING

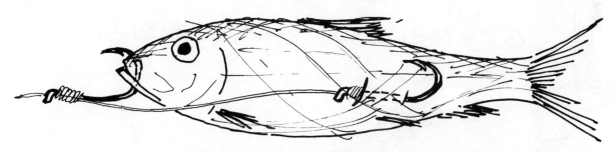

4TH METHOD WHOLE HERRING

herring when time is a critical factor, such as when the angler finds himself in the midst of a hot bite. At such times, two hooks may be used to hold a whole herring, and they may be rigged nearly as quickly as a single hook. The leading hook is simply brought up through the lower jaw until the hook-point exits from the nose, and the trailing hook is embedded on either side of the herring, about mid-way between back and belly and slightly behind the dorsal fin.

Another means of using only a single hook with a whole herring is to run the hook-point through the lower portion of both eye sockets, loop the leader underneath the lower jaw, then again thread the hook through both eye sockets—this time in the same direction but near the top of the sockets.

Still a sixth method of rigging a whole herring with tandem salmon hooks is to simply thread first the trailing hook, then the leading one, through the lower jaw until they have exited from the nose. The trailing

hook is seated mid-way between head and dorsal fin.

Among the most popular and effective salmon baits are herring which have been *plug-cut*—double beveled behind the head at an angle of approximately forty-five degrees. The result is a natural bait which swims like an artificial salmon plug but more closely resembles a wounded baitfish.

To properly plug a herring, a sharp knife is necessary. Dull knives tend to ruin the bait's swimming action, especially if herring are somewhat soft to begin with. The ideal plug-cut herring is that which is cut in a single knife stroke—no ragged edges where the head has been removed.

Plug-cut herring may be cut from either fresh or frozen baitfish, although baits which have been fresh-killed are the more desirable. As with all salmon baits, herring flesh should be as firm as possible, and only baits with their scales intact should be used.

59

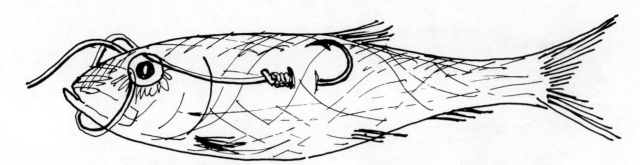

5TH METHOD WHOLE HERRING

6TH METHOD WHOLE HERRING

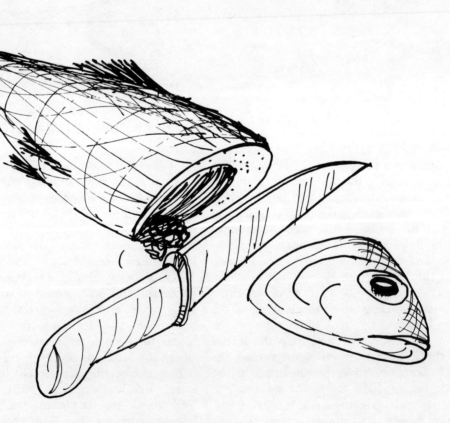

PLUG-CUT HERRING

Once a herring is properly plugged, its entrails should be removed. If bait is still somewhat frozen, it may be rigged and fished with the entrails intact for a short period of time. The water will quickly thaw the baitfish and the stomach and other innards should be removed as soon as possible.

While there are innumerable variations on hooking plug-cut herring, most hookups involve the use of double (tandem) hooks, with the trailing hook usually one size smaller than the leading one.

One popular method of using tandem hooks to rig a herring which has been plugged is to insert the trailing hook near the fish's spine where the head has been removed. The hook point should exit about an inch from the exposed flesh but about one-third down the side of the baitfish. The leading hook is run through the same channel. The trailing hook is then embedded on the side of the fish opposite that from which it exited. The hook should be seated about mid-way between back and belly but toward the rear of the fish and behind the dorsal fin. The leading hook should be embedded on the opposite side, about one-third down the side of the fish but just behind the exposed flesh.

Another method of using tandem hooks to rig a plug-cut herring is to run both hooks through a point on the exposed flesh, where the head has been removed, but near the spine, allowing them to exit as described above. In this hookup, however, only the leading hook is embedded in the flesh; the trailing hook is allowed to dangle free. The leading hook is seated approximately halfway down the side of the herring and just forward of the dorsal fin.

A third variation of the method of using tandem hooks to rig a herring which has been plugged is to run only the leading hook through the flesh. It is inserted inside the hollow body cavity and brought up through the side or back. The trailing hook is allowed to hang free, as in the above example, but is not run through the flesh of the baitfish. This type of herring hookup is often erroneously referred to as a "Westport hookup," in reference to Westport, Washington, that state's second most productive salmon port. While it is true that many charter skippers operating out of the Grays Harbor fishing village do use this hookup, it probably did not originate here. It is likely that this method of rigging a baitfish was in use before the Washington port became a charter fishing capital in the 1940s and 1950s. Still, many Westport charter operators opt for this method of rigging a herring because it is so easy and does not require a great deal of skill. This method of hooking a plug-cut herring is also one of the quickest, an important consideration when skip-

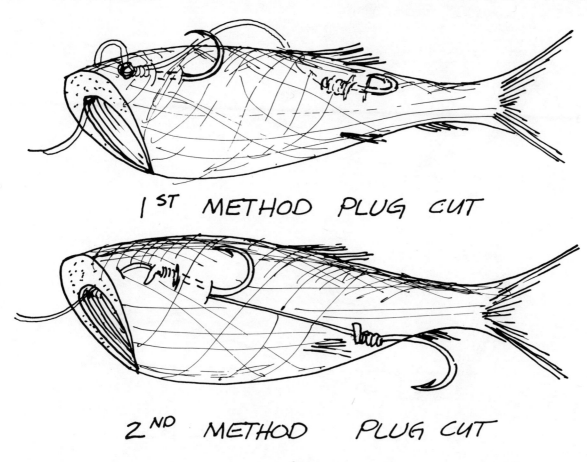

1ST METHOD PLUG CUT

2ND METHOD PLUG CUT

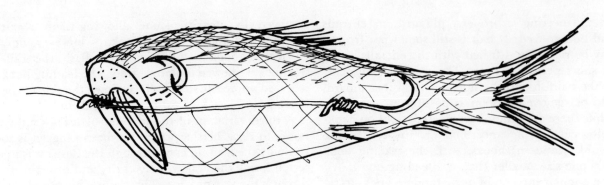

3ᴿᴰ METHOD   PLUG CUT

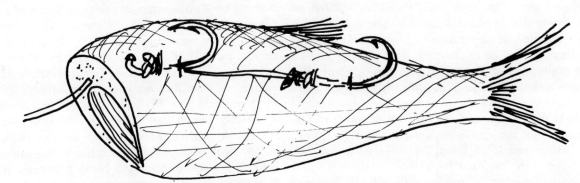

4ᵀᴴ METHOD   PLUG CUT

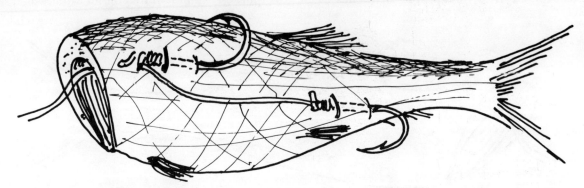

5ᵀᴴ METHOD   PLUG CUT

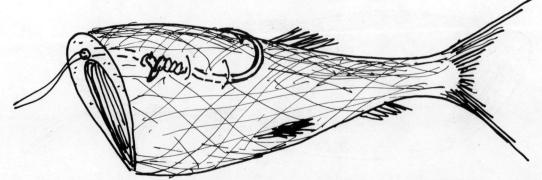

SINGLE HOOK 1ˢᵀ METHOD

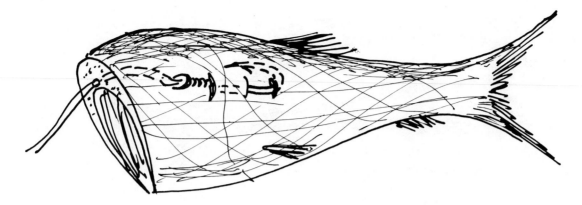

SINGLE HOOK 2ND METHOD

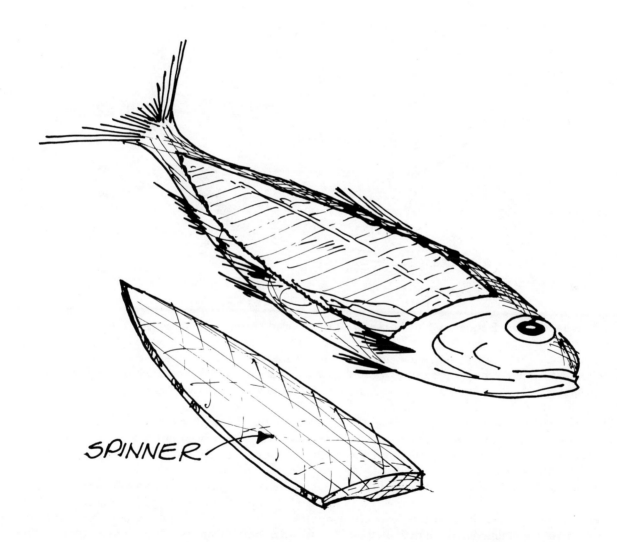

SPINNER

SPINNER CUT HERRING

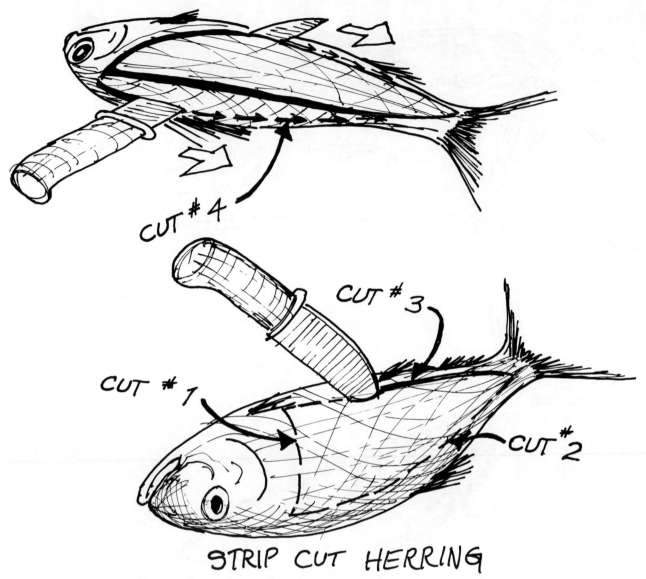

CUT #4

CUT #3

CUT #1

CUT #2

STRIP CUT HERRING

pers and deckhands must frequently bait hooks for large numbers of charter passengers.

Still another means of rigging a herring which has been plugged with tandem hooks is to thread both hooks from a point on the exposed flesh near the spine to a point about an inch behind the exposed flesh. The exit point should be slightly above the mid-point between back and belly. The leading hook is seated just behind the exit point, and the trailing hook is embedded on the same side of the baitfish but about parallel with the rear portion of the dorsal fin.

Still a fifth variation is possible. Hooks are threaded through the herring as outlined in the fourth method, except that the trailing hook is seated in the *lower* rear portion of the baitfish, pointing downward.

Plug-cut herring may also be rigged with a single salmon hook. One way of doing this is to leave the hook point exposed. In this method, the hook point is inserted into the exposed flesh at a point near the

spine and brought out approximately an inch behind the cut. It is then seated into the flesh, just under the skin, slightly above the halfway line between back and belly but in front of the dorsal fin.

Many anglers feel that baits display more life if hook points are embedded in the flesh. Another means of rigging a plug-cut herring with a single hook is to thread the hook and leader as illustrated on page 62 but to reverse the hook point and reinsert it into the skin and flesh.

Cut baits also include herring fillets which are taken from either side of a large herring. Called "cut spinners," "cut slabs," or "cut strips," these baits require an extremely sharp knife point and may be cut only from herring which is solidly or partially frozen. After they have been cut, they may be allowed to thaw, of course, but cutting them from fresh or thawed herring usually results in ragged baits which lack the proper swimming action in the water.

The illustrations on pages 63 and 64 show a cut

spinner or slab cut herring. Strip cut baits are achieved via the same cutting procedure, except that an additional cut is made from the midpoint of the leading edge to the tail end, thus dividing the slab into two parts. Only the top half should be used, and it may be rigged in a fashion similar to that shown for cut spinners below.

Hooking is an integral part of fishing cut spinners, slabs or strip baits, just as it is with whole or plug-cut herring. In order to obtain an enticing swimming motion, cut spinners or strips should be rigged with tandem hooks. The trailing hook is inserted near the top portion of the strip or slab, then pulled through. Next, the leading hook is embedded in the channel left by the trailing hook. Usually, the trailing hook is permitted to dangle free, although it may be seated in the lower rear portion of the slab or strip as long as the bait swims enticingly. Hooks may also be inserted on the flesh side of the slab or strip, then run through to the skin side.

While the above baitfish are intended to display a definite swimming action of their own and should imitate live but wounded baitfish, most baits used in conjunction with dodgers or rotating flashers should be rigged rigidly and straight and should simply follow the erratic movements produced by the leading dodger or flasher blades. Two of the most popular and effective baitfish hookups for use behind dodgers and flashers are the "candlefish cut" and the "toothpick rig."

The candlefish herring hookup is not, of course, a candlefish at all. Rather, it is a herring which has been cut and rigged to resemble the smaller, thinner baitfish species. This bait hookup is a good one for herring which are slightly too large to be fished whole.

To achieve the correct bait appearance, the head and forward belly are removed, and a notch is cut from the lower half of the forward portion of the stomach section. A single hook, run through the leading portion of the baitfish from underneath, is used to hold the bait, followed by another single, double, or treble hook. If a treble hook is used, one of the hook points may be inserted into the baitfish.

In order to properly rig a whole herring for use behind a dodger or flasher blade, a long metal or plastic threader, similar to a knitting needle, is used. The threader is notched near the point in order to hold the leader. The threader is inserted into the mouth of the herring and run through the body until the point—and notch—emerges from the anal opening. The leader, which has been tied in a loop, is then placed in the notch of the threading needle and retrieved through the mouth.

Single, double, or treble hooks may be used, although the favored rig includes a 1/0 treble hook, one point of which is firmly embedded near the tail of the baitfish. A small brass clip is used to hold the baitfish's mouth closed, and a toothpick or similar straight object is pushed into the baitfish, parallel to its spine, to keep the bait as straight as possible.

While most baits employed in conjunction with

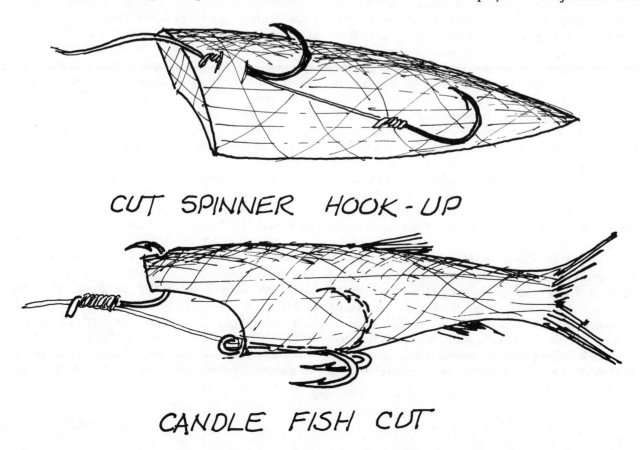

CUT SPINNER HOOK-UP

CANDLE FISH CUT

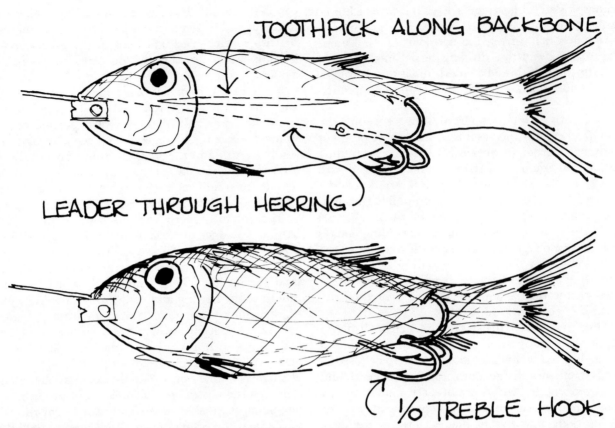

TOOTHPICK ALONG BACKBONE

LEADER THROUGH HERRING

1/0 TREBLE HOOK

salmon dodgers and/or rotating flashers are rigged to swim straight, anglers consistently elicit strikes with baits which are intended to swim on their own. Whole herring, plug-cut baits, and even cut slabs and strips all bring strikes at times when trolled behind heavy terminal dodgers or flashers. One wonders if the reason that salmon are reported to prefer one type of baitfish hookup over another is that the majority of anglers use that hookup. Like many other species, it appears as if Pacific salmon will strike almost any bait—at times. In fact, the author has examined the contents of numerous salmon and found, among other things, the *heads* of baitfish which had apparently been plug-cut! Ostensibly, these are just as delectable as are the bodies of plug-cut herring—to hungry salmon. Perhaps the best advice is that anglers experiment with different baitfish hookups. Experimentation often pays handsome rewards in the world of salt water salmon angling.

Using live baitfish to entice salmon from the salt or brackish waters is an ancient and effective method of sport fishing. Although the popularity of this technique is slowly growing throughout the United States, live bait fishing is especially popular among British Columbia's sport salmon fraternity. Live bait fishing may be conducted with herring, anchovies, or other baitfish, but herring is most popular.

Anglers using live herring or other baits should exercise extreme care when handling and hooking baitfish. Most good live bait anglers prefer hooks of considerably smaller size than those used in fishing dead baitfish. If a single hook is used, it may be run through the nose or back of the baitfish. A more effective hookup is attained by using a single hook followed by a trailing double or treble hook.

Artificial salmon lures range from long streamer flies to weighted spoons and spinners. Between these extremes lie a myriad of "wobblers," plugs and squidlike lures. Virtually any artificial salmon lure may be fished alone or in conjunction with dodgers or flashers.

Spoons and spinners are used extensively by fresh water salmon anglers. Their saltwater usage is somewhat restricted to certain geographical areas, most notably the waters of British Columbia. But fishermen also use these artificials to trick Pacific salmon in the estuarial waters surrounding numerous salmon streams.

Spoons and spinners differ greatly in size, color, and type, and their swimming actions vary significantly. Most popular are medium-sized salmon lures in stainless steel, brass, or copper finishes. These are especially effective on Chinook and are employed frequently around the mouths of California and

66

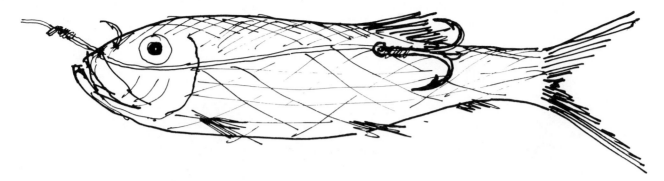

LIVE HERRING HOOK-UP

An effective artificial lure for Pacific salmon. *Author photo*.

SALMON SPOON RIG

An assortment of salmon plugs. *Author photo.*

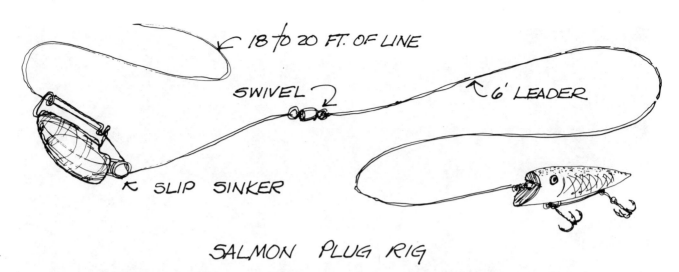

SALMON PLUG RIG

Oregon salmon rivers. Brightly colored spoons and spinners find some degree of popularity among Chinook and coho fishermen but are most effective on sockeye and pink salmon. Various shades of red or red and white combinations are favored for these species. Wobblers, similar to salmon spoons, are also extensively used.

Spoons and spinners may be weighted, in which case they may be trolled or cast from a boat, jetty, or shore. At times they are plunked—cast into the current and held in place by a heavy sinker. If greater weight is required for trolling or casting, anglers may add lead sinkers.

Salmon plugs are gaining in popularity in certain Western waters. These lures are made of wood or plastic and are shaped somewhat like a short length of broomstick. Cut and notched at various angles or molded in numerous designs and colors, plugs achieve a distinct swimming motion and are usually equipped with one or more hooks, often treble hooks. Like the other artificials, properly fished plugs are very effective in tricking salmon.

Salmon flies also come in a wide range of colors and patterns. Traditionally, these have been constructed of polar bear fur, but synthetic materials are rapidly gaining in popularity as the availability of natural hackle declines.

While flies are used fairly extensively by river and stream fishermen, saltwater fly fishing for Pacific salmon seldom includes casting. The most popular fly fishing methods revolve around the use of flies which are trolled—either on or near the surface for coho, or behind flashers and dodgers for both Chinook and coho.

Regardless in which manner flies are trolled, the same patterns and colors may be used. Most salmon flies are tied onto tubing, rather than directly onto a hook, and this permits the flies to slide freely along the leader or line. Flies may be changed quickly by simply removing them from a leader and threading another hollow-core model onto the same leader.

The best salmon flies, like flies used for almost any other sport fish, are tied sparsely. Usually they include green and white coloration, although blue and white or yellow and white hackle combinations are also popular. Frequently, salmon fly bodies are constructed of a series of brightly colored beads which may be threaded over the line or leader.

Other salmon flies are of the "tinsel" variety. These are similar to the standard salmon streamers but include metallic bodies and/or hackle. Tinsel flies are usually more brightly colored than their standard counterparts, and they find their greatest use among coho fishermen.

All salmon flies designed for use on Pacific salmon may be trolled without weight when coho are feeding near the surface, or they may be trolled behind dodgers or flashers.

Artificial squidlike lures are very popular among Western salmon anglers and have been used with great success by Canadian commercial fishermen in recent years. They have proved extremely effective on sockeye salmon, commercially taken. Plastic or rubber squid are almost always trolled behind a dodger or flasher.

Squid-type lures are available in a wide range of colors. Relatively large squid in various tones of red are effective for coho, while smaller versions in the same or similar color combinations are used for sport-caught sockeye. For Chinook, the most popular squid colors are blue or green. These lures, like most salmon flies, are designed to slide freely along the leader and may be changed rapidly.

Some plastic or rubber squid have iridescent

Assorted salmon flies for saltwater use. *Author photo*.

finishes, small flecks embedded in the artificial surface to reflect the available light. Like the other "hoochies"—squid-type lures—the iridescent varieties are extremely effective when trolled in conjunction with dodgers or rotating flashers.

4
THE TECHNIQUES

NUMEROUS techniques are employed by sport anglers to take Pacific salmon from salt or brackish water. All methods are productive *at certain times and in certain places*. Through experience and research, we have come to learn much about the habits and characteristics of the various Pacific species, and the result is that we are now able to determine or predict with some degree of accuracy the behavior of certain species.

Doubtless the best angling technique is the one which produces fish. But quite often salmon may be taken at the same time and place by fishermen employing different tackle and techniques. At other times and in other places, a single angling technique is productive. When fishing is slow, experimentation may provide the only answer.

Almost without exception, the best salmon fishermen—like their brothers on other fishing grounds and in search of other game—are experimenters. Such anglers are likely to find the most effective means of tricking fish under almost any circumstances and in virtually any locale. Other anglers, usually less successful, prefer to stick to a single technique and specific, prescribed tackle combination.

While there are variations and additions, the basic techniques employed in salt water salmon fishing are: (1) deep and/or heavy trolling; (2) flasher or dodger fishing; (3) light to medium trolling; (4) mooching; (5) fly fishing; (6) spinning or casting; (7) live bait fishing; and (8) jetty or shore fishing.

Each technique has its place and its champions. And, while it cannot be disputed that a specific technique will produce better than others at certain times and places, each method—properly learned, executed, and employed with the correct tackle combination—is effective.

Deep and/or Heavy Trolling

Deep and/or heavy trolling (sometimes called "deeplining") is one of the most effective ways of taking salmon from salt water. This is especially true when fishing for Chinook, which are usually found at greater depths than coho.

While Chinook often roam and feed in shallow water or near the surface of deep water, they are usually found near the bottom. Their shallow-water, surface-feeding treks are limited chiefly to the relatively dark hours of the day. It has been demonstrated that most Pacific salmon species—Chinook included—swim near the water's surface at night. Because of their surface-cruising habits, these fish are often found in the upper water strata during the first light of day. Similarly, they are likely to be taken near the surface at dusk.

During the brighter daylight hours, however, Chinook (and to some extent certain other Pacific species) tend to head for deeper, darker water. At such times they are sometimes found just off—or right on—the bottom, often in water of one hundred feet or more. Primarily to hook fish when they are cruising at great depth, anglers have devised and refined various techniques which call for relatively heavy gear.

There are several ways in which deep trolling may be accomplished, but all involve the use of heavy sinkers and the accompanying tackle necessary to achieve and maintain relatively great depth.

Fishing depth depends on several factors. Obviously, the amount of weight used will partially determine the depth at which the terminal tackle is trolled. So, too, will the length of line out at any given moment. But other factors, equally important, also influence trolling depth. Too often are some of these factors ignored by anglers.

The diameter of the fishing line is one such factor. Line of a small diameter meets less water resistance than does line of a greater (fatter) diameter. Because of this, a steeper line angle is possible with small-diameter line than with line which is relatively large in diameter. And a steeper line angle means a greater trolling depth.

Line material is another important consideration, because the weight of a line—like that of a sinker—will determine, partially at least, the trolling depth achieved. Nylon line, for example, is relatively light in weight when contrasted with, say, single-strand metal line, such as stainless steel. Obviously, the metal line will troll at a steeper angle—and hence greater terminal depth—than will a lightweight synthetic line.

Trolling speed also helps to determine the depth at which the terminal gear is operating at any given time. Increasing the trolling speed will mean a flatter line angle and will result in a decrease in the depth of the terminal end as water drag increases with speed. Thus, terminal tackle will be working more shallowly as trolling speed is increased.

In similar fashion, trolling against the tide or current will result in a flatter line angle—and less ter-minal depth—than will trolling with the current. Wind, too, influences the depth at which the terminal tackle is operating at any given moment to the extent that it increases or decreases boat speed and drag against the line and terminal gear.

The terminal tackle itself has a great effect upon the depth at which it is trolled. Flashers and dodgers, for example, exert greater water drag than does a simple crescent-shaped sinker and baitfish. The less water resistance, the greater will be the depth at which such tackle is operating at a given time.

All of these factors combine to determine the precise depth at which the baitfish or lure is trolled, and knowledgeable salmon anglers are not only aware of the various influencing factors but make periodic adjustments to correspond with the particular situation.

One favorite deep trolling technique is to use a relatively stout rod of about six to seven feet in length, a heavy-duty saltwater level-wind, star-drag reel of the multiplying type, and fairly hefty fishing line. Either metal or nylon monofilament line may be used. To the line is attached a heavy trolling sinker of up to about twenty-four ounces, followed by a single baitfish or lure.

A heavy rod is needed to handle the relatively heavy sinker, and the rod tip should be moderately stiff. Metal line of about fifty pounds breaking strength is recommended. Sinkers are of the oval or semiround variety to reduce drag, and relatively short leaders are used. Such a tackle combination is simply trolled slowly and at varying depths. Trolling too rapidly will result in improper bait or lure action and insufficient depth.

Another efficient means of achieving great troll-

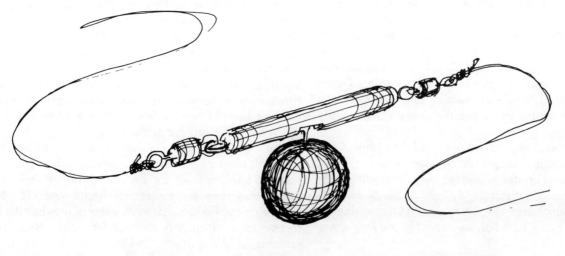

SINKER RELEASE DEVICE

ing depth is to use a sinker release mechanism instead of a standard salmon trolling sinker (while round or oval sinkers are frequently used, less drag is exerted by kidney-shaped slip sinkers or the banana-like mooching weights). Sinker release devices are designed to allow the weight to fall free of the line when a fish is hooked.

Anglers using sinker release devices may use the same tackle as that used in the various standard deep or heavy trolling techniques. The disadvantage of employing these mechanisms is that sinkers are lost (they simply fall to the bottom) when the device is tripped. For anglers to whom the pocketbook is an important consideration, sinker release devices are not the answer. Heavy lead weights costing what they do today, most salmon fishermen shy away from tackle items which result in considerable added expense.

Still a third method of deeplining is to use a downrigger. These innovations consist of large reels which hold separate lines to which are attached heavy lead weights. Lead balls may weigh eight pounds or more. Often called "cannonballs," these lead weights are lowered into the water as fishing line is let out. As with sinker release devices, downrigger balls fall free of the fishing line when tripped, as when a solid strike is encountered. Unlike sinker release mechanisms, however, downriggers allow the angler to retain his weights: when

tripped, weights are not lost but may instead be retrieved on their own lines.

Actually, modern downriggers *are* sinker release devices which permit the angler to retain the expensive lead weights for use over and again. The modern versions come equipped with handcranks which enable the angler to retrieve the heavy lead balls with greater ease than in earlier days. Many such devices also have built-in line meters which allow the fisherman to determine at precisely what depth his terminal gear is working.

Less sophisticated downriggers are also used extensively by salt water salmon trollers. All that is required is a heavy lead weight and a length of strong twine or other line material. The more primitive downriggers enable the fisherman to play his catch unhindered by the excessive lead weight once the line is tripped, and they permit the angler to retrieve his weight via the nonfishing line, which is fastened securely to both boat and sinker. Trolling depth may be varied by varying the length of the downrigger line.

Fish- and depth-finders are also increasing in popularity. These recent technological innovations are electronic devices which alert the angler to the presence of fish and baitfish schools, and they also indicate underwater features of interest to saltwater salmon fishermen. Although still relatively expensive, these gadgets are especially effective in deep

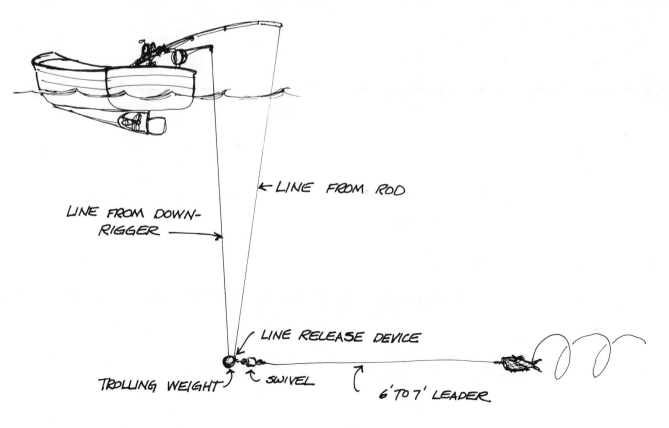

trolling. Perhaps their main advantage is their ability to show the contour of the bottom. Bottom features are of particular interest to Chinook salmon anglers, since these fish are often found over holes or foraging near underwater shelves or dropoffs.

Depth sounders and fish locators are available in a wide range of models. They range from the relatively inexpensive to those costing several hundred dollars. Depending upon the ability and willingness to pay the going rates, anglers may opt for any of a seemingly endless list of models—or they may opt to fish without any such device whatsoever! These instruments are recent inventions or relatively recent adaptations of older innovations, unknown to our grandfathers in sport use.

Flasher and Dodger Fishing

Flashers and dodgers are very effective for taking salmon from salt water. As previously noted, flashers are designed to rotate in large, lazy loops, while dodgers should simply dodge from side to side without revolving. Each may be used with a variety of artificial lures but each is most commonly followed by herring or other baitfish, squidlike lures, or salmon flies.

Dodgers are effective in fishing for both Chinook and coho. They may be trolled at great depth or near the surface. While they are effective on both mature and immature Chinook, they are used extensively to attract silvers. Thus, they are normally trolled in the top thirty or forty feet of water, where coho are most frequently found.

Dodgers require relatively stiff rods of nine feet in length or less, small- to medium-sized salt water salmon reels capable of holding up to about three hundred yards of line and relatively heavy lead sinkers of up to approximately twenty ounces, although much lighter weights are used at times. Trolling line may be constructed of metal or synthetic monofilament; usually, anglers use mono unless considerable weight is required, although metal line is preferable because it does not have the built-in elastic qualities of synthetic line and therefore does not distort the action of the dodger. Breaking strength of the line may range anywhere from approximately twenty to fifty pounds. Rod holders should be employed because of the relatively heavy drag against the water.

Some dodger fishermen use lighter tackle—especially when fishing nearer the surface primarily for coho—but the heavier gear outlined above is

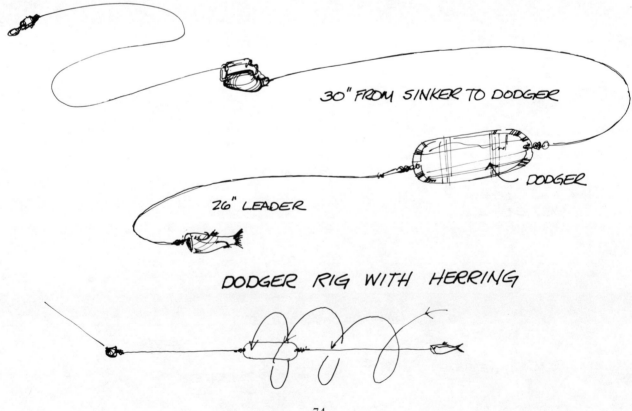

30" FROM SINKER TO DODGER

DODGER

26" LEADER

DODGER RIG WITH HERRING

74

recommended when trolling deep for Chinook.

Rotating flashers are used in trolling for both Chinook and coho, and they are trolled much more rapidly than are dodgers. The large flashers are particularly effective for taking Chinook at relatively great depths.

While some anglers eschew heavy tackle fishing (most commonly that conducted with dodgers or flashers), there are numerous advantages to using such equipment. Although both dodgers and flashers exert considerable drag against the rod tip, tackle combinations which are properly rigged and fished are amazingly sensitive. Once the angler becomes familiar with this type of gear and has gained some experience in its actual use, he will be able to determine a salmon strike on such tackle almost as easily as does a moocher or fly fisherman. Moreover, while salmon (especially Chinook) are often prone to gently nudging a trolled or mooched batifish which is fished with lighter tackle, they usually strike dodger or flasher combinations with more zest and relish: seldom will a gentle, repeated mouthing of the baitfish occur; instead, salmon strikes are apt to be singular and sudden. And dogfish, hake, and other unwanted fare are rarely

Large rotating flashers like this one are generally thought to be the most effective piece of terminal tackle ever designed for sport salmon fishing. Flies, hoochies, or baitfish are trolled behind. *Author photo, courtesy of* Salt Water Sportsman.

attracted to dodger or flasher rigs, while they may be common nuisances for light-tackle moochers who frequently work their baits just off—or right on—the bottom.

Still another advantage of using these devices is that, since they are trolled rapidly (especially flashers), anglers may cover a much broader fishing area than can moochers or light-tackle trollers in a given period of time. Rotating flashers are trolled faster than virtually any other type of salmon gear, and such rapid trolling is particularly advantageous during slow fishing periods when search-and-find tactics offer the best chance of success.

Not the least of the advantages of using rotating flashers is that, properly rigged and trolled, these devices take more salmon than does any other tackle! A bold statement? Perhaps. But consider the evidence.

In their book, *Saltwater Fishing in Washington*, authors Frank Haw and Raymond M. Buckley describe a scientific study which was conducted in that state's Puget Sound, near the Seattle-Tacoma area. The program involved the taking, tagging, and release of large numbers of coho and Chinook salmon. The authors themselves took part in the study, one of the goals of which was to determine "how many salmon were available to efficient anglers. In order to do this, rotating flasher gear was used because it is considered to be the most effective sport gear available."[1]

A total of four rotating flasher combinations were trolled over a period of forty-three days. At the end of that time, 1,100 salmon had been taken. This works out to an average daily catch of nearly twenty-six fish, all four rods included. When this average daily catch of twenty-six salmon is divided by the number of flasher combinations used, it becomes readily apparent that the researchers' use of rotating flashers resulted in an astounding overall catch: *over six salmon per rod were taken daily, on average!*

It should be noted that, at the time the study was conducted, the daily allowable salmon limit, per angler, was three fish. Thus, experimenters averaged over *twice* the allowable daily limit—consistently, over a period of forty-three days—using properly rigged and trolled rotating flasher equipment!

Haw and Buckley note that, at the time the experiment was conducted, the "average" Puget Sound salmon fisherman was taking between 0.1 to 0.2 salmon per angling day. They conclude that the "average" angler "could increase his catch by a factor of 10 by using flasher gear."[2] While flashers (and, to some extent, dodgers) are not for everyone, sport salmon anglers who would like to increase their odds of scoring might wish to try the heavier tackle.

The authors, both fisheries biologists for the Washington State Department of Fisheries, recommend that gear similar to the type described here be used:

A good flasher combination is a stout rod of about nine feet in length, a heavy-duty salt water reel, fifty-pound test single-strand metal line, and a heavy lead sinker of from ten to thirty-two ounces.

Rods used in trolling rotating flasher gear should have sufficient spine to cope with the relatively heavy terminal rig but do not have to be of the broomstick variety. In fact, while rods should have enough starch to handle the accompanying equipment, their tips must be relatively sensitive so that the angler is able to read the action of the flasher and to ensure that it is working properly at all times. Rods should have long, sturdy butt sections and metal reel seats. The guides should be strong and of the finest quality available. Nine-foot rods are recommended because of the inordinately long distance between the lead sinker and the terminal lure. (The experimenters used a Betts rod, model 5318.)

Because heavy metal line is recommended for use with rotating flashers and accompanying tackle items, heavy-duty reels are required. (The experimenters suggest a Pflueger Pakron or Penn 49.)

Although synthetic line may be used, metal line is endorsed by most flasher fishermen. As previously noted, metal line will not stretch as will single-strand monofilament line. This is important when trolling flasher gear, because synthetic line may tend to distort the action of the flasher and terminal lure. It is also much easier to reach greater depths with the heavier metal line. (The experimenters recommend single-strand Monel line of fifty-pound test.)

A three-way swivel is attached to the metal line, and the lead weight is fastened to one of the remaining swivel eyes. The third swivel eye holds a length of rubber tubing (called a rubber "snubber") to which is attached a fifty-inch length of stiff metal "piano" wire. Fifty pounds breaking strength is recommended. The flasher is then secured to the piano wire and followed by approximately thirty inches of forty- to fifty-pound test nylon monofilament. Finally, the terminal lure is fastened to the mono.

While herring, candlefish, plugs, spoons, spinners, or other natural or artificial lures may be used in conjunction with the rotating flasher gear described here, squid-type lures were used by the researchers. These are available in varying patterns and colors; one particular type of lure may produce significantly better than the others at any given time. Again, experimentation frequently pays handsome dividends when it comes to salmon fishing.

Like dodgers, flasher combinations require a stur-

Rig used to catch coho and Chinook for tagging in Puget Sound resident project. Sturdy rods and reels are needed for trolling rotating flasher gear. *Courtesy of Washington Department of Fisheries.*

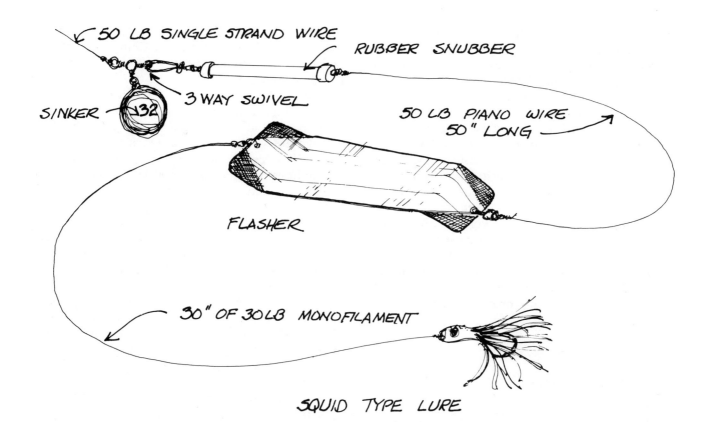

50 LB SINGLE STRAND WIRE

RUBBER SNUBBER

3 WAY SWIVEL

SINKER 32

50 LB PIANO WIRE 50" LONG

FLASHER

30" OF 30 LB MONOFILAMENT

SQUID TYPE LURE

ROTATING FLASHER RIG

dy rod holder. Those with adjustable features are preferred. They serve not only to free the angler from having to hand-hold a rod exerting considerable drag, but they are also effective for keeping terminal rigs separated when two or more fishermen are trolling from the same boat. (The experimenters recommend a Minzer rod holder.)

Because flashers are trolled more rapidly than are dodgers, a steady, metronomic beat will be apparent, and this should be reflected in the rod tip. If trolled too slowly, rotation will not be uniform; if trolled too rapidly, the rod tip will dip too quickly. Good flasher fishermen constantly adjust their trolling speed to compensate for current and wind factors which may influence the action of the flasher at any given time.

Experienced flasher anglers also vary the depth of their terminal gear until salmon are found. For this reason, it is wise to have an assortment of sinkers of varying weights at hand at all times. While as little as ten ounces may be used, sixteen-, twenty- and twenty-four-ounce weights are usually required. At times, as much as thirty-two ounces may be needed to reach the proper terminal depth.

Because depth plays so critical a role in successful

Flashers and dodgers are frequently fished from downriggers. Note hand crank in foreground. *Author photo, courtesy of* Salt Water Sportsman.

salmon angling, it is usually more efficient for two or more anglers to use the same tackle but to maintain different trolling depths until salmon are encountered. Each should know precisely how much line he is dragging at any given time. When fish are found, all hands may then place their terminal rigs at the depth at which the first strike occurs.

Both dodgers and flashers may be used with sinker release devices or downriggers. If such gear is used, anglers will be able to play their fish without the excessive weight required to reach and maintain the correct trolling depth. Perhaps the most effective technique of all is to use a large rotating flasher ahead of the baitfish or lure, a downrigger with a built-in line meter which allows the angler to ascertain the precise depth of terminal tackle and an electronic depth sounder or fish locator. Such a combination is deadly when properly trolled in search of the various Pacific species.

Light Tackle Trolling

Relatively light trolling techniques have been the mainstay of saltwater sport salmon angling throughout the years, and such techniques are especially effective for taking Chinook or coho in depths of up to about ninety feet.

Coho are frequently found at thirty or thirty-five feet, but only rarely at depths of sixty feet or more. Chinook, on the other hand, may be found at one hundred fifty feet or more but sometimes feed near the surface or around the shoreline. Thus, it is sometimes unnecessary to troll heavy terminal tackle. Additionally, light trolling is an ideal angling method for salmon fishermen who disdain the use of heavier tackle.

Standard light trolling tackle consists of a rod of from about eight to ten feet in length with a light action tip but with enough starch to permit the angler to bury the hooks past the barbs. Rods should have relatively long butt ends, metal reel seats, and high quality guides, perferably in carbaloy or lined with ceramic.

Small- to medium-sized saltwater trolling or baitcasting reels are most commonly used. The most popular are revolving spool, multiplying reels with level-wind and star drag features. Reel spools should be loaded with as much line as possible—100 to 150 yards for coho and other relatively small Pacific species, and 200 yards or more for mature, large Chinook. Nylon monofilament line is recommended; breaking strength may vary, depending on the

size of the quarry. For coho, twelve- to fifteen-pound test line is sufficient, but adult Chinook should be taken on line of about twenty to twenty-five pounds breaking strength.

While light tackle trolling lends itself to a wide variety of terminal lures, artificials are not used as extensively as are the simple natural baitfish. Most popular are whole or plug-cut herring, cut (herring) spinners, or candlefish. Anglers opting to drag artificial lures find generally good success with various spoons, spinners, wobblers, and plugs.

Crescent-shaped sinkers are used to keep drag to a minimum, and these may range in weight from about two to eight ounces. While relatively heavy sinkers are sometimes used, most light trolling is conducted with from two to five ounces of weight.

"Longlining"—light tackle trolling with a minimum of weight and a maximum of line out—is a popular method of taking salmon in some quarters. At such times, as little as one-half of an ounce of weight is used.

Diving plane sinkers may be used instead of lead weights.

Trolling speed is critical. For coho, baits should spin fairly rapidly; Chinook, however, prefer slow-looping baits. If boats will not troll down to the desired speed, it may be necessary to alternately engage and disengage the propeller (actually a form of mooching). This not only allows for slower moving baits but also permits the angler to vary the depth at which the terminal lure or baitfish is working. Salmon frequently take baits as they drift toward the bottom, or as they rise slowly upward. For this reason, it is a good idea to place the motor in neutral from time to time. Baits will drift deeper as the trolling speed is decreased, and they will rise as the forward motor position puts the boat under way again.

An alternate way to achieve this same desirable effect is to troll in erratic, zig-zag patterns instead of moving in a straight line. When boats are turned sharply, the rods fishing on the inside of the turn virtually stop their forward movement, and terminal lures or baitfish drift slowly downward. As the boat returns to its former directional course, baitfish or lures rise gradually. (Of course, the reverse is true of rods fishing on the outside of the turn; their terminal gear rises as the outside trolling speed increases, then returns slowly to the former strata as the boat resumes its forward course.)

Trolling depth is important, but anglers may not know at what approximate depth fish are concentrated. For this reason, it is recommended that anglers vary the depth of their terminal lures or baitfish at periodic intervals. Or two or more anglers

Framed by the rising sun, Ken McDonald, owner of the luxurious charter boat *Viking Star*, which fishes Puget Sound from its berth on Seattle's Lake Union, checks the action of his plug-cut herring. Harbor Island, near downtown Seattle, and the shipworks are in the distance—a favorite spot for light trollers. *Author photo.*

may fish at different depths until salmon are found. It is important to know how much line one has out at all times. When salmon are encountered, anglers may then be assured of reaching and maintaining the same depth at which strikes have occurred.

One of the primary reasons for lack of success when fishing Chinook is that most anglers troll too shallowly. The chief exceptions are early and late in the day when salmon, as previously noted, are likely to be feeding relatively near the surface. At *most* other times, however, fish are likely to be found in deeper water. For this reason, it pays to experiment by trolling at various depths. In general, trolling depth should be increased as the light source increases. In similar fashion, depth should be decreased as daylight fades to dusk.

Despite the fact that many Pacific salmon fishermen commonly troll too shallowly, there are reasons why trolling *slightly* above the water stratum in which one suspects that fish may be found may be productive. First, a salmon's line of sight is better above its body than below it, a fact which is evident by studying its anatomical structure. Second, it is easier to discern objects which are silhouetted by the background of natural light than those which simply reflect the available light and are positioned below the body of the fish. Perhaps these facts partially explain why fish often rise to take dry flies from the water's surface. In any event, it seems reasonable to believe that a lure or baitfish trolled *above* a fish is more likely to be spotted than one which is trolled below it.

Rod holders, while sometimes convenient, are unnecessary in light tackle trolling, since the drag of the terminal rig combination is minimal. But some anglers feel that the use of a rod holder prevents one from setting the hooks prematurely and thus results in more fish.

Light trollers work the tide off West Seattle's Alki Beach. *Author photo.*

If rod holders are used, reels are frequently set with the drag off and only the click adjustment used to keep the line from free-spooling. When a strike occurs, the fish may take line freely, but the clicking sound alerts the angler to the strike. Other fishermen believe, however, that the unnatural sound—and the accompanying vibration—of a clicking reel may frighten off wary fish. Many of these anglers like to place their rods in holders, but with the click feature in the off position. Instead the drag may be set very loosely—to a point at which the line will not pay out on its own, but one at which a gently nibbling salmon is able to strip line easily.

Regardless of which way a rod holder is used, it is generally agreed that anglers should not attempt to set the hooks immediately upon receiving a strike. Instead it almost always pays to let a salmon take a bait slowly, deeply. Hooks should not be set until a steady tug is felt. At that point, they should be set firmly but not in a lightning manner with undue pressure applied. Muscle-men often perform better with dumbells than salmon rods.

Mooching

Mooching is among the more popular and effective Pacific salmon fishing techniques and has gained a considerable and loyal following in recent years. The technique is employed extensively by not only sport salmon anglers but has gained popularity among certain party and charter boat operators, most notably those fishing out of the Grays Harbor area of Washington State.

While mooching indeed has a vast number of adherents and despite the claims of some authors that the technique is the most popular of all Pacific Northwest salmon fishing methods, it has been this writer's observation that the technique still has far to go in order to achieve or exceed the popularity of the various salmon trolling methods. With the exception, for example, of the bulk of Westport—Ocean Shores charter fleet members (and several of those operating off the Columbia River mouth), many of whom employ mooching to keep fuel expenses to a minimum, most Washington charter skippers prefer the time-honored methods of trolling for salmon—often with flasher or dodger gear. Similarly, the various trolling techniques are more popular than mooching throughout other salmon areas—California, Oregon, British Columbia, and Alaska.

This is not to say that mooching is not efficient or productive. To the contrary, it is not only an excellent means of taking Pacific salmon from salt water, but it is fun fishing to boot. The pure excitement and pleasure of taking trophy-sized Chinook on light mooching tackle is perhaps equalled only by taking somewhat smaller coho on fly rods.

Mooching is a term applied to bait fishing with relatively light tackle when the forces of nature—tide or current, wind and waves—give movement to the boat and bait. Mooched baits may be fished from an anchored or drifting boat or from a boat in which the operator alternately shifts the motor in and out of gear. The most common form of mooching is drift mooching, in which the boat is simply allowed to drift across a promising stretch of water, the baitfish pulled alluringly behind.

While some salmon fishermen would have less experienced anglers believe so, there is no mystique to the various mooching techniques. Any serious salmon fisherman may learn the technique within a few hours' time.

Tackle selection is very important, although there is some latitude for individual preference. Mooching rods range in length from about eight to ten feet. Most common are tubular fiberglass rods of about nine feet in length. Rods are relatively light in weight and in action; their tips must be quite sensitive, but they should possess enough spine to cope with strong-running fish. The best mooching rods have relatively long butt ends to facilitate leverage when playing a fish, high-quality carbaloy or ceramic-lined guides and sturdy metal reel seats.

Reel choice depends primarily upon individual preference. Some anglers prefer spinning (either open- or closed-face) models, although most moochers opt for saltwater trolling or bait-casting reels. Bait-casting reels, such as those used exten-

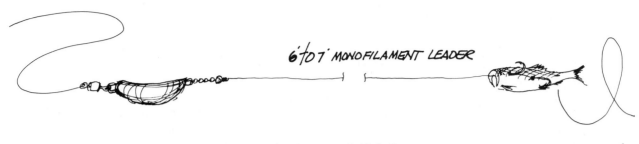

6' TO 7' MONOFILAMENT LEADER

MOOCHING GEAR

Small boat moochers ready to net a winter blackmouth.
Author photo, courtesy of Salt Water Sportsman.

sively by fresh water steelheaders, serve the purpose, but casting is seldom required and it is this writer's opinion that the best all-around mooching reels are of the revolving spool, multiplying type. If reels of this type are chosen, they may be small- to medium-sized but should display high quality drag systems (star drag is preferred) and level-wind features.

Mooching line is almost invariably made of synthetic material. Nylon monofilament is perhaps the best choice. It is easy to work with and has remarkable strength for its diameter. Breaking strength is a matter of personal preference—and experience.

Most commonly employed is mono of from about fifteen to twenty-five pound test. Reels should be loaded to capacity to ensure that anglers have plenty of line to pay out to strong-running fish. In general, at least 150 yards should be wound onto the reel spool, although 200 yards or more should be used when fishing for adult Chinook.

Mooching sinkers (the banana- or crescent-shaped type) are preferred in order to minimize drag, and these may range in weight from about one-half an ounce to four or five ounces. Normal fishing conditions call for sinkers of from two to four ounces. If wind or tide conditions are particularly strong, heavier weights may be required. In the calmest of water, an ounce of weight is usually sufficient.

Sinkers may be the stationary type—or of the sliding variety. Increasingly, moochers are coming to appreciate the outstanding merits of using sliding sinkers. They not only serve the same purpose as do the stationary, crescent sinkers, but they allow both fish and fishermen considerably more freedom. If sliding sinkers are used, some sort of swivel (usually a beaded chain swivel) is required. Most stationary mooching sinkers have built-in beaded swivels attached.

Leaders most commonly used by moochers are made of relatively light nylon and range from about six to nine feet in length, depending primarily upon rod length. Breaking strength of the leader should be equal to, or less than, that of the line so that any breakage which may occur will be restricted to the leader (or to a knot, usually a weak spot). In this manner, all terminal gear will not be lost, should line separation occur.

Mooching leaders may be rigged with a single hook for use with herring, but double-hook rigs are most commonly employed. These range in size from 2/0 to 6/0, and size selection should be made on the basis of the baitfish and the anticipated size of the target. In general, the smaller the baitfish, the smaller the hooks; the larger the quarry, the larger the hooks. Under most conditions, hook sizes of 2/0 to 4/0 are required. These will handle even the largest of Chinook and normally work well with herring of from about five to seven inches in length.

Baits may be fished whole, plug-cut or in strips. By far the most popular are medium-sized herring which have been plugged—double beveled behind the head at an angle of about forty-five degrees.

An excellent tackle combination for beginning moochers is a relatively light-action, tubular fiberglass rod of about nine feet in length, a level-wind, star drag trolling reel filled with twenty-pound test nylon monofilament line, a mooching sinker of perhaps three or four ounces (depending on weather and water conditions) and a seven-foot leader equipped with hooks sized 2/0 and 3/0 (remember, the leading hook should be one size larger than the trailing hook), or perhaps 3/0 and 4/0. Leader should be, say, seventeen pounds breaking strength. Equipped with such a tackle combination, virtually any fisherman should be able to cope with coho or Chinook of almost any size.

Next to fly trolling or casting and light tackle spinning techniques, mooching provides the lightest tackle method of taking Pacific salmon. Usually after a promising water area is chosen, the moocher moves into an *upwind* position and simply drifts with the wind (if there is little or no wind but a strong current, the boat should be maneuvered into a position up-current from the desired fishing area). After a drift, the moocher then starts his motor and returns to his original upwind (or up-current) position for another pass across the selected water expanse.

If there is no wind or current capable of moving the boat at a sufficient speed, moochers may use their motors to achieve the desired bait action. In fact, mooching is often synonymous with the lightest trolling techniques. More commonly, however, the angler simply trolls a short distance, then places the motor into neutral. By alternately engaging and disengaging the propeller, the "motor moocher" is able to achieve virtually the same effect as the drift moocher.

The depth at which the baitfish is working is varied automatically in motor mooching: the baitfish sinks in the neutral motor position and rises when the prop is engaged. This allows the angler to fish at various depths without having to reel in and pay out line. The drift moocher, however, should constantly retrieve and pay out line in order to fish at different depths. In fact, the common practice in stationary or drift mooching is to allow the baitfish to drift slowly to the bottom in water of, say, thirty to one hundred feet, then crank in a few feet of line. With sensitive rod tips, it is easy to tell when the sinker has hit bottom. The baitfish now just off bottom, the boat moves across a promising stretch of water. The angler intermittently retrieves and pays out line as the boat is allowed to drift with the forces of nature. By alternately cranking in and paying out line, the drift moocher is able to fish a variety of depths, even as the boat is in motion.

At times the motor may be used in a negative manner. By alternately engaging and disengaging the propeller, the moocher is able to control the drift rate of the craft. This is an effective means of preventing a strong wind or current from moving the boat too rapidly for baits to be effective.

Still another mooching technique, especially productive on calm, windless days or when anglers are without the use of a motor, is simply to work the rod tip up and down in a slow "jigging" motion. This is a fishing method which is employed often aboard charter or party vessels, primarily when fishing for coho. It is also a fishing technique which is particularly well suited for large angling groups fishing from the same boat because there is usually a minimum of line tangles involved.

In any mooching technique, the angle of the line is extremely important, and one of the main reasons for lack of success is that the terminal tackle is often trailed behind the boat at an incorrect angle.

Motor mooching is a popular technique for taking salmon from Washington's Juan de Fuca Strait. *Author photo*.

Relatively steep line angles of forty-five or fifty degrees are most effective when fishing Chinook, but flatter angles of thirty or thirty-five degrees may be adequate for coho. Anglers should vary their terminal gear and boat speed in order to reach and maintain the proper line angles at all times.

With the exception of the jigging technique described above, mooching methods permit the use of rod holders. If a holder is used, the reel drag should be adjusted to a very light setting or the reel click alone may be used to prevent the line from free-spooling. When a strike is encountered, rods placed in holders may be picked up without pulling the baitfish or lure from the mouth of the fish. Quick-release rod holders, which permit the angler to withdraw the rod vertically, are excellent choices for moochers.

As with hand-held rods, rods which are fished from holders should be accompanied by loosely set reel spools which allow salmon to solidly take the bait before pressure is applied. In fact, it is highly advisable to pay out a few yards of line when a gentle bite is encountered. Most veteran salmon anglers are in agreement that one of the most common causes for failing to hook an interested salmon is that the bait is too often prematurely pulled from the fish's mouth. This is especially true of Chinook, typically "munching" nibblers. Patience in salmon angling is more than a virtue. Often it spells the difference between success and failure.

While rod holders may be used in both drift and motor mooching techniques, the more experienced—and often more successful—moochers eschew them as not only unnecessary but perhaps a hindrance. The fact remains that, despite a myriad of technological advances in equipment design in recent years, nothing beats skill and experience. And to most veteran moochers, nothing can compete with a hand-held rod.

Mooching techniques have few drawbacks. Perhaps the major disadvantage of the various methods of mooching is that unwanted bottom dwellers such as dogfish, hake, ratfish, and the like are frequently hooked. These fish can cut or damage a leader so badly that it is usually unwise to use the same leader again. For this reason, moochers should never be caught without an abundant supply of pretied leaders and an equally abundant arsenal of hard-bodied baitfish.

Fly Fishing

Saltwater fly fishing for salmon, unlike techniques employed for the same species in their native rivers and streams, revolves primarily around the trolling techniques outlined under flasher and dodger fishing and rarely includes the presentation of flies by casting. An important exception is the recently devoloped and refined sport of casting to surface-cruising salmon (especially coho) in the southern portion of Washington's Puget Sound and certain other limited areas. In such instances, wet flies—similar to those used for tricking freshwater trout and/or other marine species—are used.

Aside from such pioneering efforts, relatively little fly fishing is conducted for Pacific salmon species in their salt water habitat, and purists will point out—rightly so—that such use of flies does not constitute fly fishing at all.

But there is one saltwater salmon angling technique in which flies are used extensively and without accompanying heavy or bulky terminal tackle: trolling salmon flies with little or no weight or other terminal gear. It is a technique which is highly specialized but extremely effective on occasion.

Fly trolling techniques, except those associated with flashers and dodgers, are intended almost exclusively for coho. Silvers, unlike their Chinook counterparts, are often found in the upper water strata. In fact, they sometimes feed right on the surface, and brightly colored streamer flies are often very effective during such periods.

The fact that coho may be seen leaping does not necessarily indicate that the fish are feeding on the surface. Coho, some believe, leap to clear themselves of sea lice, a theory which seems without basis in logic, since these parasites occur on salmon during their entire lives at sea. Moreover, sea lice can be expected to fall from the fish within several hours (the usually quoted period is forty-eight hours) of their entering fresh water. Indeed it seems more likely to conclude that these fish leap in order to condition themselves for their climactic and often arduous upstream spawning migrations.

The best means of determining the depth and presence of coho is to watch for patches of baitfish around which salmon are likely to be found. If bait-fish are not sighted, "working" birds—those which may be seen circling and or diving for baitfish—may indicate the presence of coho. Sometimes bait patches are so thick that thousands of birds may be seen circling, diving, or simply resting on the water. When resting, birds have probably recently gorged themselves on available baitfish, and trolling a fly near such resting bird flocks is often amazingly productive.

Coho are pelagic fish which are often found near riptides. Riptides are areas in which two opposing tidal forces meet; they are easily discerned by the profuse debris which tends to accumulate along the line separating the currents. Strong currents often concentrate baitfish, like the usual accompanying debris, along their common line, and salmon are likely to be found nearby. It is a good idea to troll along riptides if baitfish or working birds cannot be found.

As with Chinook, some of the best fishing for coho is immediately after sunrise and/or before sunset. But anglers in search of surface-feeding silvers should also know that other peak feeding periods are often found on or near the tide changes. If possible, it is a good idea to fish from an hour before to an hour after any tide change. Sometimes fish feed heavily on high tides; at other times, peak feeding may occur coincidental with low tides. Any of the various Pacific salmon species may feed on either the outgoing or incoming tide, and an accurate tide book is a valuable aid to serious saltwater salmon anglers.

Although shallow or surface trolling traditionally has been confined to a handful of well known coho areas (most notably at Neah Bay near Cape Flattery at Washington's northwesternmost tip and in a few British Columbian and Alaskan waters), the technique is gradually expanding to include other productive areas. As this unique coho angling technique expands geographically, it is also gaining a small but avid following of enthusiasts.

While most knowledgeable salmon anglers agree that the coho is the most spectacular of all the Pacific species which occur along the West Coast, relatively few have sampled such exciting sport as taking mature silvers of perhaps ten to fifteen pounds on the lightest of salmon tackle. This technique, when effective, is nearer the pure form of salmon angling than almost any other (the only exception I can think of is the revered fly casting for salmon), and coho taken in this manner are among the most formidable of adversaries. Their leaping, acrobatic runs will impress even the most ardent Atlantic salmon or steelhead fishermen.

Surface trolling for coho may be productive at various times throughout the year, but by far the most exciting action occurs during the late summer and fall. At this time of year, silvers have achieved the bulk of their optimum weight and are still adding ounces, even pounds, rapidly. Moreover, they appear to feed near the surface more consistently during the Indian summer days of late August and September than at other periods of the year.

The best surface fishing is likely to be found during overcast weather or when dense fog combines with nearly windless days. At such times, coho frequently feed just below the surface and are especially susceptible to salmon flies as they slash their way wildly through immense concentrations of baitfish, gorging themselves on herring or candlefish before beginning their upstream spawning runs.

Anglers wishing to troll flies on or near the surface may choose from a wide variety of tackle items. Most popular is a standard mooching rig consisting of a relatively light-action rod of about eight or nine feet in length, a small- to medium-sized level-wind, star drag reel with a revolving spool and one hundred yards or more of ten- to fifteen-pound test nylon monofilament line. Such tackle can easily handle even the largest of silvers. Moreover, such a tackle combination permits the addition of lightweight banana-shaped sinkers of from one half an ounce to

Jerry Ray, formerly of Mel's Resort at Neah Bay, Washington, but now a commercial fisherman, uses a small club to kill a bright fall silver which went for a surface-trolled streamer fly. Fish which are intended for the table are best killed quickly—out of kindness and because they are likely to thrash around on the deck or in the fishbox, bruising their flesh in the process. *Author photo.*

about two ounces in weight in the event that coho are unwilling to strike flies trolled right on the surface.

Flies may also be trolled from spinning or other light-action tackle. The author has often used a lightweight fresh water fly rod, intended for inland trout, for this purpose. If fresh or saltwater fly reels are used, reel spools may be filled with either floating or sinking line. Or reels may be loaded with a sufficient length of single-strand nylon line. If actual fly lines are used, salmon trollers should make certain they have plenty of backing; at least one hundred yards should be added to the fly line.

Most popular are flies of the long streamer variety. The best are those which are sparsely tied, although commercially tied streamers usually display profuse and colorful hackle. Bucktail or polar bear hair is preferred, but many commercially prepared salmon streamers are now made entirely of synthetic hackle.

Since the olfactory sense of salmon is well developed, many fly trollers add a small herring or other baitfish strip to the single (or trailing) hook as an added inducement. Others eschew the use of bait strips completely and seem to enjoy nearly comparable success trolling only naked flies on the fishing grounds. The author, however, has enjoyed the best success when a tiny baitfish strip has been added.

Flies must be trolled rapidly, since coho prefer faster moving lures than do the other Pacific species. This is particularly true when flies are trolled right on the surface. Trolling speed may be reduced somewhat when sinkers are added in order to submerge the fly, but a fly which is trolled on the surface should move quickly enough to send up a small "roostertail" behind it.

Flies may be tied directly onto the line or leader, or snap swivels or other connectors may be used. Because streamer flies seldom twist to any great extent, swivel connectors are viewed as an unnecessary evil.

It is wise to have a selection of various fly colors and patterns available at all times. If two or more anglers fish in this manner, the recommended tactic is for each to employ a different fly color or pattern until one or two fish are hooked. Anglers may then switch to the specific type of fly which has produced the most strikes. At times, coho appear finicky; at other times they may be indiscriminate feeders and will as readily strike a yellow and white color combination as one which is blue and white.

One of the mot pleasurable aspects of taking coho on the surface is that *the angler is actually able to see* approaching fish before a strike or hookup occurs. Seldom is the fly trolled more than about thirty feet behind the boat, and many anglers believe that fifteen feet is preferable, reasoning that the prop-wash actually attracts fish.

When a fin is sighted behind a trolled fly, the most effective manner of helping to increase the odds of a strike is to strip out a few yards of line. Perhaps the easiest way to achieve the same result is simply to quickly point the rod tip toward the stern of the boat. This can be accomplished easily and quickly by anglers who fish from the sides of the craft. The sudden slackening of the line causes the fly to temporarily cease its forward motion, and it is at this instant that a silver is most likely to strike. At other times, fish will strike flies which are moving at a constant speed. For this reason, rod holders may be used.

Although coho will rise to a fly presented in their parent rivers and streams, these fish appear to be enticed more readily while in salt or brackish water. This is especially true in the famed waters of Discovery Passage and Cowichan Bay off Vancouver Island, and it is one of the reasons that tricking silvers on flies is such exciting, incomparable sport.

This writer was first introduced to the fast-paced action of surface-trolling for large hooknose coho a number of years ago. Through my radio broadcasts and related work, I had met Mel and Arlene Ray, owners and operators of Mel's Resort at Neah Bay, a famous landmark for salmon fishermen over a score of years and which now operates under new ownership. I had spoken with the Rays and their son, Jerry, innumerable times over the telephone while gathering material for my "Fish Watch" programs, and I had met Mel and Arlene, but not Jerry, during several visits to the area.

Over the years, the resort owners had told me of the exciting surface sport available in August and September. Frankly, I was not impressed. Until I had the opportunity to sample some of the highly touted action, that is.

Arriving at Neah Bay, I met Jerry, who was to act as my guide for a day of fly trolling. He briefed me quickly and we loaded our gear into one of the resort's twenty-foot kicker boats.

Fog enshrouded us like cotton as we departed the dock, and I was glad to have Jerry—extremely familiar with the lay of the water, land, and dangerous rocky shoreline—along. Within a few minutes' run, we could hear the whistle buoy off Cape Flattery, and we scanned the horizon through the diminishing fog for signs of baitfish. We soon spotted an enormous flock of birds which were feeding heavily on baitfish.

We dropped our streamer flies astern and trolled them so rapidly that tiny roostertails shot up behind them. Within a few minutes, I had my first fish—a bright, mature coho of about twelve pounds. I was tolling a green streamer, and it wasn't until I picked up my second fish that Jerry switched his blue fly for one which was similar to mine.

During the hours that ensued, we caught and released a number of silvers, finally keeping three fish each, the allowable limit in Washington waters. Never have I enjoyed faster-paced salmon fishing. In all, we had taken and released, unhurt, perhaps two dozen coho—in addition to the six we decided to keep. Back at the dock, we weighed our six-fish haul: sixty-two pounds, dressed. Our keepers had averaged nearly thirteen pounds in the round.

While that particular trip was exceptionally productive, I have since enjoyed nearly comparable action. But the most exciting and coveted aspect of trolling surface flies without any accompanying weight is that anglers are confronted with a rare opportunity to take husky and brutish coho on the lightest of tackle. While Jerry and I had taken an inordinately large number of fish, what mattered most was that each hookup resulted in truly spectacular battle: this is salmon fishing at its finest, thanks to the light tackle required.

Spinning and Casting

Spinning and casting for Pacific salmon species are confined primarily to the fresh and estuarial waters of parental streams. However, angling with spinning or bait casting tackle in the small, sheltered inlets and bays found along the Pacific is both a productive and effective method of taking fish.

Spin fishing and casting are particularly popular among Californians and Oregonians. Relatively little spinning or bait casting is done by salmon enthusiasts in the more northerly latitudes, with the possible exception of that done from jetty or shore.

Lightweight fresh or saltwater spinning or bait-casting rods are used, accompanied by compatible spinning or casting reels. Most popular are rods of from seven to eight feet in length. Instead of spinning rods of the relatively short variety, longer, more limber rods are often used; rods such as those used for taking summer- or winter-run steelhead are ideal, and bait-casting reels with multiplying, revolving spools may accompany these. Most popular are those with level-wind features and star drags.

Line breaking strength is typically fifteen- to twenty-pounds when Chinook are sought, although six- to ten-pound nylon mono is adequate for coho and most other Pacific species. Leaders—if used at all—often measure three to four feet (sometimes longer) and are of the same breaking strength as the line, or lighter.

Terminal tackle for spin-casting techniques includes all the popular salmon spoons and spinners, but herring or other baitfish are sometimes cast. Similarly, trolling with spinning or casting tackle may include a wide range of artificial (or natural) lures.

Usually no more than about two ounces of weight are required for casting, and weighted spoons or spinners are often sufficiently heavy. Trolling the same lures, however, usually requires additional weight, and anglers should take this into consideration when selecting a rod.

Spinning or casting equipment may be used for light trolling or mooching but is too light for use with heavy terminal gear. As previously noted, such tackle may also be used in surface trolling with streamer flies.

At times, casting for Pacific salmon is integrated into mooching techniques. This is particularly true with Chinook in saltwater. Occasionally anglers using standard mooching tackle (but perhaps employing a bait-casting, level-wind "steelheading"-type reel) will cast baitfish a distance from the boat, often in or around seemingly productive kelp beds. At still other times, baitfish are cast into open water; the bait is allowed to settle and is then reeled in slowly.

Some of the best spin-fishing or casting opportunities are found near the mouths of salmon streams. With sometimes amazing success, casters fish the brackish mouths of rivers emptying into the Pacific and other West Coast marine waters.

Live Bait Fishing

Live bait fishing is one of the most effective techniques for taking Chinook and coho from saltwater. Since it is generally agreed that these Pacific salmon species are attracted to baitfish or lures imitative of a wounded natural bait, it stands to reason that the real item—an actual, slightly injured baitfish—most closely resembles the ideal salmon lure.

While live bait fishing may be conducted with candlefish, anchovies, and other baitfish, herring are by far the most popular. In recent years, live herring have become increasingly available at a number of retail outlets along the Pacific coast and its inland waters. Anglers are now able to obtain live herring at many coastal resort communities and, given proper care, baitfish will live for a surprising length of time.

Fisheries biologists Frank Haw and Raymond M. Buckley describe fishing with live herring in their book, *Saltwater Fishing in Washington*. They point out that, while live bait fishing is popular throughout British Columbia, relatively few American salmon anglers use this technique for taking Pacific species from salt water.[3]

But this was not always the case. During an earlier era, live bait fishing was a popular pasttime among a relatively small but dedicated angling fraternity. During a recent salmon fishing trip to La Push, Washington, I discussed live bait fishing with two old-timers, Seattle-area natives who had used the technique extensively a number of years ago. Fishing from the docks at Todd Shipyard was exceptionally productive, they told me, and this was often how they spent their "lunch" hours while working the graveyard shift. They recounted how salmon, apparently attracted to the bright industrial lights at night, were easily tricked into taking live herring. Similarly, specific fisheries existed near the various herring holding pens scattered throughout the sound. Salmon, attracted by the presence of the penned bait, were easily tricked by live bait fishermen working the peripheries of such areas.

The first thing required in live bait fishing is a container in which herring may be kept until ready for use. Haw and Buckley suggest using a plastic garbage pail of about twenty gallons capacity. (Galvanized metal is toxic to fish.)

While some charter, party, and even private boats now boast bait wells which facilitate the handling and care of live bait, even kicker boat fishermen may enjoy the technique if the garbage pail approach is taken. Such containers are sufficient for short-range trips and, provided oxygen is supplied continuously, they will keep bait alive for extended periods.

Certain plastic pails are also toxic, and the authors suggest that anglers line the pails with plastic bag liners. Pails should be filled only to the half-way mark with sea water.

Oxygen may be provided by a foot-operated air pump, or anglers may simply aerate the water by periodically filling a small bucket with sea water and pouring it back into the garbage container from a height of two or three feet. Constant aeration is required to provide sufficient oxygen to keep the herring alive.

Live bait may be fished with light tackle, such as standard salmon mooching gear. Usually, not more than an ounce or two of weight is required because the bait is normally fished from an anchored or drifting boat.

Live bait fishing requires that anglers allow plenty

of slack line when a strike occurs. Often salmon will mouth the baitfish gently and slowly before taking it firmly in tow, and live bait fishermen must exercise more patience than is required for most other salmon fishing techniques. Hooks should not be set until the angler feels a distinct and steady tug on the line.

As with other salmon angling techniques directed toward taking fish from the brine, successful live bait fishing depends largely upon obtaining the proper depth. To this end, anglers should experiment at different levels until strikes occur.

If live bait is unavailable from retail sources, anglers may dip their own bait from among the sometimes enormous patches encountered while fishing for salmon. In addition to providing fresh bait with which to fish, finding and dipping herring can be an enjoyable experience in itself.

The successful bait dipper should be constantly alert to the presence of diving or working birds. Often their presence indicates that baitfish are nearby.

Baitfish may be dipped with any long-handled net, so long as the mesh is sufficiently fine. Smelt nets like those used to take baitfish and table fare from the Cowlitz River in Washington during peak smelt runs are ideal. Many of these nets come equipped with long, aluminum handles which telescope for use but which may be collapsed for storage and transportation convenience. A good smelt net costs approximately fifteen dollars.

When baitfish are spotted, dippers should keep their nets from the water until the last possible instant. Then, in a rapid, swooping motion, nets may be plunged into the midst of herring schools. While fresh-dipped herring or other baitfish may be used whole or cut into plugs, they may also be placed into the bait well or garbage container for immediate use in live bait fishing.

Jetty and Shore Fishing

Land-bound anglers without access to a boat or who do not possess the sea-legs required by party, charter, private, or rental boat angling may still test their skill at taking salmon with their feet planted firmly on the ground. While fishing from the bank is a popular recreasport among freshwater salmon anglers, it is not necessarily limited to that pursuit. Indeed fishermen may find some surprisingly spectacular results in fishing the Pacific species, especially Chinook, in salt water.

While pier, jetty, barge, and shore fishing for other saltwater species has been extremely popular for a number of years, serious salmon angling from jetty or shore is only beginning to come into its own. Spurred on by recent success stories and the ever-increasing expense of fishing from boat, anglers are rapidly coming to realize the importance of jetty or shore fishing for salmon.

Such techniques are especially effective for taking Chinook salmon, which often feed amazingly close to shore. In many instances, kings will follow bait schools into the shallows, or they may gorge themselves on shrimp or other natural feed which is forced by tidal currents onto the rocks. At such times, the properly equipped shore or jetty angler stands a good chance of connecting. (As this is written, some truly giant Chinook are falling to jetty fishermen: only yesterday, a sixty-pound king salmon fell to a lucky or skillful angler who was fishing the North Jetty near Washington State's Ilwaco, at the Columbia River mouth!)

Jetty and shore fishing are also excellent means of providing angling excitement for the entire family. Children especially enjoy fishing from shore or breakwater. This method of fishing also precludes the expense incurred in owning or renting a boat and/or motor and in spending a relatively expensive day or half day aboard a party or charter boat.

While the tackle range for shore and jetty fishing is fairly extensive, terminal lures usually consist of herring, spinners, or spoons. If artificial lures are used, spinning or casting tackle should be used. Lures are simply cast into the surf and retrieved slowly. The technique is not unlike that employed by river fishermen in search of salmon, steelhead, or other freshwater species.

While spoons and spinners are available in a wide range of colors, finishes and designs, most popular are chrome, brass, or copper lures of relatively large size. These are often the same lures used by anglers trolling at the mouths of large West Coast salmon rivers. Weighted lures of red, red and chrome, or red and brass are also effective and, if heavy enough, do not require that anglers add additional weight.

But herring is again one of the most popular baits. These may be fished whole, plug-cut, or as cut spinners.

One recommended tackle combination for jetty or shore fishing consists of a spinning or casting rod (steelheading rods are excellent) and a multiplying, revolving-spool reel (level-wind types are recommended). Nylon monofilament line is loaded onto the reel spool, followed by a crescent-shaped sinker of from one to three ounces. Sinkers should be the stationary type, replete with built-in bead-swivels. A

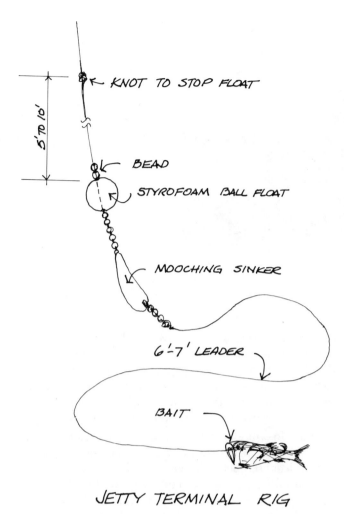

KNOT TO STOP FLOAT

5' TO 10'

BEAD

STYROFOAM BALL FLOAT

MOOCHING SINKER

6½-7' LEADER

BAIT

JETTY TERMINAL RIG

nylon leader, like those used for mooching or light trolling, is fastened to the other end of the swivel-sinker combination. Leaders may be tied with either a single hook or a double-hook rig, depending on personal preference. Herring—whether whole, plug-cut or cut spinners—are then rigged in accordance with previously described instructions (just as they might be hooked for mooching).

Usually a bobber or float of some type is attached to the line to keep the baitfish from sinking to—and resting on—the bottom. Bobbers may be placed at any point along the line, depending on individual angling situations. If the water is deep within casting distance, floats should be placed several feet above the sinker. Conversely, they should be attached only a short distance above the bitter end of the fishing line when shallow-water casting conditions prevail.

But using a standard clip-on float may result in problems. Depending upon fishing conditions, the distance from the baitfish to float may be as much as

fifteen feet or more—too lengthy to accomodate the recommended tackle and technique.

To solve this problem, a floating bobber with a hollow core may be used. Such a device permits the float to slide freely between the sinker and a predetermined point on the fishing line. When the rig is cast into the surf, the sinker will take the bait down only as far as desired, since the bobber will stop at the desired point along the line. To get the bobber to stop, a small knot, large enough only to stop the float, is tied at the predetermined point on the line at which the float should stop when cast, and small beads of any type may be added to keep the knot from slipping through the bobber.

Bobbers may be fashioned from any material which will float. Most popular are bobbers which are crudely constructed of cork or styrofoam. A small, hollow core is made through the float, and the homemade device is threaded onto the fishing line before the line is tied to the sinker.

The terminal rig is cast into the surf, and the homemade bobber keeps the bait off the bottom. Tide or current action should make the bait revolve enticingly.

As in any other technique for taking Pacific salmon species from salt water, the depth at which the baitfish is working is critical. For this reason, it is wise to vary the point at which the bobber-and-bead combination are stopped by the knot.

Jetty or shore fishing requires patience and restraint when a strike is encountered. Since this method of fishing is most commonly employed for Chinook, it is a good idea to let the fish have plenty of time to take in the baitfish before pressure is applied to drive the hooks past the barbs. As is usually the case with Chinook, salmon taken from jetty or shore are likely to be slow nibbling fish and not those which hastily slam the presented baits. Like successful moochers, good jetty or shore fishermen make it a practice to pay out a few yards of line when a bite is felt.

Notes

1. Frank Haw and Raymond M. Buckley, *Saltwater Fishing in Washington* (Seattle: Stan Jones, 1973), p. 83.
2. Ibid., p. 83.
3. Ibid., p. 80.

5
PRIME SALT WATERS

ILWACO, Westport, Depoe Bay, the Farallons, Campbell River, and Yes Bay—all are familiar names to saltwater salmon fishermen. Yet these are only a handful of the West's most renowned salmon areas. Indeed, from Alaska to California, the Pacific coast and its multitudinous harbors, bays, and inlets offer innumerable opportunities for serious and casual angler alike.

While it would be virtually impossible to touch on each and every area, the following are descriptions of, and noteworthy tips on, the major Pacific salmon waters.

Washington

Washington State heads the list of salmon fishing regions. That state produces nearly as many sport-caught salmon as are taken each year from all other Pacific coastal waters combined. In fact, figures released by the Washington State Department of Fisheries a few years ago disclosed that Washington's sport salmon harvest actually *exceeded* that of Alaska, British Columbia, Oregon, Idaho, and California combined!

In addition to providing the bulk of the West Coast sport salmon catch each year, Washington hosts a vast number of sport salmon fishermen. Statistics show that during 1976 (the latest year for which figures are available at this writing), for example, a total of nearly 1.9 million angler trips took place in the waters of that state. Each of the over six hundred thousand anglers who fished in Washing-

ton waters during 1976 averaged three outings. Included were both residents and nonresidents of the state, as well as foreign sport fishermen from Europe, Australia and Japan. As is pointed out in the "Washington State Sport Catch Report—1976," that state "truly has an international sport fishery."*

Nor do anglers fishing Washington waters have much about which to complain: the state, despite recent legal setbacks, has been producing an astounding number of sport-caught salmon. Figures show that 1976 was a record year in terms of the sport harvest. Just under 1.75 million salmon were taken by sport anglers. This number exceeded the previous record catch of just under 1.4 million salmon by approximately 350,000 fish.

Washington boasts five major salt water salmon areas, each including several spots which are heavily fished each year. The main areas are: (1) the Pacific coast; (2) the Strait of Juan de Fuca; (3) Puget Sound; (4) Hood Canal; and (5) the San Juan Islands. (A sixth major sport salmon fishery, that of sockeye, occurs during years in which there is a relative abundance of adult fish returning to the Lake Washington system. A description of the tackle and techniques used for taking sockeye from Lake Washington is included in Part III, "Fresh Water Salmon Fishing".)

Fisheries change with the times, and Washington is no exception. That state has seen a dramatic reversal in angling patterns in the last quarter century. The emphasis has been in a concentration of angling effort away from the various inland marine waters

*All statistics for Washington are from Gene D. Nye, W. Dale Ward, and Lee J. Hoines, *Washington State Sport Catch Report-1976* (Olympia, Washington, Washington State Department of Fisheries, 1976).

and toward the Pacific coast. Twenty-five years ago, for example, Puget Sound boathouses offered rental skiffs numbering into the thousands; today only a few hundred rental boats exist. The number of inland marine resorts and boathouses has declined dramatically during this period, no thanks to better and faster highways leading from the major population areas to the coast and an increase in the popularity of ocean charter and party boat fishing.

During this twenty-year period, Washington's sport salmon fishing scenario has turned from one in which approximately ninety percent of the catch occurred in Puget Sound and adjacent inland waters to one in which roughly two-thirds of all sport-caught salmon are now taken from the Pacific ports. In fact, state fisheries statistics for 1976 show that approximately sixty-four percent of all sport-caught salmon taken from salt water were harvested from or near the four major coastal resort areas. During the same year, the waters of Juan de Fuca Strait and northern Puget Sound produced only approximately nineteen percent of the sport harvest, while about seventeen percent, the remainder, came from lower Puget Sound.

Washington's sport salmon fisheries are aided greatly by information supplied by anglers via salmon "punch cards." Until recently, punch cards

A Pacific coast party boat deckhand applies the twine to a fine salmon. *Photograph by Bob Peterson courtesy, of Fish Watch.*

were free of charge. At this writing, there is now a small charge (three dollars for state residents) to fish salmon in state waters. Punch cards are required, along with the fee stamp, of both residents and nonresidents alike. Information included on these cards relate primarily to where and when salmon were taken. By studying the information obtained through these cards, biologists are able to arrive at a surprisingly detailed picture of what has taken place on the salmon scene during any given year.

Gordon Sandison, Director of the Washington Department of Fisheries, the agency responsible for salmon management in that state's waters, notes in his foreword to the "Washington State Sport Catch Report—1976": "Many users of this book may be unaware that it is probably the most comprehensive statistical summary ever published on any major recreational fishery anywhere on the West Coast. It contains tables and charts that detail where and when catches were made, the number of anglers and angler effort."

By examining data included in this report, the author has been able to construct an accurate and detailed account of what readers may expect at the various salmon fishing areas of Washington.

Before venturing into specifics, however, it might be interesting to note the growth of Washington's sport salmon fishery. During 1964, the first year in which salmon punch cards were used, slightly over one million marine angler trips were made. In 1976, marine trips numbered nearly 1.9 million. At the present rate, about twenty-five thousand new anglers are joining the ranks of Washington's sport salmon aficionados each year.

Such growth has occurred not without reason: figures for the 1976 season show a record year, in terms of angler success. Fishermen averaged .88 salmon per trip, and the average catch per angler was 2.79 salmon over the course of the year.

It is perhaps not surprising that a relatively small number of fishermen account for a large number of sport-caught fish. In any area and with any species, such is likely to be the case. These anglers are the "pros"—those who not only possess the skill and experience to score consistently but who spend a larger-than average share of their leisure time in pursuit of their favorite quarry. It may surprise some, however, to note that a full forty-five percent of salmon punch card holders either did not fish or were totally unsuccessful during the latest year for which figures are available. Of this number, fifteen percent did not even wet their lines. But nearly thirty percent of these fishermen *did*—and came up skunked! Obviously, there is more to taking Pacific salmon than merely spending a day on the water.

Not surprisingly, angling pressure builds to a veritable frenzy during the peak summer months. In Washington State, for example, only between eight and ten thousand angler trips take place in any given week during the first four months of the year. Pressure builds rapidly beginning about May and reaches its peak during August. In 1976, there were an average of approximately 135,000 trips per week at mid-August. While the success ratio may not be any greater at this time of year than at certain others, the angling-vacationing hordes flock to the water in droves. That fishing during mid-summer is not for the claustrophobic is more than a wry understatement.

Before citing specific catch statistics, it would be prudent to mention that the figures, while helpful, fail to tell the whole story. Average catches per angler, for example, are greatly influenced by the fraction of charter boat fishermen in the total landings. Charter trips are essentially *guided* trips and the average catch per charter angler at Neah Bay, for instance, far exceeds the average catch per kicker boat angler. Inside Puget Sound, the fleet is made up almost entirely of do-it-yourselfers with many novice fishermen among them. The average fisherman trying his skill at Sekiu from a rental or private boat is far more experienced than the average fisherman working out of Puget Sound. Similarly, the San Juan Islands attract boaters who tend to be incompetent, casual fishermen, and the area is much better than the numbers indicate. Thus it is apparent that the figures cited should not be viewed as the sole criterion for selecting the "best" salmon spot.

The Washington coast offers four major salmon fishing ports.

Ilwaco, near the mouth of the vast Columbia River system, is one of the most important areas—not only to Washington fishermen, but also to Oregon anglers and, in fact, all the various salmon fisheries interests up and down the West Coast. The Columbia and its tributaries account for one of the most productive offshore fishing grounds to be found in the Pacific. Indeed Ilwaco has consistently been at or near the top of the salmon success ratio list in recent years. During 1976, for example, Ilwaco lead the state in sport fishing productivity with an astounding 2.16 salmon per angler trip! Anglers fishing the famed waters of Grays Harbor out of the highly touted Westport (and lesser known Ocean Shores) area placed second with an even 2.00 salmon per trip.

From the protected harbor of Ilwaco near Washington's southwesternmost tip ply a large number of sport fishing vessels each year. Here

Captain Jack McNeal, veteran fisherman and skipper of the famed *Hobo* out of Ilwaco, Washington, prepares to scoop a scrappy coho from the Columbia River mouth. *Author photo, courtesy of* Salt Water Sportsman.

charter and private boats venture into the Pacific in search of both Chinook and coho. The 1976 season saw a total of more than 200,000 marine angler trips, most of which were highly successful. Of the over 400,000 salmon which were boated, most were coho. In fact, silvers numbered just over 370,000 and outnumbered Chinook by about 6 to 1. Fishing here peaks during July and August, but excellent success is enjoyed throughout the entire May—October season. In fact, some of the best action during the latest year for which figures are available at this writing took place during June and September. During the first week of June, Ilwaco sport fishermen averaged an amazing 2.87 salmon per trip! Such a success ratio is indeed impressive in a state in which the daily allowable salmon limit is three fish.

Despite the excellent success posted by Ilwaco anglers, it is necessary to cross the legendary Columbia River "bar" to reach the Pacific (often fish are taken right on the bar or inside the river mouth). This bar can be extremely hazardous, and at times even the largest of charter or party craft hasten or delay their usual early-morning departure times to suit then-current bar conditions. If small boat fishing is to be attempted oustide the Columbia, only thoroughly experienced boatmen who are certain

Westport charter anglers with their day's catch. *Author photo, courtesy of* Salt Water Sportsman.

of prevailing water, weather, and tide conditions should make the bar crossing. It is the inexperienced—or irreverent—skipper who too frequently causes problems for the U.S. Coast Guardsmen stationed near Cape Disappointment.

If weather is questionable, charter or party boats offer an excellent alternative to small boat fishing in the ocean, and these are found in large numbers at Ilwaco. Additionally, there are small boat launching ramps, sling lifts, and camper and trailer facilities. Motels and restaurants are found at both the Port of Ilwaco and at Long Beach, about three miles north of the boat harbor.

The Westport-Ocean Shores area is actually comprised of two distinct fishing ports which straddle Grays Harbor. The harbor itself spans only a relatively short distance, but roads leading between the communities require a lengthy drive. These are Washington's second and third coastal fishing ports.

In recent years, salmon fishing out of Westport-Ocean Shores has nearly equalled—and sometimes even exceeded—that found near Ilwaco and the Columbia River mouth. In fact, the 1976 season saw an even 2.00 salmon average per marine angling trip, slightly under that experienced by Ilwaco anglers. The Chinook-coho ratio for Grays Harbor party boats is approximately the same as for the Ilwaco fleet, with a slightly higher percentage of Chinook boated.

The Westport charter fleet numbers perhaps two hundred craft. While a larger number may be obtained by including part-time boats, this is about the maximum number of boats in operation at any time, with the possible exception of August. Ocean Shores currently boasts only a single charter office and books trips for about a dozen craft. Actually, Ocean Shores is more of an all-around resort community than a simple fishing village. Modern condominiums and motels flourish, and there are a number of restaurants, as well as a golf course and seasonal razor clam digging. Westport, in contrast, is founded primarily on fishing—both sport and commercial—although there are motel, restaurant, and other recreational facilities. Camper and trailer

93

A scene repeated thousands of times annually on Pacific charter boats. *Courtesy of Washington Department of Fisheries.*

sites also abound, and there are launching facilities for private boats.

La Push, situated about one-third of the way down the Washington coast, is the fourth Washington port to face the Pacific. It is another popular and highly productive salmon area. In fact, La Push fishermen averaged a solid 1.52 salmon per angling trip during the same recent season for which catch figures are shown for the other areas.

La Push does not have a large, dangerous bar to cross, such as those found at Ilwaco and Westport-Ocean Shores (the Grays Harbor bar is second only to that of the Columbia, in terms of the respect it commands). Located at the mouth of the Quillayute River, which is known for its exceptionally large Chinook salmon, this small resort area has a limited number of motel, charter, and rental boat facilities but offers some of the most scenic saltwater surroundings to be found anywhere in the state. Restaurants and launching facilities are also available.

La Push fishermen find a higher proportion of coho to Chinook than do anglers fishing out of Ilwaco or Grays Harbor. According to 1976 catch statistics, coho outnumbered Chinook by approximately nine to one. While August ushers in the angling crowds, as is the case in most other Northwest salmon areas, the best fishing actually occurred during the first half of June. In fact, anglers fishing from La Push during the first week of June averaged slightly better than 2.7 salmon per trip.

Coho are abundant from May through October. Perhaps the best fishing for Chinook is during July and August. During this time, moochers and trollers frequently connect on large, mature kings. One of the best areas for large king salmon is found near The Needles—tall, spirelike rocks rising majestically from the sea.

Neah Bay is located on the Strait of Juan de Fuca, just inside Cape Flattery at the state's northwesternmost tip. Its unique position has given the area its reputation as the salmon "crossroads" of Washington. Here fish make their way both north and south along the Pacific coast. Additionally, however, salmon pass Neah Bay during their migratory runs into Juan de Fuca Strait and Puget Sound. Although the port is situated on the strait, and does not face westerly into the Pacific, much of the fishing actually takes place in the ocean.

Located on the Makah Indian Reservation, Neah Bay boasts the third highest per-trip salmon success

The legendary Cal McKenney, longtime charter skipper who operated out of La Push, Washington, unhooks a coho which fell for a "hoochie"—a squid-type lure—fished behind a flasher. Cal was killed in an auto accident not long after this photograph was snapped. *Author photo, courtesy of* Salt Water Sportsman.

ratio with approximately 1.5 fish per angling day. Aside from the outstanding salmon fishing, a major attraction of the area is its ability to afford both ocean and strait fishing: often the usually calmer waters of Juan de Fuca Strait may be fished when ocean conditions warrant caution. Moreover, some of the best action is found *inside* Cape Flattery—especially for large feeding king salmon.

Charters (most of which are six-man boats), skiff rentals, and launching facilities are available at Neah Bay, but motel and restaurant accommodations are limited. Like Ilwaco, Grays Harbor, and La Push, Neah Bay offers both Chinook and coho sport from May to October, although the waters of Juan de Fuca Strait have remained open to salmon angling during the fall-spring months of recent years.

Like fishing at the other areas, Neah Bay action peaks during July and August. The best fishing, however, is anytime between mid-May and late September. Coho are abundant from late May to late September; Chinook begin to come on strong during June. Some of the best fishing for mature king salmon occurs during the first half of July.

A higher proportion of Chinook to coho occurs at Neah Bay than at any of the Pacific salmon harbors. In general, anglers may expect about one fish in five to be a king or blackmouth. Over the years, this area has been one of the premier king salmon spots of Washington.

Hooknose silvers—large, adult coho displaying their distorted upper jaws at maturity—are especially abundant near Neah Bay during late August and September. It is during this period that surface trolling with streamer flies is most productive and exciting. Anglers who have been introduced to this coveted sport are likely to become less enamored with even the largest of king salmon—such is the thrill of taking large coho on flies!

Sekiu (prounounced "C-Q") and Pillar Point are found on the Strait of Juan de Fuca and receive heavy fishing pressure throughout the year. Unlike at the ocean ports, anglers fishing out of these two areas are able to fish salmon during each month of the year. Practically speaking, however, accommodations are rare between about mid-October and mid-February. During the early part of the February-October season, blackmouth or immature Chinook make up the bulk of the sport catch. February typically offers some of the best Chinook fishing, in fact. Catch statistics for 1976 show that anglers enjoyed a success ratio as high as 1.44 during mid-February. Coho are relatively scarce until June, but the best silver fishing occurs during August and September.

Beginning at Sekiu and heading eastward along the Strait of Juan de Fuca and into Puget Sound and adjacent waters, overall fishing success drops drastically. The 1976 figures show, for example, that anglers fishing Sekiu-Pillar Point averaged only .60 fish per trip. Compared to the 1.55 fish-per-trip average at Neah Bay and similar, high-success fishing enjoyed at the four major Pacific ports, fishing at Sekiu-Pillar Point (and other more easterly areas) is *less than half as productive*, in terms of pure fish numbers, as Neah Bay or the coastal areas.

But while catch statistics here are not nearly as impressive as those reported for the previously detailed areas, this is Chinook country. In contrast to Neah Bay, La Push, Grays Harbor, and Ilwaco—which produce from five to nine times as many coho as Chinook—anglers fishing the Sekiu-Pillar Point area take considerably more Chinook than coho. In rough numbers, approximately 40,000 Chinook were boated here during the 1976 season, while only about 25,000 silvers were reported in the catches. In other recent years, Sekiu-Pillar Point fishermen have taken as high a Chinook-to-coho ratio as four to one!

Hog-sized lingcod—excellent table fare—are often taken incidentally by Pacific salmon fishermen. While ling numbers have dwindled recently in certain inland waters, fish are still numerous along the coast. *Courtesy of* Fish Watch.

Jerry Ray nets a 12-pound coho taken on a surface-trolled streamer fly. *Author photo, courtesy of* Salt Water Sportsman.

The best fishing for mature king salmon is normally found during June to around mid-August. Perhaps the "hottest" bite occurs during the first two weeks of July, but two- and three-year old Chinook are taken in good numbers from about mid-March through mid-September. Most prevalent here are light trollers and moochers who work plug-cut herring near the shoreline. Late summer and fall silvers are taken anywhere along this stretch of Juan de Fuca Strait, usually a mile or more from shore.

Sekiu offers motel, charter, restaurant, boat rental, and launching facilities, but rental motors are practically nonexistent. Only camping, trailer, and launching accommodations are currently available at Pillar Point.

Eastern Juan de Fuca Strait is made up of an area which stretches roughly from Agate and Crescent Beaches, about fifteen miles west of Port Angeles, to Anacortes, north of Seattle. While the entire general area is heavily fished from spring to fall, angler trip catch figures show only about .6 salmon on average. The two main salmon areas are Port Angeles and Agate and Crescent Beaches (although the future of the latter is uncertain at this writing; an existing campground-fishing port may be closed).

Port Angeles, situated at the base of the magnificent Olympic Mountain range, is a moderately large town which caters to both industry and tourism. As a main jumping-off point for ferry-bound passengers visiting British Columbia's beautiful Victoria, Port Angeles boasts waters which are fished heavily throughout the vacationing season. There are numerous motels, restaurants, and shops, in addition to a limited number of charter or party boats, skiff rentals, and launching sites.

Fishermen working the waters of eastern Juan de Fuca Strait take about equal numbers of Chinook and coho. The strait is open to fishing year around, although—as elsewhere—the heaviest fishing pressure occurs during the peak summer months. By far the best fishing, in terms of catch numbers, is found from about the first of February through the middle of March when large numbers of immature Chinook show throughout the area. Figures for the 1976 calendar year, for example, show that anglers consistently averaged better than one fish per rod during this period. In fact, fishermen averaged two to two and one-half times the salmon per trip total of .58 posted over the course of the year.

The best fishing for mature king salmon typically occurs from late June to mid-August. At this time, moochers and trollers often find productive sport near Ediz Hook, Green Point, and the garbage dump (euphemistically dubbed "Can Can Cove" by a local radio station). Coho show sporadically throughout the year, but the heaviest concentrations invariably occur from July through September.

The San Juan Islands see heavy fishing pressure during the peak summer vacation months. The waters surrounding this maze of scenic islands produce only about .4 salmon per angler trip, however. But here, too, Chinook usually outnumber coho. The 1976 season produced approximately three times as many Chinook as coho, in fact.

This is private boat country, for the most part. Charter and party boat accommodations are difficult, if not impossible, to find. Skiffs, however, are available at certain points along the islands.

The San Juans are famous more for their beauty than for their angling opportunities and thus comprise a favorite family cruising and vacation playground.

Still, fishing may be good at times. These waters are open to salmon fishermen throughout the year, and the only factor determining whether fishing may or may not take place is the weather. During the 1976 calendar year, the best fishing occurred during the week ending January 4, when anglers averaged an even 1.0 salmon per marine trip. Of course, winter weather separates the men from the boys, thus making for better catches among more seasoned anglers.

The area between Skagit Bay and Deception Pass

Vence Malernee hauls tackle toward a kicker boat moored at a rain-soaked Sekiu float. *Author photo, courtesy of* Salt Water Sportsman.

Winter salmon fishing isn't often cozy sport, but the results can warm the heart. Here small boat fishermen take an immature king, a "blackmouth," from the frigid waters of Juan de Fuca Strait. *Author photo.*

also produces salmon, though in fewer numbers than the areas already described. The 1976 figures showed an average catch of only .19 salmon per angling day. Here the ratio of Chinook to coho is approximately two to one. Another popular inland marine area lies between Admiralty Inlet and Possession Sound and provides slightly better salmon fishing success. In fact, the 1976 figures show that anglers fishing this area averaged *over twice* the number of salmon taken by fishermen in the Skagit-Deception area. Both general marine areas see some of the best angler success during January and February.

The Puget Sound area which lies between Seattle and Bremerton offers only about one-fourth of a salmon per angling trip but enjoys very heavy fishing pressure. This area, too, may be fished year around. Normally, Chinook outnumber coho by about three to two. Typically, the best fishing for large, mature Chinook is found during August and September. Blackmouth fishing may be expected to peak from about December through February. Resident coho

Early morning is usually the best time to fish for Pacific salmon, especially Chinook. Here a solitary angler trolls Puget Sound in the gathering daylight, framed by a sleepy Seattle skyline. *Author photo.*

Young angler displays a hefty king salmon. *Courtesy of Washington Department of Fisheries.*

—silvers bred to remain inside Puget Sound during their entire lives—may be taken during every month of the year, but the largest number of coho is seen from July through about mid-October.

Salmon success is somewhat better in the southern Puget Sound area, near Tacoma and Olympia. Anglers fishing these waters average about .4 salmon per trip. Here, too, coho may be found at virtually any time of the year, and the same is generally true of immature Chinook.

By far the most impressive catches taken from these waters occur during the winter months. Most productive is the period from about December to mid-February. In fact, catch statistics for 1976 show that, during January, southern Puget Sound fishermen averaged from 1.50 to 2.14 fish per outing. Most of these salmon were three-year-old Chinook.

Fishing for four-year-olds typically peaks from about May through July. The largest numbers of coho are taken from mid-July to late August.

Hood Canal, west of Puget Sound, provides fishing which is comparable to that enjoyed in southern Puget Sound. This, too, is small boat territory for the most part. A number of resorts, skiff rentals and launching sites are found along the canal. Typically the best fishing here occurs during late winter and early spring. Both coho and immature Chinook may be found almost anytime during the year.

Puget Sound and adjacent waters have catered to the small boat angling fraternity for decades. Only recently have charter or party boats begun to take an active interest in inland marine fishing. Partially out of economic necessity, many of the charter craft working out of such coastal ports as Ilwaco and Westport now offer off-season salmon (and sometimes bottomfishing) trips to Puget Sound residents and visitors.

But a handful of charter and party boats carry anglers on salmon and bottomfishing runs during the summer months also. The number is increasing gradually, spurred on by the success of such pioneer efforts as those of Seattle's Viking Charters, most notably the modern, fifty-eight foot *Viking Star*. It appears that other charter operators will soon recognize the potential offered by operating close to the major metropolitan areas, even if the fishing is not what it is at, say, Ilwaco—or the other major Pacific ports.

Recent state fisheries department punch card returns dispel all doubt about Washington's salmon fishing opportunities. In terms of pure numbers, the best bets are the major coastal ports which face the Pacific—and Neah Bay, at the northwest tip of the state.

But coastal anglers take far more coho than

Saltwater salmon plant, made from the deck of a Washington State ferryboat, to enhance Puget Sound sport fishing. *Courtesy of Washington Department of Fisheries.*

Chinook and, while most veteran anglers would prefer fighting the former than the latter—even when size is a factor—the majority of fishermen, steeped in tradition and myth and forever hoping to do battle with a king of lunker proportions, opt for the quarry which is typically larger in size. For kings and blackmouth, therefore, it is difficult to beat the waters of the western Strait of Juan de Fuca. For smaller Chinook and coho, the protected waters of Puget Sound, Hood Canal and the San Juan Islands—in addition to Admiralty Inlet—provide ample sport.

Washington's sport fishery depends heavily upon artificial hatchery production, and it is apparent that here, as elsewhere, the future of the Pacific salmon species will become even more heavily dependent upon the expansion of hatchery facilities. Of course, the constant and (at this writing) seemingly incessant legal battles and the crippling effects they have upon fisheries management will also determine the future of the resource. But through the efforts of state and federal agencies, organized sport groups, and concerned individual sportsmen, it is hoped that the fishery will continue to survive, if not unscathed, then at least uninterrupted.

In recent years, the Washington State Department of Fisheries has been striving to enhance various phases of that state's salmon resources. One area of concentration has been the Puget Sound Sport Fishing Enhancement Program, the main success of which to date has been to rear coho and Chinook which remain within the general confines of the sound and are thus available to anglers on a year-round basis. Fish are retained at the hatcheries about three months longer than normal, and these late releases display a proclivity toward cruising the

waters of Puget Sound, rather than migrating to the ocean. These are the resident fish which are rapidly becoming an important facet of the state's "in-sound" program.

While artificial production and other fisheries management efforts have aided sport fishing success, the liberalization of regulations permitting anglers to take smaller salmon (in some instances there is *no* minimum size requirement at all) has also contributed to increased angling success.

On the other hand, Frank Haw, Deputy Director of the Washington Department of Fisheries, wisely notes: "Our Chinook minimum size in Puget Sound is the largest in history (20 inches). Even so, catches are near the historic highs experienced in the 1950s (when the size limit was 12 inches). Few coho now taken in Puget Sound are less than twelve inches, even though there is no size limit."

Oregon

Oregon offers excellent salmon fishing for both Chinook and coho. Unlike Washington, Alaska, and British Columbia, however, Oregon does not have a myriad of inland marine waters. Thus, most saltwater salmon angling is done along the state's four hundred-mile coastline.

Anglers fishing Oregon waters for Pacific salmon take approximately one-third the number of fish which are taken from Washington waters. Statistical data are obtained from salmon-steelhead tags; approximately twenty percent of these tags are returned each year. Information derived from these tags is supplemented by statistical port check and creel samples to improve the total annual catch estimates. Nonresponse bias is corrected by various statistical methods, and it is believed that the estimates arrived at are quite accurate.

Oregon's Fish Division of the Department of Fish and Wildlife has provided figures for salmon sport catches in recent years. The latest year for which figures are available at this writing is 1976. This is the same calendar year for which figures are provided for Washington, and anglers may wish to note differences in sport fishing information furnished for the two states.

The 1976 salmon year was a bumper one for Oregon: statistics show that an estimated total of 656,374 salmon were taken. Of this number, ocean-caught fish totalled nearly 568,000, while "inland" (primarily freshwater-caught fish) salmon numbered approximately 88,000.*

As in Washington, coho outnumber Chinook. But Oregon's combined ocean and inland coho-to-Chinook ratio is significantly higher than is Washington's. During 1976, Oregon's sport salmon fishery included about four coho for each Chinook, in contrast to Washington's roughly two and one-half-to-one ratio.

Considerably fewer anglers fish Oregon's waters than those of their more northerly neighbor. During 1976, it is estimated that slightly more than 272,000 fishermen tried their luck while fishing from Oregon, while about 625,000 fished out of Washington. Overall angler success, however, appears to be similar: while daily catch averages are not available for Oregon, sport fishermen averaged an annual catch of 2.85 salmon per angler, slightly above Washington's 2.79 average.

Perhaps not surprisingly, the Columbia River—which forms the natural boundary between Washington and Oregon—is the foremost producer of salmon for rods working out of Oregon. Nearly thirty percent of all ocean-caught fish taken from Oregon ports were boated near the mouth of the Columbia. Perhaps the most productive of all West Coast salmon areas—particularly because of its large number of coho—the Columbia-Pacific area offers excellent fishing throughout the spring-fall season. The best fishing is found from June through September, with action peaking during August and early September when coho mill around the mouth of the river before beginning their upstream migrations. Chinook are also available in good numbers at this time of year.

While Washington's Ilwaco is the jumping-off spot for anglers fishing the Columbia River mouth from that state, Oregon offers three major Columbia-oriented ports. Warrenton, Astoria, and Hammond each provide access to the river via launching facilities, and extensive charter or party boat fishing facilities are available at each point as well. Nearby restaurants, motels, and camper-trailer parks round out the accommodations.

Until recently, there was no charge to fish salmon from Washington, but there was a fee to fish out of Oregon. For this reason and others, many Oregonians crossed the Astoria-Megler Bridge to fish out of Ilwaco on the Washington side. While there is no longer free fishing from either state, thousands of anglers continue to trek to Ilwaco, where there is a more extensive charter fleet.

*All statistics for Oregon are from R. L. Berry, comp., *Oregon Salmon and Steelhead Catch Data, 1967-1976* (Portland, Oregon, Oregon Department of Fish and Wildlife, Fish Division, 1976).

Brad O'Connor, Seattle *Times* Outdoor Editor and son of the legendary gun writer, Jack O'Conner, with a Columbia River spring Chinook. *Courtesy of Washington Department of Fisheries.*

Irregardless of the state from which one fishes, the same Columbia River bar must be crossed in order to reach the Pacific, although fishermen sometimes score impressive catches in the tidewaters of the river itself. As previously noted, extreme caution is required of any bar crossing—but especially of the Columbia's.

Nehalem Bay is another popular ocean fishing port. Some of the best offshore fishing here is encountered during September and October, but good fishing is found throughout the season in the bay itself. In fact, both trollers and bank fishermen take salmon from the brackish bay waters. Chinook enter the Nehalem River about August and are available until late September; coho begin to show in the river about mid-August but may be taken as late as mid-October. Most of the fishing here is done by trolling from the Nehalem bar upriver. Rental boats and launching facilities are available at Nehalem Bay, and commercial fishermen will often carry salmon parties.

Tillamook Bay offers good salmon fishing from about mid-April through December. The best fishing for spring Chinook is from about mid-April to mid-May, although some fish are taken earlier in the year. Fall Chinook fishing is at its best from mid-September to mid-October, while coho are abundant from September on. Nearby Garibaldi offers charter and party boat accommodations.

Offshore fishing in the Tillamook-Garibaldi area reaches a frenzy during August, when peak summer angling-vacationing crowds flock to the area. In fact, figures for the 1976 season show that nearly 24,000 salmon were taken here during August; July, in contrast, was the second most productive month but offered only about one-fourth the number of fish as were taken during August.

Pacific City-Nestucca Bay provide excellent Chinook fishing during June and July, but fall fish begin to show about early August and are available through September. Coho normally enter the Nestucca and Little Nestucca rivers about September 20 and remain available until the end of November. Offshore fishing from Pacific City begins about late June and continues throughout the summer. Plugs and wobblers are popular, as is mooching and (occasionally) surface-trolling with streamer flies for coho. Charters, launching, and rental boats may be found at Pacific City.

Siletz Bay also offers some top summer salmon fishing opportunities. Large, mature Chinook enter the Siletz River during August, with peak fishing occurring during September. Coho show in late September and are abundant during October and early November. Trolling is most productive in the bay and the tidewaters of the river. Guides and launching facilities may be found at Siletz Bay.

Depoe Bay offers a large number of party and charter boat accommodations and is a favorite Pacific port among Oregon anglers. There is easy access to the Pacific for both charter and private craft, and both Chinook and coho are available. Offshore fishing peaks during June, July, and August, although a few fish are taken as early as April and as late as November.

The Yaquina Bay-Newport area is still another popular Pacific salmon fishing area. The best fishing here is during June, July and (especially) August. But salmon show as early as April and may be taken as late as November.

Chinook are taken from Yaquina Bay and off Newport during August, and coho are abundant, too, during this period. Charters, rental boats, and launching are at Yaquina Bay, and Newport offers an extensive party boat fleet.

Alsea Bay-Waldport is another productive stretch of the Oregon coast. Trolling for Chinook peaks during August and September. Coho begin to show in numbers about mid-September, although the best silver fishing is normally found during October.

Pacific salmon fishing isn't just for the boys. Here a West Coast charter skipper nets a distaff-hooked silver. *Author photo.*

Boats may be rented on the Alsea River at Waldport.

Siuslaw Bay-Florence-Mapleton is productive for both Chinook and coho from about the middle of July through November. Offshore charter fishing peaks during July and August, although fish may be taken from the brine anytime between April and November.

Winchester Bay and its offshore waters are second only to the Columbia River mouth in terms of the Oregon sport salmon catch. During the 1976 season, over 90,000 salmon were taken here. Both Chinook and coho are abundant in the Pacific, but charters and guides also fish the bay. Trolled herring bring strikes from both Pacific species from June through September. Spring Chinook begin showing about mid-March and may be taken through June, but fall Chinook arrive during August and early September. In terms of salmon numbers, July is the best month here. August is also extremely productive. Boats, guides, tackle, and other salmon-related facilities may be found at the town of Salmon Harbor, near Winchester Bay.

Coos Bay-Charleston anglers find excellent offshore fishing from early June to early September. Limited fishing for fall Chinook and coho occurs inside Coos Bay itslef. As at Winchester Bay, the most productive month for offshore fishing at Coos Bay-Charleston is July. Some of the best bay fishing takes place during September and October.

Gold Beach at the mouth of the famed Rogue River is another popular Oregon port. Here offshore fishing for both Chinook and coho gets under way during the summer, with action peaking during August and September. July is also a very productive month. Boat launching is available, and charter or party boat accommodations may be found at Gold Beach, on the south side of the Rogue River mouth, or at Wedderburn, on the north side.

Brookings, at the mouth of the Chetco River (which the Oregon Department of Transportation calls "by far the best salmon and steelhead stream south of the Rogue"), offers access into the Pacific via charter or party craft. Large numbers of Chinook and coho enter the Chetco. Chinook begin their upstream migration about September but may be available as late as mid-November; coho arrive at late September but may show through December. July is the peak month for ocean fishing: during 1976, over twice as many salmon were boated during July as August, the second most productive offshore fishing month.

California

California waters, for all practical purposes, provide the southernmost limits of the Pacific coast salmon range. While it is true that coho have been spotted as far south as Mexico, relatively few fish are encountered south of Monterey. But recent efforts to establish a salmon fishery in southern California waters have been sufficiently successful to generate great enthusiasm among the more southerly residents of the state.

The California Department of Fish and Game does not keep extensive records on the sport salmon fishery, as do Oregon and Washington. The reader may find this somewhat surprising, since Chinook and coho salmon are an important part of the recreational fishery occurring throughout the northern portion of the state. In a recent letter to the author, Mr. Joe Sheehan, information officer in the Sacramento office of the California DFG, notes: "There are no 'catch statistics' on salmon in rivers and streams."

Yet northern California waters offer some outstanding opportunities for both salt and freshwater salmon fishermen. From Monterey north, nearly any moderately large Pacific community offers charter, party boat, or skiff fishing

throughout the bulk of the angling season.

Both Chinook and coho are native to northern California streams. While Chinook runs occur primarily in the larger, glacial river systems from San Francisco Bay north, these fish sometimes spawn in the smaller connecting tributaries. And coho spawn in many of the state's smaller coastal streams—and sometimes in the tributaries of the larger river systems.

California salmon charter and party boat facilities have improved considerably in recent years. Offshore fishing, such as that which takes place near the Farallon Islands and other popular and productive Pacific salmon digs, usually incorporates the use of relatively heavy trolling tackle. Often heavy sinkers of twenty or more ounces are used.

But light-action tackle is also used and appears to be gaining a greater following. At this writing, light angling techniques are popular especially in the more northerly offshore waters. Live bait, too, has made for more exciting fishing aboard charter and party boats operating from the Bay Area north.

While salmon are sometimes fished from Avila and Morro Bay, catches are sporadic. Typically, the best salmon action occurs during the spring. Charter or party boats and rental skiffs are available at both ports, and private boats may be launched into the Pacific.

Somewhat more consistent fishing is found near Monterey Bay. Usually the best catches are posted during the spring months, but fishing may be fair into the fall. Charter or party boat accommodations are available at Monterey, Moss Landing, and Santa Cruz. Rental boats are available at these three communities, and at Capitola, located a few miles east of Santa Cruz. Private boat launching is possible at all four Monterey Bay communities.

Half Moon Bay, just south of San Francisco's expanse of the Pacific, offers fair salmon fishing, although most charter or party boat runs originating from Princeton are targeted on bottomfish. Rental boats are also available at Princeton.

Point San Pedro offers the only launching and skiff rental facilities between Princeton and San Francisco Bay. Both Chinook and coho are taken here.

The San Francisco Bay area is the hub of California's sport salmon fishery. A vast number of charter and party boats operate out of Fisherman's Wharf, Gas House Cove, and other San Francisco points, as well as from the Sausalito and Berkeley Yacht Harbors. Skiff rentals, however, are practically nonexistent.

While Chinook which make their upstream spawning migrations through several bays en route

Sunburst from the sea! A Pacific salmon clears the ocean's surface and is brought to net by a party boat deckhand. Scenes like this one are common along the northern California coast from spring through fall. *Author photo, courtesy of* Outdoor Life.

to the Sacramento and San Joaquin systems may be taken infrequently from the waters of northen San Francisco Bay, they are rarely boated in the Delta or San Pablo Bay. By far the most productive salmon runs are those made to promising offshore points outside the Golden Gate—the Farallons and other salmon feeding areas.

Most popular among Bay Area charter and party boat fishermen is heavy tackle trolling, in which sinker relase mechanisms are coupled with weights of thirty-two ounces or more. At times, lighter tackle is used to advantage, but skippers who know both the areas in which fish may be found and their feeding habits usually opt for the heavier gear. Salmon fishing here may begin as early as February and continue into the late summer or fall months.

Tomales Bay waters provide a relatively short-lived salmon season during most years. Typically, coho are taken near Point Reyes and Inverness beginning about October. Chinook may be found in limited numbers during most months of the year; some of the best king fishing takes place near the bay entrance when Chinook follow baitfish schools into the bay. There are hazardous waters here, however. Outgoing tides may bring large breakers to the bay entrance, and small boat fishermen should exercise caution at all times. Public launching is at Nick's Cove.

Bodega Bay is fished heavily by skiff fishermen. Boats may be launched at Doran Park, near the harbor entrance on the east side of the bay. Both Chinook and coho are taken.

Point Arena, situated along the Pacific coast between Bodega Bay and Fort Bragg, offers good salmon fishing, with action peaking during July and August. Both rental skiffs and boat launching

Albacore tuna are occasionally hooked by coastal salmon anglers, but the best bet is to book a charter or party boat trip slated strictly for the longfins. *Photograph by Ron Jones, courtesy of* Fish Watch.

facilities are available. Charter or party boat accommodations are found at Albion, between Point Arena and Fort Bragg. Here, too, the best fishing for both Chinook and coho usually occurs during mid-summer. Albion also boasts rental boats and launching facilities.

The Humboldt Bay area is heavily fished for salmon. Chinook show in fair numbers throughout the spring and early summer, and both Chinook and coho are taken from July through September. Party boats are available at Buhne Point, located between Eureka and Fields Landing. Charter runs to offshore grounds are made regularly throughout the summer season. Rental skiffs may also be found at Buhne Point.

During the summer months, there is often outstanding salmon fishing to be found at the entrance to Humboldt Bay. At such times, drifting or trolling with anchovies, herring, or sardines may be especially productive.

The summer months also provide topnotch salmon fishing near Fort Bragg and Shelter Cove. Both Chinook and coho are abundant. Charter or party boat accommodations are available near the entrance to Noyo Harbor, and avid salmon anglers frequently launch skiffs from the beach at Shelter

Cove. Rental boats are also available at Fort Bragg. Most popular fishing techniques here revolve around the use of trolled baitfish or artificial lures.

Charter or party boats also operate out of Trinidad, between Eureka and Crescent City. Skiff rentals and launching are also found at Trinidad. Salmon fishing peaks during July and August, when both Chinook and coho are taken in impressive numbers.

Crescent City charter and party boats work the mouth of the Smith River with excellent success at times. The Smith is California's northernmost coastal stream and sees good runs of fall Chinook. Action peaks during mid-summer, when both Chinook and coho may be taken. Rental boats and launching facilities are found at Crescent City.

The California Department of Fish and Game has experimented with a stocking program designed to enhance the salmon runs occasionally found off that state's southern coast. At times, coho show in moderate numbers as far south as Santa Barbara and Ventura Counties. Perhaps such enhancement efforts will pay dividends in future years. While salmon have been taken with some regularity off the southern coast over the years, catch numbers are quite low. In order to rectify the situation and to provide a new and exciting sport fishery, stocking programs have been conducted near Oxnard and Oceanside. Although the ultimate outcome is still in doubt, it is hoped that the DFG's considerable efforts will meet with success and that the southerly range of Pacific salmon may be expanded.

Alaska

Alaska is salmon country. The state boasts an astonishing thirty thousand plus miles of coastline—more than that of all the lower forty-eight states—and the continental shelf adds another half million square miles of productive marine waters. Larger than Texas, California, and Montana combined, Alaska is roughly equal in size to one-fifth of the lower forty-eight states.

Alaska first became a possession of the United States when it was purchased from Russia in 1867 for slightly over seven million dollars. It became a territory in 1912 and was admitted to statehood in 1958. Throughout its varied existence, Alaska has been a premier region for sportsmen, salmon anglers included.

Despite Alaska's vast coastline, most saltwater salmon fishing opportunities are found in the southeastern part of the state—frequently called the "Panhandle." This area is comprised roughly from Haines to Skagway on the north to Ketchikan on the south. It is a region lacking adequate roads and highways in many places, and the primary means of travel is by boat or airplane.

Alaska's charter or party boat industry has grown rapidly in recent years. Boats now operate out of such diverse places as Ketchikan, Juneau, Seward, Homer, Kodiak, Whittier, and other points. Because of sometimes hazardous weather and water conditions, however, rental skiffs are not abundant throughout Alaska.

All Pacific salmon species are found in Alaskan waters, but—like elsewhere in the West—Chinook and coho provide the most coveted angling opportunities. The state boasts some of the largest Chinook salmon catches. In fact, the world record Chinook, a fish weighing 126 1/2 pounds, was commercially trapped near Petersburg. Favorite Bay yielded an 87-pound "soaker" in 1971, and the more popular and productive salmon waters of the state consistently turn out impressive Chinook catches.

In general, Chinook are abundant throughout the southeastern part of the state from about April to July. They show in the largest numbers off southcentral Alaska during the May-July period. Coho are present along the southern and central coast from about July through September. Sockeye appear on the southeast coast during July and may be taken through August, but fishing for this species is best in the more northerly latitudes from about June through July. Pink salmon become abundant during July and August and chums may be taken anytime between July and September.

Saltwater salmon fishing techniques vary throughout the state, but the best fishing is invariably from boat. Trolling with baitfish and artificial spoons and spinners is most common, but mooching with herring baits is increasing in popularity and proving just as productive in the northland as throughout the more southerly Pacific salmon range. In southeastern Alaska, Chinook may be found feeding year around but are taken in the greatest numbers immediately before they begin their upstream spawning migrations.

Because of Alaska's vast marine system, it would be folly to attempt to list each and every productive salmon area. Instead there follows a listing of some of the more heavily fished and productive salmon angling spots:

The Ketchikan area offers numerous top sport fishing opportunities. The Unuk River, among the West's most populous salmon streams, enters the Behm Canal about sixty miles north of Ketchikan

Silhouetted by a shaft of rare winter sunlight, a small boat fisherman plays a Chinook salmon. Such scenes are common throughout Alaska's salmon-rich waters. *Author photo, courtesy of* Salt Water Sportsman.

and accounts for a large number of fish taken from this general area.

Yes Bay, located on the Behm Canal about fifty miles northwest of Ketchikan, is among Alaska's most popular sport salmon fishing areas. In fact, Yes Bay furnishes perhaps the best fish-per-angler average of all Alaska salmon spots. The area is accessible by float plane from Ketchikan and offers good fishing for Chinook, coho, pinks, and chum. The largest Chinook ("soakers") usually appear about the third week of May and are available until late June. Humpy, coho, and blackmouth fishing peaks during July, although feeder kings are available at all times during the spring-fall season. Halibut, cod, snappers, shrimp, and crab add to the resources of this area.

Alaska Tour & Marketing Services, Inc., which provides sport fishing packages throughout the state, recommends that anglers heading for Yes Bay bring both mooching and spinning or casting tackle. For mature Chinook, mooching rods of at least six feet in length and which will handle sinkers of up to twelve ounces are needed. Star drag, multiplying or spinning reels and no less than two hundred yards of twenty-pound-test (or heavier) nylon monofilament are required. Many anglers here use leaders which are *heavier* than the line: thirty- to forty-pound-test is common.

Fishing for pinks and coho requires light-action tackle consisting of an eight-and-one-half foot steelhead drift rod used to cast one-quarter to two ounce lures or baits. Free-spooling casting reels or spinning models are recommended. Fifteen-pound-test line is popular; anglers should load at least two hundred yards of mono onto their reels. Herring and salmon spoons bring most strikes in salt water.

Clover Pass, situated about fifteen miles north of Ketchikan, is a famous saltwater area and is located in the calm, protected waters at the head of Behm Canal. The area is accessible by road and boasts excellent salmon fishing. Adult Chinook are most abundant from late May until late June; pink runs peak during July; coho fishing is normally hottest during August and September. Feeder Chinook are available from spring until fall. The same tackle used at Yes Bay will bring strikes here—and, in fact, at most of Alaska's popular salmon haunts.

Glacier Bay, home of the oldest, largest and most active of glaciers, offers good Chinook fishing during May and June. Chinook are also available during August and September. The best fishing for silvers is found during August and September, too. Feeder Chinook are taken throughout the spring-fall season, along with occasional catches of sockeye and pinks. Most of the fishing here is conducted from twenty-four foot covered cruisers. Salmon moochers may connect with an incidental halibut or other bottomfish species.

Bell Island, forty-five miles north of Ketchikan, offers top king fishing during May and June. A fall run also occurs during August and September, and coho are most plentiful during these months.

Blank Inlet, seven miles south of Ketchikan by boat, provides good summer angling for Chinook, coho, pinks, and chum. Mountain Point, seven miles southest of Ketchikan by road or by boat, also

Floating fish camp! Remote resorts like this one, accessible only by boat or plane, are common throughout the Northland. *Author photo.*

furnishes action from the same four Pacific salmon species.

The Sport Fish Division of the Alaska Department of Fish and Game has been kind enough to provide information relating to a number of that state's other salt water salmon areas. The agency notes that the following areas are worthy of anglers' attention:

Point Alava, situated about twenty miles southeast of Ketchikan and accessible by boat, is a productive area for several Pacific salmon species. Peak fishing for Chinook occurs during May and June, while coho, pinks, and chum become available beginning about July and extending through September.

Point Sykes is another popular salmon area. Located about twenty-five miles southeast of Kethcikan, Point Sykes is accessible by boat. Alaska DFG officials recommend that anglers seek the aid of fishing guides here. The area produces king and feeder salmon, as well as coho, pinks, and chum.

Chasina Point is still another possibility for salmon fishermen based near Ketchikan. Accessible by boat, Chasina Point is found twenty-two miles southwest of Ketchikan. The use of a guide is recommended here, too.

Grindall Island, twenty miles northwest of Ketchikan, is accessible by boat and, like Chasina Point, offers seasonal fishing for Chinook, coho, pinks, and chum. Guide services are also recommended here.

Vallenar Point produces good catches of Chinook, coho, pinks, and chum in season and is located eleven miles northwest of Ketchikan. The area may be reached by boat. Nearby Caamano Point offers similar opportunities for taking the same four salmon species.

Admiralty Island, also accessible via Ketchikan, offers boats, motors, and guide services, as do Klawack Inlet and Big Harbor, both of which are reached via Craig. Admiralty Island boasts several extremely productive salmon spots. Among the more popular are Point Retreat, reached by boat from Juneau, Auke Bay or Tee Harbor, and Piling Point, accessible via the same three routes. Point Arden, Doty's Cove, Mitchell Bay, and "Tyee Area" are other Admiralty Island points which are fished heavily from May through September. All spots offer exceptionally good fishing for Chinook, coho, pinks, sockeye, and chum.

The waters surrounding Juneau offer still other highly desirable saltwater salmon fishing possibilities. Echo Cove, about forty miles north of Juneau and which may be reached via the Glacier Highway, provides sport for Chinook, coho, chum, and pinks during the late-spring-to-late summer season. North Pass, about twenty-five miles northwest of Juneau, may be reached by boat from Juneau, Auke Bay, or Tee Harbor. Chinook, coho, sockeye, pinks, and chums may all be found at North Pass.

The Breadline, also accessible by way of Juneau, Auke Bay, or Tee Harbor, is very heavily fished and produces large numbers of all five Pacific salmon species. Nearby Aaron Island and Lena Point offer similar angling opportunities.

Point Retreat, Favorite Reef, South Shelter Island, and Barlow Cove are reached by boat from Juneau, Auke Bay, or Tee Harbor; each turns out good numbers of Chinook, coho, sockeye, pinks, and chum during the spring-fall season. Auke Bay, only twelve miles north of Juneau, may be reached by car via the Glacier Highway. All five Pacific species are taken here, as well as from the waters surrounding Piling Point and Outer Point.

Middle Point, on the western side of Douglas Island, is still another Juneau-area spot which sees heavy fishing pressure during the summer months and which produces all five Pacific salmon species. The White Marker and Point Hilda, just south of Middle Point, provide action on the same species. Icy Point, Marmion island, Dupont, Point Salisbury, Point Bishop, and Point Arden, all accessible from Juneau, Auke Bay, or Tee Harbor, furnish similar action.

Yakutat Bay, off the Gulf of Alaska, is extremely productive for Chinook and coho. Fishing guides are available at Yakutat. The nearby Situk River is considered to be one of the top fishing spots in all of Alaska. Best fishing in the bay is between spring and fall.

Kodiak Island offers outstanding salmon fishing during the spring and summer months. Monashka Bay, about five miles northeast of Kodiak on the Mill Bay Road, produces both coho and pinks, and both pinks and chum are taken near Anton Larsen Bay, about fourteen miles northwest of Kodiak. The bay also provides a boat launching site. There is fishing off the Chiniak Road at Women's Bay, about nine miles south of Kodiak. Again pinks and coho are taken here.

Middle Bay, located eighteen miles south of Kodiak, is a favorite among coho and pink salmon fishermen, and the same two species are taken at Kalsin Bay, twenty-five miles south of Kodiak on the Chiniak Road.

Bristol Bay is famous for its vast commercial fishing fleet but is also extremely productive for Chinook and sockeye sport anglers. Coho, pinks and chum may also be found scattered throughout the area. Rental boats and guide services are available

Small, dependable float planes are used extensively throughout Alaska and British Columbia, where access to prime fishing grounds is often restricted. *Author photo.*

out of Bristol Bay.

Kachemak Bay, near Homer, and Homer Spit are productive for coho and pink salmon during the summer and fall, as are the waters off Anchor Point, Ninilchik, Clam Gulch, and Kenai. Coho and pinks are abundant from spring to fall at Resurrection Bay, near Seward.

Anchorage is another productive Alaskan salmon port, and excellent guide and charter services are available here. Near Homer, China Poot Bay also boasts good guide and charter services, as well as rental skiffs. While Chinook are not taken in great numbers here, fishermen score respectable catches.

Wrangell Harbor offers some of the finest small boat fishing opportunities to be found in the entire state. Both Chinook and coho are available here, and rental skiffs may be found. Norton Sound, out of Unalakleet, offers boats, guides, and a full range of

marine facilities. Kings, feeder Chinook, silvers, and chum may be taken here from spring through fall.

Cook Inlet and Prince William Sound hold vast numbers of salmon. Here, too, the spring, summer, and early fall months are the best fishing periods.

British Columbia

Canada's westernmost province features some of the most spectacular saltwater salmon fishing imaginable. The upper half of British Columbia remains relatively undeveloped, and salmon anglers with access to private boats and aircraft are able to explore at leisure a myriad of pristine bays and inlets. While the lower portion of the province also holds many waters which have been only lightly fished to date, the majority of the most productive salmon spots have been documented.

Chinook salmon are the largest and most sought-after species in British Columbian waters. They are found in all coastal waters and may be taken during every month of the year. Typically, however, Chinook fishing peaks during July, August, and September, with late July and early August probably the most productive period for mature spring salmon. They range in weight from about three to seventy pounds (fish under three pounds are termed *grilse*). *Jack* Chinook mature one year earlier than normal and make up a relatively large proportion of British Columbia's Chinook catch.

Coho are typically three years of age at maturity and run from about three to twenty pounds. The larger fish are known as *Northerns*, while smaller silvers of three pounds or less are often called *bluebacks* in the Gulf of Georgia where they are found in abundance during the spring months. The best coho fishing throughout the province usually occurs from July to September.

The Fisheries and Marine Service, Pacific Region, under the auspices of the Department of Fisheries and the Environment and the Economics and Special Industry Services maintains and compiles extensive records relating to British Columbia's sport salmon fisheries. A copy of the "1976 Salmon Sport Fishing Catch Statistics" was provided to the author, and it forms the basis for much of the information outlined in this section.[*]

Statistical data show that sport anglers took an estimated 539,550 salmon and grilse from British Columbia tidal waters during the 1976 calendar year—twenty-one percent more salmon than were taken during the 1975 season and thirty-six percent greater than the average yield for the ten-year period covering 1967-76. Catches of Chinook were up thirty-nine percent over those of the previous year, and the number of Chinook grilse was fifty-seven percent higher than that taken during 1975.

Chinook accounted for about one-fourth of the total salmon sport catch, while coho accounted for a slightly higher percentage. Pinks, sockeye, and chums were down approximately twenty-five percent over the previous year.

Sport fishing statistics show that, during 1976, anglers experienced a good success rate—1.4 fish per angling day. The top-producing areas were Comox-Courtenay, Victoria-Sooke, and Campbell River.

By far the greatest number of mature Chinook and grilse were caught in the Victoria-Sooke and Comox-Courtenay areas. In fact, these catches com-

Charter fishing has become increasingly popular in British Columbia in recent years. Here a deckhand hefts a nice salmon over the rail as the lucky angler looks on. *Author photo.*

prised about forty percent of the total spring salmon harvest. The best fishing was experienced during the month of August. (An exception was the Saanich Inlet area, which saw its best fishing during September, when a large number of Chinook were taken.)

The greatest number of coho was taken from the Comox-Courtenay and Campbell River areas, with July proving the most productive month.

In terms of fishing pressure, the heaviest concentration of angling effort was expended in the Comox-Courtenay area, followed by Victoria-Sooke and Vancouver-Howe Sound. Of all major saltwater salmon areas, the waters surrounding Port Hardy and Alert Bay were the most productive: the average daily catch here was an astounding three fish per trip! In contrast, the poorest success was noted in the Queen Charlotte Islands, where only about one-half of a salmon per boat day was averaged.

It is interesting to note catch numbers, sizes, and peak fishing periods for each species at each particular major saltwater salmon area. This is indeed possible, since British Columbia's sport fishing sampling and statistical data are among the most complete anywhere on the West Coast.

[*]Statistics for British Columbia are from (Compiled & edited by: Micheline Ann Taylor) (Staff of) Economics and Special Industry Services Directorate, *1976 Salmon Sport Fishing Catch Statistics for British Columbia Tidal Waters* (Vancouver, B.C., Department of Fisheries and the Environment, Fisheries and Marine Service, 1976).

Jack Bolton, well-known Boise radio executive and on-air personality, admires a fine rockfish catch. These bottom dwellers often strike herring which are intended for salmon. *Author photo, courtesy of* Outdoor Life.

Over ninety percent of the sport salmon harvest in British Columbia waters occurs between the Victoria-Sooke area of the Strait of Juan de Fuca and Campbell River on the north. Thus, the major thrust of the sport fishery extends the length of the Gulf of Georgia.

In terms of pure catch numbers, the Victoria-Sooke area is most productive during December, when spring Chinook of about eight pounds, on average, are taken in the greatest numbers. In fact, catch statistics for the 1976 calendar year showed that the average catch per boat day at this time of year was 2.3 fish. January is the second most productive month for springs. (Jack Chinook are found in the greatest numbers during December, then January.)

Somewhat larger Chinook are available here during July and August, when the typical fish averages about ten pounds. But Canadian fisheries personnel recommend fishing for Chinook during May, September, and October in the waters off Victoria.

For coho, Victoria-area waters are most productive from May through September, while the best grilse fishing is found from September to June.

The best Chinook fishing in the Strait of Juan de Fuca off Sooke Harbour typically occurs during June and July. Coho peak during September, as do pinks in odd-numbered years. For grilse, the best fishing is found between September and May.

Swiftsure Bank, located northwest of Washington's Cape Flattery and stretching along the west coast of Vancouver Island, is an extremely productive salmon haunt. Large Chinook frequent the continental shelf to feed during both their ocean and returning migrations and are available here from spring through fall.

The west coast of Vancouver Island also affords innumerable fishing areas which have become highly popular among sport salmon anglers. Especially along the northern part of the island, one may find numerous bays and inlets. Many such areas now house developed resorts and other fishing-related facilities. But many are still available only to anglers arriving by boat or plane. It is apparent that many new areas will be opened up as roads are expanded up both sides of Vancouver Island. Naturally, this will mean new and exciting salmon water to be tested—and savored.

Port Renfrew, west of Sooke Harbour on Juan de Fuca Strait, is another popular salmon fishing area. The same general seasons for the various Pacific species apply here.

Bonilla Point lies north of Washington's Cape Flattery at the western end of Juan de Fuca Strait. This area, too, is highly productive for both Chinook and coho. Some of the best fishing for the former occurs from late June through early August; for the latter, peak action takes place in August and September.

Barkley Sound, Toquart Bay, and Alberni Inlet, all on the west side of Vancouver Island, are fine salmon areas. Chinook are taken in good numbers during August and September, and coho are likely to show in abundance during the same period. The Port Alberni area produces spring Chinook in the greatest numbers during August, but the best per-trip averages—despite the relatively light angling interest—occur during the November-April period.

The Tofino section of Vancouver Island, with such excellent salmon spots as Cox Point and Rafael Point on Clayoquot Sound, provides topnotch salmon fishing during August and September, when both Chinook and coho may be taken.

Nootka Sound, including the waters of Estevan Point, Escalante Point, and Ferrer Point, are lightly fished, as are the waters of Esperanza Inlet. But all provide fair to good salmon fishing at certain times of the year. The May-July period is most productive for springs, while the best coho fishing occurs during June and July.

Quatsino Sound may be amazingly productive at

times. In fact, figures for the 1976 calendar year show that sport anglers averaged 3.7 salmon per boat day during July, when coho made up the bulk of the catch. August was nearly as good, with an average catch of 2.9 salmon per boat day. There are large Chinook to be found in these waters, and July is the peak month for mature fish. At this time of year, springs average fifteen pounds, but the *average* size of Chinook taken during August is about twenty pounds. There is also good fishing—but extremely light fishing pressure—throughout the waters of Kyuquot Sound, off Lookout Island, Clerke Point, Cape Cook, and Lawn Point.

The waters of Saanich Inlet, northwest of Victoria on the eastern side of Vancouver Island, produce good catches of spring salmon from May through August, and coho show in numbers beginning in July but may be taken as late as December. Silver fishing reaches its peak during September.

Cowichan Bay sees generally good fishing throughout the entire calendar year. The best fishing for springs takes place in July. Coho are taken in the greatest numbers during July and August. Perhaps not surprisingly, some of the best fishing here occurs during the winter and early spring months. Figures for the 1976 season show an average catch per boat day of 3.3 salmon between January and April, many of them jacks and grilse.

The Nanaimo-Ladysmith area is excellent for Chinook from July through September. Coho fishing here hits its stride during July and August. Grilse are available in large quantities from January through June.

The Comox-Courtenay stretch of the Georgia Strait, as previously noted, leads the list of British Columbia salt water areas in terms of both fish numbers and angler effort. Here the best fishing for Chinook invariably occurs during July and August. Coho are abundant from June through September.

Veteran salmon fisherman Paul Vauchelet braves a sudden downpour to do battle with a coho. *Author photo.*

Pinks are taken during both odd- and even-numbered years, with the best fishing to be found during August and September. Prime fishing for grilse occurs anytime between May and September.

Campbell River, also on the east side of Vancouver Island, is heavily fished and very productive. Canadian fisheries officials say the best time to fish Chinook here is from June to September. Closer scrutiny shows that Chinook fishing peaks during July but is nearly as good in August. Coho may be taken anytime between June and August, with July seeing the peak runs. The best fishing for pinks occurs during August and September, and grilse may be taken anytime between May and September. The best fly fishing for silvers is found during the first half of September. Campbell River offers a full range of marine services, including rental boats, resorts, restaurant, and boat launching facilities.

Although Campbell River is fabled for its large *Tyee*—Chinook weighing upwards of thirty pounds—it is interesting to note that springs taken here are not as large, on average, as are those taken from the Comox-Courtenay area. Typically, Campbell River springs average eight to ten pounds during the peak summer angling season, while those taken from the waters of Comox-Courtenay range between about fourteen and seventeen pounds. (Neither area compares with Rivers Inlet when it comes to average Chinook weights!)

On the mainland, the Vancouver-Howe Sound area enjoys good Chinook fishing from June through September, while coho fishing peaks during July and August. Grilse are abundant from January through September, but the best fishing for pinks is during August.

Chinook offer topnotch action at Pender Harbour during July, and coho fishing here reaches its climax during August and September. Pink salmon runs peak during August, but grilse may be taken from January through September.

The Powell River area provides good fishing for Chinook during July. Coho offer top sport during June, July, and August. As elsewhere, grilse are available from January through about September.

The Queen Charlotte Islands offer enormous potential but sporadic fishing. By far the largest angling crowds flock to the islands during August, but fishing success at this time of year is not always good. In fact, catch statistics for the 1976 season showed that the average catch per boat day during August was only 0.2 salmon! The best Chinook fishing here typically occurs during May, when fish of about thirteen or fourteen pounds are tricked. Coho fishing peaks during September.

The waters of Prince Rupert may be productive for Chinook from January to July, with the best action taking place during June and July. At this time of year, springs are likely to weigh about fifteen pounds. Coho fishing here peaks during July and August, when silvers average about seven pounds. The waters north of Prince Rupert (Nass River-Arandale) are lightly fished, but the Grenville-Principe area to the south provides fair to good fishing for Chinook during June through October; silvers are taken here from July through September.

The Kitimat area, including the waters of Caamano and Laredo Sounds, as well as those of Butedale, the Gardner Canal, and Kitimat Arm, see considerably heavier fishing pressure. Here Chinook are taken in large quantities from May through September. Coho fishing peaks during August but continues into September.

Somewhat smaller Chinook are taken near Bella Bella, with the best fishing occurring during May. Coho are tricked during July and August. Large spring salmon provide good angling in the Bella Coola area, which stretches from Bella Coola on the east to Nama, Fitzhugh Sound, and Calvert Island on the west. Here springs typically average twenty pounds during the August peak. Silvers of from five to nine pounds, on average, may be found scattered throughout the area from late July through October.

Of all of British Columbia's more popular saltwater salmon fishing areas, those waters lying

Here's an example of the kind of *Tyee* salmon taken consistently by Rivers Inlet anglers. *Author photo.*

Rivers Inlet *Tyee* weighing over 60 pounds is held by Brian Chernoff of Canada's Department of the Environment. Chernoff and fellow Canadian biologists helped Washington Department of Fisheries personnel obtain sperm from legendary Rivers Inlet Chinook (king) salmon for cross-breeding with Puget Sound fish. *Courtesy of Washington Department of Fisheries.*

north and east of Vancouver Island's northwesternmost tip are the most productive in terms of the sport harvest. The Port Hardy-Alert Bay area stretches to Johnstone Strait, Knight Inlet, and Kingcome Inlet on the east and produces outstanding action. Springs averaging between about ten and fifteen pounds are taken in large numbers from May through August; the best fishing usually occurs during August (1976 figures show an average catch per boat day of 4.9 salmon!). Silvers show from July through October, but the best coho fishing coincides with the peak Chinook runs of August.

Rivers Inlet, about 250 miles north of Vancouver, hosts a limited run of the largest Tyee salmon British Columbia has to offer. From the standpoint of average weight, Rivers Inlet cannot be topped: *Chinook taken here typically average between 32 and 36 pounds* (fisheries statistics reveal that, during 1971, Chinook taken from Rivers Inlet averaged

40.8 pounds)! The inlet may indeed host the largest race of king salmon to be found anywhere.

Despite the expansion of the fishing season because of a heavy and growing influx of American sport anglers, the best fishing for large Tyee salmon occurs during the last week of July and the first half of August. At this time of year, anglers may expect an average catch per boat day of about 1.3 salmon. While springs are available virtually year around, they are likely not only to be more abundant during this late July-early August period, but also larger than at other times of the year.

Rivers Inlet has grown rapidly as a sport fishing mecca during the past fifteen years, as witnessed by the number of licenses issued annually. In 1961, only 228 sport fishing licenses were issued; during 1976, 2,344 anglers applied for fishing licenses here, a nearly tenfold increase in the sport fishing effort. As new resort facilities are opened, and existing ones expanded, fishing pressure will undoubtedly continue to grow.

Of all Pacific salmon spots, Rivers Inlet is *the* place to head for trophy-sized Chinook. During the past fifteen years, the heaviest Chinook taken during any given season has ranged from a low of 60.0 to a

Large *Tyee* salmon are standard fare at Rivers Inlet. *Author photo*.

Long and girthy, these Rivers Inlet *Tyee* (kings) fell for plug-cut herring. *Author photo*.

high of 77.5 pounds. During the latest season for which figures are available at this writing, the largest Chinook recorded was a seventy pounder.

Rivers Inlet is accessible only by boat or plane. Float planes depart Alert Bay, Vancouver, and Seattle daily during the July-August Tyee runs. A half dozen fishing resorts dot the inlet, and two or three "floating resorts" — large cruisers replete with small fishing boats for their guests — anchor near the head of the inlet each summer. Moorage and other marine services are now difficult to obtain unless anglers are registered guests of the resorts, thanks to the rapid commercialization process which began about 1970. Moreover, peak Tyee weeks see generally overcrowded conditions.

But Rivers Inlet also offers excellent fall coho fishing, with the best action found from September to early November. Herring, or herring and flashers or dodgers, are most commonly used by trollers, although "hoochies" — artificial squid — and streamer flies also produce strikes.

For giant Chinook, large chrome or chrome and

brass salmon spoons are used as alternatives to the favored herring baits. Trolling for Tyee is done exceptionally close to the shoreline—sometimes as near as fifteen or twenty feet. The inlet's rocky cliffs drop almost vertically in many areas and offshore fishing for Chinook is usually unnecessary. The best fishing is likely to occur during tide changes, although local anglers seem to favor the early morning and late evening hours. Standard mooching or light trolling tackle is recommended.

PART THREE
FRESHWATER SALMON FISHING

6

THE EQUIPMENT

THE selection of tackle for taking Pacific salmon species from fresh water is as important a facet of the sport as is choosing the proper equipment for saltwater use. Because river and stream fishing is somewhat more restrictive than the various techniques employed in fishing salmon in the brine, there is far less room in which individual opinions and preferences may operate.

With the exception of fishing for salmon species in freshwater lakes, sport angling techniques used by freshwater salmon anglers are limited to three general but basic areas: "big water" trolling, spinning or casting, and fly fishing. Of the three basic methods, the first two are most commonly employed.

Big water trolling is a term used to refer to a specific salmon fishing technique employed extensively throughout the West's larger river systems— the Sacramento, Columbia, and others—and in the brackish or estuarial waters of certain coastal rivers and streams. Baitfish or artificial lures may be trolled. Spinning or casting techniques may be employed from either boat or bank and, like salt water trolling, either natural or artifical lures may be used to entice salmon. Fly fishing is a sport unto itself; while it is a method used rarely by Pacific salmon fishermen, fly casting can be extremely productive at times.

Freshwater salmon fishing as a sport is relatively new below the Canadian border, although Roderick Haig-Brown and a handful of knowledgeable and enlightened anglers have extolled its virtues for years. Although the various freshwater tactics have been employed extensively throughout British Columbia and Alaska for some time, they are only now beginning to find a considerable following in such states as Washington and Oregon.

Perhaps one of the roadblocks to the proliferation of freshwater Pacific salmon fishing techniques is the fact that these fish stop feeding when they enter their parent streams during upstream spawning migrations. With some reason, anglers have long surmised that to attempt to take them with any degree of consistency and success is something short of folly. To the contrary, however! Despite the fact that most Pacific salmon species *do* stop feeding actively when they near or enter their fresh water streams of origin, many will readily take baits and lures which are properly presented. In fact, it has been scientifically demonstrated that not all salmon stop feeding at this time. Washington State Department of Fisheries' Deputy Director and biologist Frank Haw tells of a female spring Chinook which was examined a few years ago: the salmon, checked while in the Columbia River near Washougal, Washington, had "at least seven smelt in her stomach."

The above notwithstanding, most salmon *do* stop feeding as they near their cradle streams. And for those which do not stop altogether, there is a definite slowdown in feeding as fish reach sexual maturity. This fact has profound consequences for the sport salmon angler in search of freshwater action. That is, ripening Pacific salmon cannot be expected to strike presented baits and lures with the great degree of reckless abandon which they often display while in their saltwater habitat, where they feed heavily and voraciously in preparation for their upstream journeys.

But some positive conclusions may be drawn, too. Not only will mature salmon strike baits and lures while in fresh water, but they do so with surprising gusto at times. In fact, ichthyologists have given sport anglers a valuable tip, thanks to scientific studies: in general, Pacific salmon are apt to take baits or lures more readily while in the lower reaches of their natal rivers and streams than near their spawning grounds. And not only are fish taken low in their parent streams more likely to be cooperative than are those taken high near their gravel redds; they are also likely to be brighter, fresher, scrappier, and firmer of flesh. Suffice it to say that serious freshwater salmon anglers had best stick to the lower reaches of salmon streams, leaving the upper portions of such waters to procreation and predation.

But the eagerness with which a fish strikes a properly presented bait or lure is not limited to the distance from its spawning grounds alone. Indeed some salmon runs produce fish which are extremely cooperative with sport anglers, while other runs produce fish which are frustratingly reluctant to strike. In general and where Chinook are concerned, *the earlier the run, the better the chances that fish will readily take baits and lures.* Spring Chinook, such as those occurring in Washington-Oregon's Columbia River, are typically more cooperative than are their later-running summer or fall sibling groups. In fact, biologists have demonstrated that Columbia River spring Chinook "bite eight times better" than do members of that system's fall runs! Thus, early-season success is more likely than that which may occur later in the summer and fall months—at least in the Columbia.

While sockeye and chum are sometimes taken by river and stream fishermen, freshwater anglers are content to concentrate on three of the Pacific species—Chinook, coho, and pinks. As previously noted, the latter occur only in the odd-numbered years south of an area consisting roughly of an imaginary boundary marked by British Columbia's Fraser River; in their more northerly range, they may be taken during both odd- and even-numbered years. Of the Chinook and coho taken each year from many of the West's more popular and productive salmon streams, many are *jacks*—two-year-old, sexually mature fish.

Chinook jacks typically weigh two to six pounds, while coho are likely to weigh only half as much. Because jack salmon, like their larger, older counterparts, are sexually mature, they die after spawning. For this reason, it is desirable from a fisheries management standpoint that jacks be harvested by sport anglers. Ichthyologists are in general agreement that there is usually a sufficient number of larger, older males to fertilize the eggs laid in the spawning redds by females.

Fisheries biologists further argue that freshwater salmon angling makes better sense than that conducted in salt water—from a conservation standpoint. In the first place, virtually all fish which are hooked in fresh water are adult, sexually mature salmon, and not immature, growing fish, as are many of those which are taken at sea. Secondly, specific *races* of salmon cannot be either identified or protected while in the brine, as can those which are returning to their cradle streams. This can be extremely important to fisheries managers who must often attempt to compensate for exceptionally small returns in any given river at any given time. For example, how is it possible to protect a dwindling Chinook run from, say, River A when offshore fishing is permitted? Obviously, it is not possible, since *all* Chinook are fair game while at sea. But salmon races can be protected both easily and effectively upon their return to fresh water, where angling restrictions may be imposed for their protection if necessary. Additionally, *in terms of pure poundage,* freshwater salmon fishing makes better conservation sense than does fishing them in salt water. Fish returning to their native streams (with the exception of the precocious jacks) are at their maximum weight; those taken from the brine are often far from maturity, still in the growing stages.

Whether for Chinook, coho, or pinks, the selection of the specific tackle to be used in fresh water will depend on the anticipated size of the target and the technique to be employed.

Rods

Rods used for taking Pacific salmon species from fresh water range from lightweight fly casting models to the type used for relatively heavy trolling by saltwater anglers, but most common are those between the extremes.

When trolling is employed around the brackish mouths of salmon rivers and streams, "standard" saltwater tackle may be used. Typically, water encountered in such instances will be relatively shallow; hence the heavier trolling rods and accompanying gear (such as downriggers and heavy sinkers) are usually unnecessary.

Most popular estuarial trolling techniques call for relatively light-action rods of about eight to nine feet in length. These are usually sufficient to handle from one to six ounces of lead, about the maximum required in such instances. Rods of this type should display medium-action tips but enough starch to permit the angler to bury the hooks. Most popular are tubular fiberglass rods.

West Coast flycasters have adapted tackle and techniques which now produce some fine salmon catches, but the sport is still in its infancy. *Author photo.*

Somewhat lighter versions are adequate when only an ounce or two of weight is needed. In such cases, standard mooching rods are ideal. These should measure about eight to ten feet in length, have relatively light-action tips, long handles, and metal reel seats. As with all salmon rods, only those to which are fastened the best line guides (usually carbaloy or ceramic) should be purchased. Both the medium- and light-action rods may be used to troll baitfish in shallow water and without excessive weight.

At times, forms of "bucktailing" or "flashtailing" — rapid trolling with flashtails or streamer flies — are productive near the mouths of salmon streams. Under such circumstances, anglers may use mooching rods — or even spinning, bait-casting, or fly rods. Here the goal is to troll the artificial lure rapidly in the propwash of the boat, and rarely is more than an ounce of weight required. In fact, anglers sometimes use no weight at all, preferring to let surface-cruising coho rise to the flashtails.

Conventional steelheading rods are frequently used by freshwater salmon anglers. These are especially effective when fishing small- to medium-sized salmon and where casting is necessary. If large, mature Chinook are the quarry, such steelhead rods may be too light, however. In such cases, anglers are advised to opt for the heaviest casting rods available. Few fishermen can handle a forty or fifty pound king on a standard steelhead rod — especially if current and underwater obstructions lessen the odds of beaching such a catch. Steelhead rods, usually about nine feet in length, are normally capable of handling coho and smaller species, such as pinks.

But coho and pinks may also be taken on standard freshwater trout tackle. Usually the choice is a trout casting rod of about six or seven feet in length. These are teamed with spinning or bait-casting reels and may be fished either from boat or from shore.

Fly casting techniques call for perfectly matched equipment, and manufacturer's suggestions and

121

specifications are the best guide for anglers who do not already possess such a fly combination. A bit more latitude exists within the confines of "strip-casting" with fly rods, however. This technique calls for anglers to use a fly rod of about eight to nine ounces. A herring strip and one or one-and-one-half ounces of weight are cast, then retrieved in short, fast bursts of about two to three feet at a time.

Reels

Light trolling techniques permit the use of almost any good saltwater reel. Most popular are the multiplying, revolving-spool models such as those used for ocean trolling or saltwater mooching. Usually, light trolling is done around the mouths of streams, but it is a popular and productive fishing technique wherever there is sufficient room to maneuver a boat in slow-moving water.

Spinning reels are frequently used by trollers, but most freshwater models will rust quickly if used in salt or brackish water. Spinning reels are better left to accompany anglers working more productive waters upstream, where corrosion by the brine is not a factor.

Either open- or closed-faced spinning reels may be used. Most popular are open-faced models used in conjunction with trout or steelhead rods. These are ideal where casting distance is important.

Bait-casting reels with revolving spools are also excellent choices to accompany trout or steelhead tackle and provide a good means of getting the bait or lure to an optimum distance. The best reels are those which multiply on the retrieve and which have high-quality star drags.

Direct-drive reels, such as the old "knuckle dusters" or "knuckle busters," may also be used, although they are poor choices for any but trolling techniques. Good fly reels capable of holding a sufficient length of monofilament line or fly line with backing may also be employed. In general, anglers should opt for those with high-quality drag features. While these may be used in trolling, they are most frequently used in stripcasting and fly casting methods.

Line

Virtually all freshwater salmon fishing—both trolling and casting—is done with nylon monofila-ment line. An exception, of course, is fly casting, where wet lines specially matched to the rod and accompanying tackle are used.

If Chinook are the quarry, anglers should opt for high-quality mono of, say, fifteen to twenty-five pounds breaking strength. A good all-around line for Chinook is twenty-pound-test.

Coho require lighter breaking strengths; eight- to twelve-pound test is ideal for both trolling and casting techniques. Pinks, which seldom run larger than five or six pounds at maturity, may be easily handled on nylon mono of five- to eight pounds breaking strength.

Nylon monofilament line is easy to work with and has superior strength for its diameter. It must be checked frequently for nicks and abrasions, however; such blemishes may result in line separation.

Leaders

Nylon is the most common leader material for use in freshwater salmon fishing. Like nylon fishing lines, leaders must be checked periodically for nicks and abrasions but provide considerable strength for their diameter.

When trolling near river mouths or in the larger expanses of fresh water, anglers may wish to vary the length of their leaders. As most knowledgeable steelheaders know, leader length may be critical at times. In general, clear water conditions call for leaders of generous length, while murky water conditions require shorter—and sometimes lighter—leaders.

If saltwater trolling techniques are employed, standard trolling or mooching leaders of nylon mono may be used. Typically these measure six to nine feet in length and may be rigged with single, tandem, or double-barbed (sometimes treble) hooks or combinations thereof. If baitfish, such as herring, are used while trolling near estuarial mouths, leader-and-hook combinations may be those used by saltwater anglers. These have been described in an earlier section of the book.

Metal leaders are sometimes used by salmon fishermen in salt or brackish water but are usually unnecessary. At times, however, metal leaders can be very effective, especially when the targets are large, mature Chinook which have sharp teeth. In all fresh or brackish water techniques which revolve around trolling, metal leaders may be used. They are poor choices for casting and retrieving, however.

Their primary value is to withstand the razor-sharp teeth of dogfish and other bottom species found in the brine.

In general, leaders should be lighter than the accompanying fishing line so that any breakage which may occur will take place along the leader or at the leader-connector knot. This will result in considerable savings for river and stream fishermen especially, since, in most instances, only the leader and terminal bait or lure will be lost—and not a considerable length of fishing line, swivels, or other connectors and lead sinkers.

Anglers using, say, twenty-pound-test nylon mono while fishing for large Chinook salmon may opt for leaders of fifteen or seventeen pounds breaking strength. Those using ten- or twelve-pound-test line may find leaders of eight or ten pounds breaking strength sufficient. At times, no leaders are used—especially when artificial spoons, spinners, and other commercial hardware are cast from bank or boat. Such items may be tied directly to the fishing line. In many instances, the less terminal tackle involved, the better.

Fly casters must select leaders which are suitable to their individual needs and the accompanying tackle.

Snaps and Swivels

While there are several types of snaps, swivels, and other connectors which may be used by freshwater salmon fishermen, most popular by far are the combination snap-swivels which appear similar to safety pins. The swivel end is fastened to the fishing line, and the leader may simply be inserted into the snap-end. Snap-swivels allow for the rapid changing of leaders, thus their popularity.

Many artificial lures have built-in swivels which eliminate the need for additional swivel connectors. If such lures are used, no other swivel connectors are necessary, and such terminal lures should be fastened directly to the fishing line.

Barrel swivels, however, are sometimes used— even when terminal lures do have built-in swivels to help keep the line from twisting. One typical rig is such a barrel swivel, which is fastened to the fishing line on one end and the leader material on the other, preceded by a "drop" sinker (typically a pencil lead sinker) and followed by the artificial lure at the end of the leader.

Three-way swivels may be used in a similar fashion. One eye of the swivel is used to hold a drop-per and sinker; the fishing line is attached to a second eye; the third eye holds the leader and lure.

Three-way swivels used as above are effective for casting from shore or boat, or they may be used in plunking techniques. "Plunking" is a term used to describe a method of fishing in which the terminal rig is cast into some promising salmon travel lane and left anchored there by a heavy lead sinker. Pyramid-shaped sinkers are often used because they hold exceptionally well in gravel or soft silt, such as that which is frequently encountered in the more productive salmon streams of the West.

In plunking, one swivel eye holds the fishing line, another holds the leader and terminal lure; the third eye holds a dropper length of leader material to which is fastened the sinker. The length of the dropper may be varied to suit then-current water and fishing conditions; eighteen inches is about average. The terminal rig is cast into a salmon travel lane, the sinker digs into the bottom, and the terminal lure spins in the current (nonspinning bait, such as salmon roe, is also used). The angler simply sits back and awaits a possible strike from a cruising salmon.

Sinkers

Almost any type of sinker may be used by freshwater salmon fishermen. In fact, if weighted spoons or spinners are used, anglers may require no additional weight whatsoever.

Except when trolling in big water or near the mouths of parent salmon streams—where the same sinkers which are used in saltwater trolling techniques may be used—freshwater salmon anglers normally require a relatively light weight to take their terminal lures to the desired depth. At times split-shot sinkers are even employed to take salmon flies to the proper depth. The best sinker is the one which gets the job done.

Pencil lead sinkers—straight, tubular lengths of solid lead—are popular with the various casting techniques employed in river and stream fishing. These sometimes have small holes near one end and into which a length of line or leader material may be inserted to secure the sinker to the swivel. Or, if pencil leads lack holes, they may be inserted into a short length of surgical tubing. The tubing serves to hold the sinker in place; yet pencil lead weights may be easily removed when more—or less—weight is required and a change in sinker length is necessary. Such sinkers may be cut with a wire-snipping tool to suit each particular circumstance.

3 WAY SWIVEL

30 LB NYLON 24" LONG

10 LB LEADER 20" LONG

BANK SINKER

SPINNER LURE

TERMINAL RIG for BOAT PLUNKING

LUHR JENSEN FIELD TESTING BOAT #4

Drift boats are especially handy for fishing salmon streams with poor bank access. *Author photo.*

Bank sinkers—somewhat egg-shaped in appearance—are sometimes used by plunkers instead of pyramid-shaped weights. These are effective but lack the sharp, distinct angles of pyramid leads and therefore do not hold as well in soft or muddy river bottoms.

Ancillary Equipment

Salmon fishermen trolling baitfish near the mouths of salmon streams require all the equipment used by saltwater trollers, except for downriggers, sinker-release devices, dodgers or flashers, and the like. Usually such items are reserved for offshore, deep water trolling but may be used on occasion near estuaries, since there is no precise or distinct point at which salt water becomes fresh. More typical, however, is equipment similar to that used by light trollers at sea; at times such gear will produce results just as efficiently at river mouths as it does miles offshore.

Boats and motors are necessary for trolling, whether offshore on inside a river mouth. But "drift" boats such as those used extensively for steelheading purposes may be used when taking Pacific salmon species from fresh water. Often these boats are put in at a point affording promising downstream action and pulled out at another point at the end of a day's drift. Between the launching sites, anglers may stop to fish productive stretches of water which would be otherwise inaccessible.

Tackle boxes, sunglasses, proper clothing (including good raingear), and the like are just as important to the freshwater salmon fisherman as to his saltwater counterpart. And if casting is to be done from shallow water areas, hip boots or waders are a necessity. As is true of saltwater excursions, freshwater salmon angling trips are much more enjoyable—and often successful—if anglers arrive properly equipped.

7
BAITS AND LURES

BAITS and lures employed to take Pacific salmon species from fresh or brackish waters are both as widely varied and as innumerable as are those used in tricking fish while they are in the brine. They range from such simple natural baits as a single salmon egg or egg cluster to plugs, spoons, spinners, and wobblers so brightly colored and gaudy as to make nonbelievers of all but those who employ such items.

Baitfish—especially whole or plug-cut herring or herring strips—are used extensively near the mouths of rivers and streams. In general, the same baits and hookups used in trolling for salmon in salt water are effective for taking fish from the brackish waters of their native streams. In fact, both the baits and techniques employed while trolling near river mouths are often identical to those used in offshore trolling.

But fishermen working the pools and riffles of upstream waters are likely to use baits and lures quite different from those which are employed in salt or brackish waters. In fact, it is not unusual to see freshwater anglers fishing with the same equipment, including terminal lures, as do trout or steelhead trout fishermen.

Regardless of where or when freshwater salmon fishing is to be attempted, there is one piece of advice which should not be ignored by anglers who are unfamiliar with the specific fishery and the waters in which it occurs: *almost without exception, anglers will be rewarded handsomely if they will only take the time and make the effort to ask local fishermen for their bait or lure recommendations.* Local anglers, guides, and tackle shop personnel are good sources for such vital information. They know the waters and the fisheries, and they may be of enormous benefit to anglers who lack their knowledge. Moreover, local anglers may know that Chinook prefer egg clusters, for instance, during early morning or when river conditions are murky but will take a certain artificial spoon in a specific color combination during mid-day and when the water is clear. Such tips are usually elicited easily if newcomers to the scene ask pertinent questions in a polite fashion. It is almost always the highly opinionated, bashful, or know-it-all fisherman who has the least amount of success. Generally, local anglers are extremely helpful when it comes to giving advice to newcomers.

If local sources of information cannot be found, anglers may be well advised to phone or write the state agency which is responsible for the specific

126

fishery. Each such agency has an "Information and Education" staff whose function it is to inform the public regarding the resource and to answer pertinent questions. In most cases, "I & E" officers, as they are called, are only too happy to help. Such persons are usually well-versed, if not intimately familiar, with most major salmon streams and can advise inquiring anglers as to the best tackle to use. Information sources for Alaska, British Columbia, Washington, Oregon, and California are listed at the back of this book, along with their addresses and telephone numbers.

Certain baits and lures are much more effective on some streams than on others. For this reason, it is a good idea to obtain local advice. The Columbia River, for example, produces a large number of salmon for anglers using flatfish-type lures, but fishermen using spinners with feathered treble hooks typically fare better on Oregon's Nehalem River.

Certain Pacific species are taken much more easily on one type of bait or lure than another. Streamer flies, for example, are more productive for coho than Chinook, although recent innovations in Chinook patterns have begun to reverse the tide. Pinks may strike a simple strand of colorful yarn when other species may pass it by. The list of examples is extensive, but the point is singular: it pays to know the water and the preferences of those fish which are being sought.

Perhaps the most effective of all baits for taking salmon from fresh water is salmon roe. Egg clusters are simply threaded onto the hook and cast into likely salmon haunts. Roe may be "plunked"—i.e. cast into the current and left anchored in place by means of a heavy bank or pyramid sinker. Or it may be drifted just off the bottom of the river or stream, the pencil lead sinker touching the bottom as the current carries the terminal rig downstream. Whether drifted or plunked, salmon eggs are best kept on the hook if the leader or line is tied to the hook in such a manner that it can be threaded back through the hook eye. By tying hooks in this way, a natural loop is formed; eggs can then be secured to the hook not only through the point but may also be held in place by the loop, which becomes taut after the eggs are in place.

The Washington State Department of Fisheries has provided instructions for the proper preservation of salmon eggs taken from fresh-caught, ripe females. Unless eggs have been commercially treated, it is necessary to treat them to preserve their freshness and to keep them from rotting.

For single eggs, individual ova should be placed in a solution of salt water. This solution should be saline enough so that a chicken egg or medium-sized potato will float. The solution is then simmered (not boiled) until the eggs attain the desired texture.

Egg clusters may also be preserved. Skeins should be removed carefully from the salmon or steelhead so that the encasing membrane is left intact, then wrapped in paper and allowed to refrigerate for several hours. This ensures proper drainage of the accompanying liquid. When the eggs have dried, the skein should be split. Anglers should try to leave the eggs attached to the membrane. Egg clusters are then cut from the skeins and covered thoroughly with Borax powder. They may be placed in containers, with Borax added to the clusters as they are layered into the containers, then either refrigerated or frozen. Treated eggs will remain fresh for about a month while in the refrigerator, but those which will not be used for some time should be stored in the freezer.

An alternative method to preserving salmon eggs is to substitute cornmeal for Borax. Food coloring and sugar may also be added, but the preferred baits are unsweetened eggs which have been covered with Borax and left their natural color.

Still another treatment method is offered. Skeins may be split and allowed to dry on paper towels, then sprinkled with Sodium Sulfite (Merk No. 5201). The chemicals should be applied sparingly because excessive amounts will cause the eggs to become too dry. Eggs may then be wrapped in paper towels, placed in a plastic bag or other container and frozen. Treating eggs in this manner results in bait which will "milk" when submerged in water. Some anglers think the egg-milk attracts fish more readily than do eggs which have not been treated in this fashion.

One of the major drawbacks in using salmon roe is that it is difficult to keep eggs or egg clusters on the hook for any period of time. Clusters are loosened by immersion into the water, and river or stream currents, as well as occasional bumping along a rocky river bottom, cause the bait to fall from the hook.

A good solution to this problem is to encase the eggs in a fine mesh fabric before placing them on the hook. Eggs may simply be placed in the middle of a piece of such fabric, the fabric ends tied securely around the bait with yarn or twine. Encased eggs may be kept on the hook easily. This technique permits the angler to use either fresh eggs or those which have been treated for preservation. Egg clusters may be inserted into the cloth before freezing or refrigerating and will thus be ready for use at any time.

Artificial eggs or egg clusters may also be used for taking salmon from fresh water. There are now plastic eggs on the market, replete with oils and juices which give the bait a "natural" odor. And artificial egg clusters, such as those used extensively by

Steelhead are often found in the same streams—and at the same time—as Pacific salmon. Vence Malernee traveled to Washington's Satsop River to fish coho but came up with this fine steelie instead. Here he inspects his catch in the crowding dusk. *Author photo.*

steelhead fishermen, are also popular. The latter have proved extremely effective on certain salmon streams. There are boreholes in their centers through which the line or leader may be threaded. They come in a variety of sizes and colors, the most popular of which are various shades of red or orange. Like the genuine article, these artificial egg clusters are drifted along the bottom.

Bobber-type lures are also used. Often these display tiny wings—propellerlike blades which cause the lure to spin or rotate in the river current. Like natural and artificial egg clusters, such bobbers are either drifted along the stream bottom or plunked in the current. Winged bobbers come in a wide range of colors and patterns. Orange, red, and green tones appear to be the most effective, and often these are spotted in black.

Various lures of the "flatfish" variety may also be employed. These are extremely effective and may be either trolled slowly or cast and retrieved from bank or boat. Flourescent red and orange are generally the preferred colors.

Salmon plugs, too, are effective. Like the flatfish-type lures, plugs may be either trolled or cast but are most commonly trolled in the larger river systems or around the estuarial mouths of the smaller coastal streams. The range of colors and shapes of salmon plugs is so extensive that it would be folly to attempt to describe them in detail. In general, anglers may be well advised to adhere to the proven producers.

Salmon spoons have long been a favorite of river and stream fishermen and have produced excellent results in virtually all of the West's major salmon streams. Often spoons are weighted so that no accompanying sinker is required. While spoons may be trolled, many anglers prefer to cast them from shore or boat.

The larger spoons are frequently effective for taking relatively large Chinook, but most anglers use lures which would be better suited for tricking billfish. It does not necessarily follow that "the larger the lure, the bigger the fish." To the contrary, even mature Chinook of thirty pounds or more frequently take small spoons and other artificial lures such as those often employed by trout fishermen. And the smaller Pacific salmon species—especially pinks—may indeed be frightened off by lures which are too large.

Salmon spoons should be trolled or retrieved slowly, especially if Chinook are the quarry. Too many anglers have a tendency to retrieve spoons too rapidly. In general, it is the slowly wobbling spoon which will bring the most strikes. This is particularly true when lures are fished near the bottom. As in steelheading, if anglers do not feel their lures bumping bottom occasionally, they are probably not fishing correctly. Slower retrieves or additional weight may be necessary to take the lure to the proper depth. Most popular are spoons of chrome, copper, or brass, sometimes painted with red or red and white.

Salmon spinners may also be highly effective and these, too, may be trolled or cast and retrieved. If there is sufficient current, spinners may be plunked from shore or boat. Most common are bladed, beaded spinners which are weighted so that additional sinkers are not required. Spinners should be cast in the same manner as spoons and retrieved slowly. Like spoons, they should be allowed to work near the river or stream bottom in most instances (the exception is when used in slow-moving pools or sloughs, where they should *not* be fished just off bottom).

Numerous other baits and lures are used—often successfully—by freshwater salmon anglers. Fishermen sometimes find that salmon will take even a single hook baited with an inch or two of colorful yarn (this is a favorite among freshwater humpy anglers). New products are forever arriving on the market. A few of these not only do the job but do it consistently; others are designed to attract more anglers than fish.

For the angler wishing to take Pacific salmon from fresh water, the best advice is to use that which produces results for *other* anglers. And in the same waters and at the same time!

8

THE TECHNIQUES

ALTHOUGH there are variations of each method, freshwater salmon fishing revolves around three angling techniques—boat fishing, casting, and plunking. Of course, casting and plunking may also be done from boat.

Trolling is a popular and productive means of taking Pacific salmon species from the larger river systems. It is also employed extensively to trick salmon near the mouths of smaller rivers and coastal streams. When trolling takes place near the mouths of freshwater rivers or streams, the techniques may be similar—even identical—to those used in trolling for salmon in open salt water.

Brackish water trolling may be conducted with relatively heavy tackle, although most trolling in tidal estuaries involves the use of relatively light-action gear. Standard light trolling or mooching rods of from eight to ten feet are frequently employed. These are accompanied by small- to medium-sized saltwater reels capable of holding one hundred yards or more of relatively light monofilament line. Most popular are multiplying, revolving spool reels. Those with high quality star drags and level winds are recommended.

Breaking strength of the fishing line will vary with the size of the quarry being sought. If fish are small pink salmon, six- or eight-pound test may be sufficient. Coho require nylon mono of between eight- and twelve-pound test, while breaking strength of line intended for mature Chinook may run twenty or twenty-five pounds. It is important to remember that fish which are returning to their native streams are much larger and stronger, on average, than are those taken randomly at sea. Upstream migrants have attained their maximum size: not only have

fish stored up considerable body fat for their sometimes lengthy upriver journeys, but the females are ripe with eggs and the males full of milt. Moreover, fish which are returning to their rivers of origin are much stronger when taken near the river mouth than after an upstream trek of many miles. They are bright, scrappy fish and should be regarded accordingly.

The exceptions, of course, are jacks—almost invariably males which have reached sexual maturity earlier than most members of their race. Throughout the West's coastal rivers and streams, jacks comprise a large segment of the freshwater sport salmon harvest. But the angler who is equipped for larger fish will have no problem tackling a jack.

Angling expertise and experience should also be taken into account when deciding what breaking strength of line to use. It would be just as ridiculous for a novitiate to the sport to begin with ten-pound-test line when seeking large spring Chinook as it would for the veteran angler to use forty-pound-test for coho. Each fishing line has its place, each angler his own requirements.

Some anglers use lightweight spinning tackle when trolling in the brackish waters off native salmon streams. While tackle such as this may be sufficient for pinks—and maybe even coho—it is ill-suited for doing battle with mature Chinook which may tip the scale at thirty pounds or more.

Baitfish are used extensively in trolling near river mouths, and mooching or light trolling tackle is an excellent choice to accompany whole, plug-cut or slab-cut herring or other baitfish. The usual procedure is simply to troll near the stream mouth in hopes that salmon milling around the river entrance

Trolling is a productive salmon fishing technique—whether in fresh-or salt-water. *Author photo*.

will be enticed to the bait.

Mooching is another effective means of taking salmon in the brackish waters of the tidal zone. Here the angler either drifts with the wind or current, paying out and retrieving line as he does so, or he uses the motor intermittently to give action to the bait. The primary consideration is that the baitfish moves in a desirable fashion, and it matters little by what means the fisherman achieves the desired effect.

Trolling salmon spoons, spinners, plugs, wobblers, and other artificial lures may be equally productive when salmon have moved into fresh water. This is a popular practice on many of the West's larger coastal streams and is employed extensively along California's Sacramento River, Washington-Oregon's Columbia, and a number of other rivers which are wide enough to permit proper trolling. Depending on the current at any given point of the river, anglers may troll either with or against the water flow. While coho prefer fairly rapidly moving baits, Chinook typically like to strike lures or baits which are moving in large, lazy loops or a fluttering motion. For this reason, it is often a good idea to troll *with* the current when seeking Chinook.

But boats have uses other than simply to provide a means for dragging a baitfish or lure through promising stretches of water. They are also used extensively as something similar to "floating platforms," that is, they provide an efficient base from which an angler may work. Salmon fishermen using boats to fish the freshwater rivers and streams where runs are found are more apt to score than their land-bound counterparts. Besides providing a platform from which casting or plunking may be accomplished in areas where bank access would be virtually impossible, boats also permit anglers to seek—and thoroughly fish—new waters. Almost any of the major salmon rivers may be fished more thoroughly by boat than by foot access; many of those which are large enough to accomodate small motor-propelled or drift boats are the same streams which afford generally poor access by ground. The fortunate angler is the one who has access to a boat in such circumstances. Not only will he be able to cast or plunk from his floating platform, but he will also be able to fish large stretches of water which would otherwise be inaccessible.

If boats are used to troll baits or lures, it is extremely important that anglers experiment by trolling in various directions. If dragging the bait or lure against the current does not bring results, anglers should reverse their heading and troll in the same direction as the water is moving. Or it is advisable for fishermen to troll across the water's grain at times, or in zig-zag patterns. Depending on the particular stretch of water trolled, one or more of these directions may bring results where others fail. This is especially important where the current is significant; in slower-moving pools and backwater sloughs, directional changes are not nearly as important (with some exceptions, which will be discussed later).

Often boats are used to troll in a *negative* manner. In such instances, the current may be moving too swiftly to permit proper trolling—in any direction. A very effective way to trick salmon in rapidly moving water is to allow the bait or lure to work *ahead* of the boat. The boat may be used to slow the forward movement while the lure works through the holes and pools downstream. Downstream motion may be regulated by the motor or oars. Here, too, it generally pays to experiment. Sometimes salmon will take lures which move quickly through a pool; at other times, it is best to work slowly downstream, allowing the lure to flutter lingeringly through the more promising water stretches.

While negative trolling may be productive with a variety of lures, it is a technique used by many salmon and steelhead guides when fishing with diving-type plugs. The diving plugs bite into the water much as do the diving plane sinkers used in offshore trolling, and, in most instances, no additional weight is required. Some of the more effective colors are silver, green, blue, and red.

Negative trolling, of course, is effective only in water which is moving at a relatively rapid clip. It is a technique which is best used on a moderately rapid river where the bottom is sand or gravel, and it is most productive for Chinook, which often hold near the main current. In fact, Chinook frequently lie on the bottom in relatively deep water near the head of a pool. Coho and pinks are most commonly found in the slower-moving pools and sloughs.

Finally, boats may be used simply to transport anglers to a suitable streamsite where angling will actually be done from the bank. Many very productive salmon holes are found near such isolated areas but would be impossible to reach without a boat. For this reason, it is a good idea to have boots, hip-boots, or waders on hand at all times.

Casting for salmon is not unlike casting for trout or steelhead. In fact, many of the same techniques are employed. Salmon spinning or casting techniques, however, parallel steelhead drift fishing more closely than they do trouting.

Spinning tackle may be used to take pinks and coho, but it is generally regarded as undersized when mature Chinook are the targets. Six- to seven-foot spinning or bait casting rods are accompanied by lightweight spinning (either open- or closed-faced) or revolving spool, casting reels. Breaking strength of the fishing line may run from as light as, say, four or five pounds for humpies to as heavy as fifteen or eighteen pounds for adult coho.

Since salmon casting techniques require placing the bait or lure at a predetermined spot, often at a considerable distance, only the finest equipment should be used. This is especially true of casting or spinning reels. Whenever possible, only those with the highest quality drag systems should be employed. Rod guides should be constructed of ceramic or carbaloy, and fishing lines should be checked frequently for nicks or abrasions which may—in addition to parting at the wrong moment—impede the smooth flow of the line through the rod guides.

Like the best steelheaders, salmon casters must be able to "read" the water. This is because the same species often travel through, and hold in, the same *kind* of water. It is important to know what type of water attracts which species, then to search for that particular type of water.

Chinook, as noted above, tend to lie in relatively deep, swift moving water near the head of a pool. But coho and pinks, on the other hand, are rarely found in such areas. Instead, these species generally prefer the deeper, slow-moving or almost still pools and sloughs. Where Chinook are typically found near the *head* of a pool, coho are more likely to lie near the *tail* of a pool. Obviously, it makes good sense to know in what type of water the various species are most likely to be found, since it is not that often that all three Pacific species will be found in the same stream at the same time.

Chinook rarely show on the surface. But both coho and pinks are frequently seen rolling or splashing. It should go without saying that anglers should fish any area or stretch of water in which salmon are seen.

Salmon, like their anadromous cousins, the steelhead trout, have certain travel routes and holding areas where they are likely to be found. Each of the three major freshwater species—Chinook, coho, and pinks—has its own habits and characteristics, and knowledgeable anglers may put such information to practical use in order to score.

While coho and pinks, for instance, are rarely taken from rapidly moving water, Chinook are frequently found in the faster currents. It makes little sense, therefore, for anglers in search of brute-sized king salmon to waste their time fishing the slow-moving pools and eddies of any salmon river or stream. Likewise, if coho or humpies are sought, anglers should concentrate only on the slower-moving or still pools and eddies, disregarding fast water found between likely coho or pink salmon spots. This is not to say that there are no exceptions to the rule. Rest assured that some Chinook *are* taken from backwater sloughs and some coho and pinks from the riffles. Yet there is a sufficient number of holding areas and travel routes for each species, and the angler who concentrates on the water most likely to produce the fish he is seeking is usually the angler who proves to be most successful.

Coho are often found near underwater obstructions, and it pays to fish such slack water areas thoroughly. Look for fish to be found near boulders, submerged or partially submerged logs, under cutbanks, and the like. Many fish are taken from slack water beneath overhanging trees and brush, and such areas are prime spots for coho sport. Too frequently, anglers decline to fish such "difficult" water because terminal tackle may be easily snagged or lost or because casting among underwater obstructions or overhanging brush requires a greater degree of both effort and skill than simply fishing open water stretches. Such anglers are passing up perhaps the most productive coho holding areas of all. Angling isn't always for the lazy—or the cheap! Fishermen should expect to lose some terminal tackle; if they don't, they are probably not fishing properly. And if napping is intended, spinning or casting techniques should be discarded in favor of the more relaxing plunking methods.

Fishermen who are aware of the habits displayed by the various Pacific salmon species and look for water in which fish may be reasonably expected to be found are in a much better position than are those who are either unaware that certain species prefer certain types of water or those who do not stop to read the water. The successful salmon angler must both know his quarry and pay attention to his surroundings, much like any other hunter. If, after working each promising water stretch for, say, half an hour, no strikes have been encountered, it is time to move on to the next drift.

Fishermen should attempt to place their baits or lures at virtually every point within casting distance before proclaiming a particular section of the river or stream unproductive. In general, it is a good idea to begin by casting to the opposite bank, especially if the targets are coho, which are often found lying close to the streambank. The angler can then shorten the length of each cast until the entire area has been covered thoroughly.

One very effective method of taking salmon on spinning or casting tackle is to cast the bait or lure out and slightly *upstream*. This technique is particularly effective for Chinook and when the current is moving rapidly. Apparently these fish like the fluttering downstream motion displayed by baits or lures cast in such a manner; perhaps they appear more natural than do lures which are suspended in a somewhat stationary fashion in the current. In any event, upstream casting, while extremely effective, may result in the loss of more terminal tackle than simply casting across the current, because the terminal bait or lure has time to float toward the bottom as it drifts downstream. Frequently, hooks, lures, leader, and sinkers become embedded between rocks or tangled around downfallen logs and the like.

Weather and water conditions play an important part in the freshwater salmon angling scenario. Typically, the best fishing is found when the water is slightly murky. Often new runs of fish are triggered by freshets, and the angler who finds his particular river or stream slightly discolored often stands the best chance of connecting. When water levels are low and clarity great, the best fishing is normally found at dawn and dusk.

Water conditions also dictate the use of terminal gear, to a certain extent. In general, clear water calls for longer—and usually lighter—leaders or line, while murky conditions dictate that leaders be shorter and perhaps heavier.

Tide conditions frequently influence success, too. Especially when anglers fish the lower reaches of a river or stream, action is likely to occur immediately before or after a tide change, most commonly an incoming tide. Although most salmon stop (or slow down on) feeding once they have entered fresh water, tide changes frequently coincide with—if not cause—salmon strikes. Perhaps it is a habit, learned at sea but not easily forgotten, which remains with the fish after they have reentered fresh water. Tidal conditions have little if anything to do with peak action periods farther upstream, out of the brackish zone.

Anglers fishing the backwater sloughs, eddies, and slow-moving pools for coho and pink salmon must cast and retrieve as if they were fishing a lake. Since they have relatively little, if any, current with

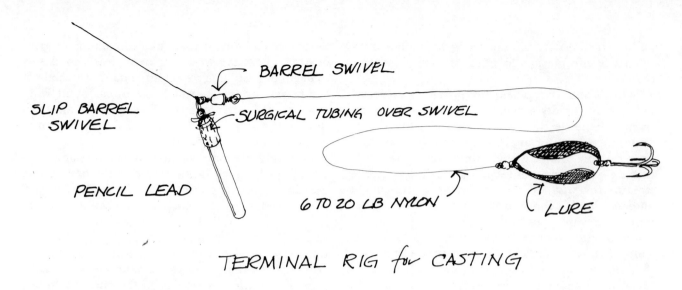

BARREL SWIVEL

SLIP BARREL SWIVEL

SURGICAL TUBING OVER SWIVEL

PENCIL LEAD

6 TO 20 LB NYLON

LURE

TERMINAL RIG for CASTING

which to contend, spinning or casting techniques are primarily a cast-and-retrieve matter. But here, too, it is advisable to work every inch of water. Generally speaking, anglers should work from left to right, or vice versa, casting to the more distant spots at first, then shortening their casts as they approach the same spot at which they began. It is more difficult to read water which has little or no current; hence, fishing for coho or humpies generally requires more patience and time than does angling for Chinook, which have distinct holding areas. For this reason, slow-moving pools and eddies should be fished at least as thoroughly as the faster-moving water and, in fact, more thoroughly.

Whether casting to Chinook, coho, pinks, or other Pacific salmon species, it pays to experiment with depth. As in saltwater salmon angling, freshwater techniques are heavily dependent upon fishing depth. If, after a while, no strikes have been encountered in a certain section of water, it may be a good idea to either add or subtract weight, in order to vary the depth at which the terminal gear is working. The same effect may often be accomplished simply by speeding up or slowing down on the retrieves.

Perhaps the best tackle for casting to Chinook or coho is a steelhead rod, a level-wind, star drag bait casting reel of good quality, and fifteen-pound-test nylon monofilament line. Such a combination is ideal for both bait and lures.

But casting techniques vary with the terminal lure. With bait, which is apt to come off the hook if jerked suddenly, the best type of cast is a forceful lob—gently but accurately placed so that the bait does not whip from the hook. Anglers casting artificial spoons, spinners, and the like usually find the greatest accuracy by letting the rod tip do much of the work.

Fly casting for salmon may be extremely effective at times. The angler who casts to salmon should have a tackle combination specially suited for the task, and manufacturer's guides are recommended for properly matching the various equipment items. Most fly casting for salmon involves the use of wet flies and sinking lines—especially for Chinook, which are frequently found in swift-moving water near the bottom.

Like spin fishermen and bait casters, fly anglers should learn the habits of the various salmon species and apply their knowledge to searching out the proper water. And, with flies, it is just as important to *thoroughly* work a stretch of promising salmon water as it is with other terminal tackle. Because so many of the better salmon holding areas are found along brushy shorelines and in areas which are difficult if not impossible to reach by foot, fly casters stand the best chance of connecting if they have the use of a boat.

Plunking, in which a bait or artificial lure is cast into a likely looking salmon travel lane and anchored in place by the use of a heavy (usually pyramid-shaped) sinker, may be both productive and enjoyable. In fact, it is as relaxing as offshore trolling with the use of a rod holder.

Plunking is the only method of taking Pacific salmon species from fresh water in which the angler waits for the fish to come to his bait or lure. Typically, the reverse is true: most stream and river fishermen try to take their bait or lure to the fish. As such, there is relatively little work to this technique of fishing. All that is necessary is to find a promising spot, plunk the bait or lure into the water, then sit back and wait for the action to begin. Occasionally, fishermen have to check their terminal rigs to make sure that baits and lures are in order, but that's about all there is to it!

134

Plunkers work the lower Columbia River for spring Chinook. *Courtesy of Washington Department of Fisheries.*

Because plunking success is dependent solely on the whims of salmon (only salmon passing by the plunked bait or lure while that bait or lure is working stand a chance of being hooked), *it is the least productive method of taking salmon from fresh water.* But because the technique is so simple, it is an ideal way for the novice angler to wet his feet. Once the bait or lure is cast into the desired position, rods may be propped into crudely crafted holders and anglers may sit back and relax. Plunking is also an ideal freshwater fishing technique for the elderly who can no longer negotiate the rapids and pools as they did in their younger years.

In plunking, it is more important to know *where* to place the bait or lure than how to cast properly. The most productive plunking efforts are made by Chinook fishermen. Because a relatively strong current is required to hold the bait off the bottom or to give action to the lure, plunking is a technique which is best suited for Chinook, which frequent the deep, faster-moving stretches of a river. While coho are sometimes taken, the prescribed method is to plunk the bait into a large, deep hole about halfway from the head of a pool to its tail. These are the "travel lanes" most commonly used by Chinook.

Salmon taken from fresh water may be either netted or "beached" by bringing the fish, head first, to the angler's feet, then gently working it onto the bank. If nets are used, both salt and freshwater fishermen should scoop the fish from the water in one swift motion. *It is extremely important that salmon be lead head first into a net.* If they are netted from behind, they are apt to have just enough punch left that they may be able to dart *from* the net instead of *into* it. Of course, fish should be played thoroughly before attempting to net or beach them. Too many anglers have learned the hard way that "green" salmon—those still full of fight—are not to be beached or netted. Only when a fish has rolled onto its side and the angler is sure that it is exhausted should the twine be applied.

9

PRIME FRESH WATERS

SALMON fishermen may take all five major Pacific species—Chinook, coho, pinks, sockeye, and chum—from an almost endless list of West Coast rivers and streams. Of the five Pacific salmon species available, Chinook and coho are the most sought-after targets. They inhabit numerous freshwater systems in each state and province in which they are found—Washington, Oregon, California, Alaska, British Columbia, and Idaho.

While it would be virtually impossible to list each and every stream in which Pacific salmon are found, the author has attempted to provide information for most of the major (and many of the minor) freshwater systems which host substantial salmon runs. The reader may be familiar with many of these—who has not heard of the fabulous salmon fishing on the Fraser, the Columbia, or the Sacramento, for instance?—but even more numerous are the smaller coastal rivers and their less well known tributaries. Many such waters provide fishing opportunities to equal—or even surpass—those found on the legendary rivers of the West.

NOTE: *Anglers should carefully check current regulations to determine whether or not the species listed here may be taken from the waters and at the times suggested.*

Washington

As is true of the saltwater sport salmon harvest,

Washington State produces a large number of Pacific salmon from its freshwater systems each year. During the latest calendar year for which catch statistics are available at this writing, over one hundred thousand salmon were taken from the various fresh waters of this state.

The combined sport harvest included 25,966 Chinook; 28,815 coho; 44,130 jacks (both Chinook and coho) and a few hundred chum, sockeye, and pinks. From these figures, it is readily apparent that jacks—almost invariably males which reach sexual maturity before most members of their species—account for a substantial portion of the state's freshwater salmon fishery. In fact, jacks accounted for about forty-five percent of the freshwater sport harvest during 1976.

Of all Washington fresh waters, the Columbia River System is by far the most important in terms of its salmon numbers. Even though the river itself was closed during the months of April, May, June, and July, the Columbia *system* yielded an amazing *sixty-two percent* of the total freshwater sport salmon taken during 1976. The tributary Cowlitz River led the way, with twenty-nine percent of all freshwater-caught salmon.

Thanks to Washington Department of Fisheries salmon punch card efforts, there is a surprising amount of information available concerning each particular river or stream. Additionally, when individual catch results are tabulated, it becomes easy to see the entire picture. From the latest statistics available at this writing, for instance, it can be learned that, while the Columbia and its tributaries produced sixty-two percent of the sport harvest, about twenty-five percent of all freshwater-caught salmon were taken from the rivers and streams of Puget Sound and the Strait of Juan de Fuca. The Pacific coastal streams accounted for only thirteen percent of the sport harvest.

But other interesting facts are also brought to light by the tabulation of punch card data. For example, from all of Washington's fresh waters combined, nearly forty-eight thousand anglers averaged one fish per day. The number of individual sportsmen who took two fish in a day was slightly over twelve thousand.

Several Puget Sound-area rivers and streams are worth examining. Among the more productive of these is the Skagit River, which produced nearly four thousand salmon during 1976. Chinook fishing here typically peaks during July and August, although some fish are taken from as early as June to as late as December. The best coho fishing occurs during October, but there is fair action during August, September, and November. Jacks are avail-

able from June through December; the best fishing takes place during August.

The Snohomish River offers fair fishing for fewer salmon. The best Chinook catches here are made during September, while coho provide peak sport during October. October is also the best month during which to take jack salmon from the Snohomish.

So few salmon are taken from the Snoqualmie River that it does not rate angling effort (the few fish taken are jacks), but the Skykomish turns out respectable catches. Chinook fishing here reaches its peak during September. Coho are taken from September through December, but the hottest action invariably occurs during October. Jacks are also most abundant during October.

The Stillaguamish River produces a limited number of mature Chinook salmon, with the best fishing occurring during October. Coho are slightly more abundant than Chinook and furnish the best sport during October, too. Jack salmon fishing

Riverbanks teem with anglers when the action is hot.
Courtesy of Washington Department of Fisheries.

"Humpies" (pinks) attract large crowds when they arrive at their natal rivers to spawn. Due to low numbers, pink salmon fishing has been curtailed somewhat in recent years. *Courtesy of Washington Department of Fisheries.*

reaches its zenith in September, but good numbers of fish are also taken into October.

The Puyallup River is one of Puget Sound's most productive. Large kings are taken during October and early November. Enormous runs of coho enter the river in September, but the best fishing is during October. Jacks are also most numerous during October.

The Nooksack River is another top salmon stream. Chinook may be taken here as early as August and as late as October; September is the best month. Coho fishing peaks during October, but fish are available from August into November. Jack fishing is good in September and October.

The Green (Duwamish) River produces Chinook from May through October, but action peaks during September and October. The best coho fishing is found during October, but fair catches are made during September and November. By far the best

jack sport occurs during October.

The Samish River is extremely productive. Large numbers of Chinook are taken from the Samish during the latter half of September and October, and peak coho fishing occurs during October. Jacks are most abundant during September but also provide plenty of angling opportunities during October.

The Skokomish River boots out fair catches of Chinook from August through late September. The best silver fishing here takes place in October. Jacks are taken during October and November.

The Quilcene River produces few Chinook, but there is fair coho fishing during November. The Dewatto, Tahuya, Dosewallips, Deschutes, Cedar, Nisqually, California, and Carbon rivers all hold salmon at various times of the year, but catches from these streams are minimal.

A handful of rivers running into the Strait of Juan de Fuca also produce salmon. Most notable is the Dungeness River, which turns out mostly coho. The best silver fishing here occurs during October, although fish are also taken during September and November. Only a few Chinook are boated or

Research program to capture adult Elwha River Chinook for hatchery spawning, as an effort to restore the Washington State river's legendary run of giant-sized kings. *Courtesy of Washington Department of Fisheries.*

beached each year. The Elwha and Sekiu Rivers, together with Deep Creek, produce salmon during the late summer and fall months, but fishing on these waters is generally less productive than on certain other Washington streams.

Washington's coastal streams account for a large number of the sport-caught salmon taken from that state each year. The leading producer is the Chehalis River, which enters Grays Harbor.

Typically, the best Chinook fishing in the Chehalis occurs during October, when mature king salmon enter the lower river. For coho, anglers should count on fishing the river between late September and early December; the best action normally takes place during October. Jacks are most numerous during September and October.

The Wynoochee River turns out a few mature king salmon each September through December, with the best fishing expected in October. More numerous here are coho and jacks: coho hit their stride between October and early December; jacks are available during the same period but provide fast-paced sport especially during October.

The Willapa, between Grays harbor and the Columbia, offers Chinook angling opportunities in September. Coho are tricked from September to early November, while jacks provide sport from September into November but are most numerous during September.

The Nemah River is more productive than the Willapa. In fact, it is among the more productive coastal salmon streams. Here the best Chinook fishing typically occurs during October, although mature kings are taken from as early as June to as late as November. Coho fishing, too, peaks in October, but silvers may be taken anytime between August and early December. The best fishing for jack salmon normally occurs during September and October.

The Quinault River turns out a few large Chinook each year, usually during August and September. But this river is better known for its large steelhead trout. Silvers are taken during May and November.

The Hoh River provides one of Washington's longer salmon seasons. Here Chinook may be found from April through November, with action reaching its peak between July and October. A limited number of coho are also taken from the Hoh; the best silver fishing opportunities normally occur during September, October, and November. Jacks may be found from as early as May through as late as October, but the best fishing is during September.

The Quillayute River, which enters the Pacific at La Push, is another productive salmon stream. Large king salmon are taken from the Quillayute from April through October. The best fishing usually takes place during May and September. Coho provide alternate sport from late August through October, and jacks are available from June through October, with the best fishing normally occurring during September and the first half of October.

The Bogachiel produces only a few adult Chinook each year, and relatively few coho. But the "Bogey" *is* a fair producer of jack salmon from July into November.

The Soleduck offers top angling for large, mature kings from April through late June (a relatively small number of Chinook are caught from March through December). Coho become available in June, but the best fishing is usually during October and November. Jacks may be taken from June through September.

The Naselle River in southwest Washington is a good bet for hefty king salmon during September and early October, and fair numbers of silvers are taken during October and November. Jacks may be found anytime between August and November, with September and October usually producing best.

The Satsop River produces some large Chinook each fall. Kings are available from about September

Vence Malernee targeted on large fall coho but wasn't disappointed when he hooked this 12-pound steelhead instead. *Author photo, courtesy of* Outdoor Life.

through December. Both coho and jack salmon are taken during the same period. The Humptulips, a sister stream, turns out excellent catches of mature kings in October and November. Coho offer good sport from October through year's end, and jacks are taken from August into November, with action peaking during late September and October.

The Satsop and Humptulips Rivers rate special mention because of their excellent coho fisheries. Not only are good numbers of silvers taken from these two streams during the fall and early winter months, but silvers—all native fish—comprise a late run which typically enters these twin streams from late October to around early December. These late fish are larger than their earlier-arriving counterparts because they spend an extra two or three months in the Pacific before beginning their upstream migration. At sea, they add weight rapidly.

The late Satsop-Humptulips fish comprise perhaps the largest genetic strain of coho in Washington waters. Typically they average about fourteen pounds, but twenty-pounders are not uncommon. Hank Wendler, veteran biologist with the Washington Department of Fisheries, says that he has seen coho to twenty-seven pounds (equal to the state sport-caught record) come out of the Satsop. For the best fishing for these larger coho, anglers should head for these rivers during November and December. It is a much overlooked fishery, in fact, and one which is well worth the angling effort.

Certain other coastal streams produce salmon in relatively small numbers. Among these are the Queets, Clearwater, Calawah, Dickey, Copalis, Salmon Creek, Bear, North, John, Wishkah, and Smith systems.

The Columbia River system, as previously noted, is by far the most important of all Washington fresh waters. Here catches are made during every month of the year.

The lower Columbia River itself is among the state's top-producing salmon waters. During the 1976 calendar year, nearly seven thousand salmon were taken here. Spring Chinook enter the river in March and are available through mid-May, with the best action usually occurring during April. Fall Chinook fishing continues good throughout August and early September. Coho, expecially abundant, are taken from as early as March through as late as December; the best silver fishing occurs in September and October. Peak jack salmon catches are made from August through October.

The upper Columbia also produces large numbers of sport-caught salmon. Chinook fishing is generally excellent from about May through October. Coho are taken in the greatest quantities during Novem-

ber. Jacks are found from May through November, but the best fishing is invariably during late September and October.

The North Fork of the Lewis River, a lower Columbia tributary entering the main river system near Woodland, is among the most important fall Chinook streams in the state. The best fishing usually occurs in August and September. Spring catches are made during April and early May. Coho may be taken from March through December, but peak action takes place during September and early October. Jacks are available from April through December but typically offer the most significant angling opportunities during September.

The Lewis' east fork sees relatively few salmon, but peak angling periods here are similar to, or coincide with, those found on the north fork.

The Cowlitz River, which enters the Columbia below Kelso, is currently the most productive of all Washington salmon streams. Here Chinook (mature kings) outnumber coho by about three to one. Additionally, there are large runs of coho and Chinook jacks.

The Cowlitz offers action on both spring and fall Chinook. The best spring fishing usually occurs during April, May, and early June. Fall Chinook angling peaks during September, but fish are available in good numbers from July into October. In fact, Cowlitz River Chinook may be taken during every month of the year.

Coho, too, may be found in the Cowlitz from January through December. But the best fishing is invariably during September, October, and early November. Jacks are abundant from April into November, but the peak fishing period is from late April to early August.

The Toutle River, which enters the Cowlitz near Castle Rock, produces good catches of fall Chinook during September. Likewise, coho fishing peaks during September, the same month in which jacks are most abundant.

The Green River offers good Chinook fishing during September and the first week or so of October. Silvers are most numerous in September but provide plenty of sport into October. Jack fishing peaks during October.

The Wind turns out fair catches of spring Chinook during April but offers relatively few coho or jacks. The Klickitat, another Columbia tributary, contains spring Chinook, the best fishing for which typically occurs during late April and May. Jacks are taken in the largest quantities during January and February. A small number of coho are tricked each September.

The Kalama River, which enters the Columbia

Wading a promising "drift" is a popular and productive means of fishing for Pacific salmon. Here the author uses chest-waders to reach water which would be otherwise inaccessible. *Author photo*.

near the town of the same name, contains fall Chinook, as well as a large run of hatchery-reared coho. Spring Chinook are taken during April and May, while the best fall fishing occurs in September. Coho runs provide action from September through the end of the year. Jacks may be found during virtually every month of the year, but the fishing peaks during September.

The Icicle River turns out salmon during June, a mixture of large Chinook, coho and jacks. The Ringold provides fair Chinook fishing during May, June, and September. Coho here are relatively scarce, but jack fishing is good in late June and July.

The Washougal is another extremely productive Columbia River tributary. Here Chinook are taken in relatively small numbers during September and October, but coho and jacks offer top sport from September into November. A special section of the river, located near the salmon hatchery, provides

large numbers of coho from September through December, with action peaking in November. Chinook and jacks are also taken during the same period.

The Elokomin River is a small tributary of the Columbia and hosts fair runs of coho during October and November. Jacks are found in the greatest concentrations here during October. Nearby Grays River produces both coho and jacks during October and November. Other rivers which hold salmon are the Cispus, the Coweeman, the Tilton, the Snake, the Methow, the White Salmon, the Little White Salmon, and the Yakima.

While pink salmon runs have been disappointing in recent years, several Washington rivers and streams host humpies in the odd-numbered years (1979, 1981, etc.). Among the most significant runs are those which enter the Skagit, the Puyallup, the Nooksack, the Nisqually, and Dungeness. Best fishing is in July and August.

Important sport salmon fisheries also occur in a number of Washington's inland lakes. Perhaps the

Successful angler with large late-run coho taken from
Washington's Washougal River during a special snag
fishery. Each year the Fisheries Department opens a
special area in which, for a month or so, snagging is legal
for these late-arriving coho returning in harvestable
numbers to the state salmon hatchery. The fishery is
generally restricted to the handicapped, although this
angler is a Fisheries Department technician. *Courtesy of
Washington Department of Fisheries.*

Seattle's Lake Washington produced these sockeye during a rare sport fishery. *Courtesy of Washington Department of Fisheries.*

most notable angling opportunities are those found in Lake Washington, Lake Sammamish, Capitol Lake, and Drano Lake.

A unique fishery has developed in Lake Washington in recent years. This large body of water, twenty-five miles in length and located just east of Seattle, offers excellent sockeye salmon fishing during some years. Although these fish begin entering the lake as early as April to spawn in the tributary Cedar River during October, the best fishing is invariably found during June and July. During late summer and early fall, sockeye are past their prime and lose much of their value as both a sport fish and as table fare.

Unfortunately for sport fishermen, the Lake Washington sockeye runs have been disappointing in recent years, and the fishery has been closed because of inadequate escapement. Because of the 1974 flooding of the Cedar River, a return of only 144,000 adult sockeye was anticipated for 1978. More than 350,000 fish are required before a sport fishery is permitted, so the lake remained closed to anglers during the 1978 season. It is hoped that a sufficient number of sockeye will return to the Cedar in the future so that a resumption of the sport fishery

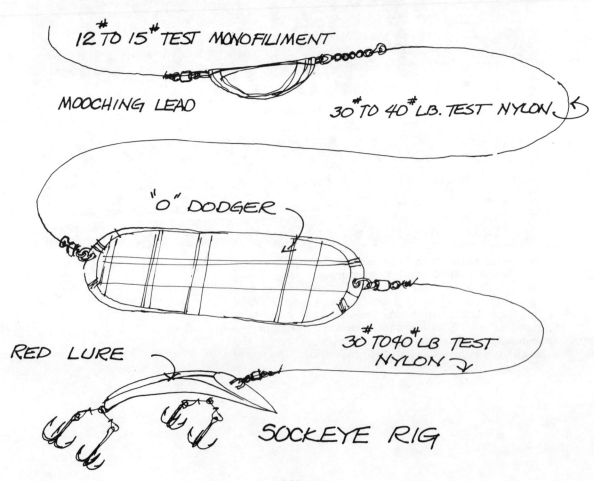

144

will take place. Special information is included here because the Seattle-based sockeye season—when permitted—is so popular and receives so much angling attention and pressure.

While the proper angling depth is important in fishing for any of the Pacific species, it is absolutely critical in determining sockeye success. These fish are extremely sensitive to water temperatures and prefer a mild stratum at which temperatures are about fifty five degrees Fahrenheit. Lake Washington's surface temperature during a typical June or July exceeds this figure considerably. Consequently, the most productive fishing is almost invariably found between about forty and sixty feet—usually at about fifty feet.

Sockeye gear consists of a small salmon dodger and spinner or flatfish-type lure. Most popular are wooden lures fitted with treble hooks, such as those used for trout. The most effective colors appear to be various tones of red, especially the brighter, flourescent colors.

Heavy sinkers are used to achieve and maintain the proper trolling depth. Sinker release mechanisms or downrigger devices are often employed, but heavy mooching or trolling sinkers of from about eight to sixteen ounces are also commonly used. Or anglers may opt for lead core line and diving plane sinkers.

Standard saltwater trolling tackle is adequate, but the lighter mooching rods may be too soft to handle the relatively heavy weights required to take the terminal combination to the proper depth. Reels are loaded with twelve- to fifteen-pound-test nylon monofilament (although metal or braided synthetic lines may be used). The sinker is followed by a length of heavy monofilament line. Length of the sinker-to-dodger line depends on the size of the dodger being used; a "0" or "aught" dodger is usually accompanied by about twenty inches of mono. Another length of the same heavy mono is fastened between dodger and terminal lure (again length varies with the dodger being used); twelve to fifteen inches are usually sufficient to accompany the "0" dodger. Lures are trolled very slowly for the best results.

The Lake Washington sockeye fishery is really little more than an adaptation of certain commercial trolling techniques which have proven effective for Canadian fishermen; thus, terminal gear is similar to that used by many commercial anglers. Until recently, it was generally assumed by would-be sockeye fishermen that these fish, being essentially plankton eaters, would not strike artificial lures. But the adaptation of commercial tackle and techniques, and the development of new methods and gear, changed the minds of many an opinionated hand.

Now believers flourish where once there were only skeptics. The sockeye-for-sport crusade is truly one of the crowning achievements of twentieth century sport salmon angling.

But Lake Washington also hosts other salmon runs. Fall Chinook are found near the mouths of the Cedar and Sammamish rivers, with the best fishing occurring from late August through early October. Coho are also taken in limited quantities from spring through fall, with action peaking during October. A few jacks are also tricked here during September and October.

Lake Sammamish, east of Bellevue, produces a few large Chinook each September. Coho are taken from late October through November. The best jack salmon fishing here is during September and October.

Capitol Lake, an artificial water formed by a dam at the mouth of the Deschutes River at Olympia, now offers excellent salmon fishing during certain periods of the year. Large Chinook or kings are taken in numbers during the fall; the best fishing occurs during September and October. The best fishing for coho occurs during October. Jacks are tricked from July into November but provide the most consistent sport during late September and October.

Drano Lake, at the mouth of the Little White Salmon River, turns out fair catches of both spring and fall Chinook. Trolling produces strikes from late August through early October.

Oregon

Oregon rivers and streams produce nearly as many sport-caught salmon as do those of Washington. For the latest calendar year for which catch statistics were available at this writing, freshwater salmon anglers took a remarkable 88,390 inland Pacific salmon.

Catch data indicates that the Columbia River system is just as important to Oregon's freshwater salmon anglers as to Washington's. In fact, during 1976, the Columbia system accounted for approximately one-third of all freshwater salmon catches posted in Oregon. Nearly thirty thousand salmon came out of the Columbia and its tributaries in that year, a not unusual occurance.

The Columbia River system is comprised of a number of waters, including those of both the lower and upper Columbia itself. The latest catch statistics provided by the Oregon Department of Fish and

Sockeye, which provide off-again, on-again sport when numerous enough, thrash near Seattle's Ballard Locks. An escapement of 350,000 fish is required before the popular lake sport fishery is permitted. *Courtesy of Washington Department of Fisheries.*

Wildlife show that, during 1976, the lower Columbia was among the most productive of that state's waters, with over four thousand salmon recorded. By far the best fishing was for spring Chinook, which offer peak action during March. Typically, fishing for springs remains quite productive until melting snows in the mountains cause the river to rise to a level which is unsuitable for angling. Near the mouth of the river, there is actually little spring fishing conducted (primarily because of water conditions); the best fishing near Astoria occurs during late August and early September. During this period, the fall runs of Chinook and coho offer top sporting opportunities.

The upper Columbia does not host large spring runs, but there is good fishing for fall Chinook and coho during September. The portion of the river lying between Bonneville Dam and Rainier is especially productive during the fall, when trolling, casting, or plunking techniques bring strikes.

The Clackamas River is a Columbia tributary which turns out respectable salmon catches from March through December. The best fishing for Chinook is during May, but anglers working the Clackamas during mid- to late April may also connect on spring Chinook. Fall Chinook and coho fishing peaks during September.

The Deschutes, another Columbia tributary, produces a large number of Chinook, coho, and jack salmon from August through the end of the year, but the best fishing takes place during September. Eagle Creek offers top fall fishing for the same species during September and October, the former being the most desirable month for angling here.

The Sandy River, near Portland, boots out both spring and fall Chinook. The best fishing during the spring occurs during April; fall fishing is good during September and October, especially the former.

Pacific salmon may be found in a number of West Coast Lakes. This fisherman nailed a large Chinook while working Washington's Capitol Lake at Olympia. The rotunda is in the background. *Courtesy of Washington Department of Fisheries.*

The Santiam River, still another Columbia tributary, produces a limited number of spring Chinook during May, but better catches are scored in September. The South Santiam also proves productive during May and September, while the North Santiam sees only spring fish.

Other Columbia system streams which hold salmon are the Calapooia River (very few fish), the Clatskanie, Hood River, John Day River, the Klaskanine River, the McKenzie, the Molalla, Big Creek, and Gnat Creek.

Pacific coastal rivers and streams yield large numbers of salmon each year. Of all such streams the fabled Rogue River and Alsea River (and bay) are most productive.

The Rogue, legendary for its steelhead, hosts large runs of Pacific salmon. The upper river above the Applegate to Savage Rapids Dam, a short distance above Grants Pass, and the lower river from the dam to its mouth at Gold Beach are the two sections of interest to salmon anglers. Typically, action in the lower river does not get under way until April. By mid-March, spring Chinook begin to show near Grants Pass, and fishing along this stretch of the river continues good into June. Most angling here is done from bank or boat—or from piers built out from the shore. The preferred technique is to cast copper or nickel spoons.

Along the lower Rogue, spring Chinook fishing is productive from the mouth to about thirty miles upstream by fishing from boat. The best time to fish the Rogue for spring Chinook is during May or June. Fall fishing peaks during September, when coho are available, but action continues good into early November.

Chinook fishing in the Alsea River Bay is best in August and September. Coho show in numbers from September through November, with the best fishing invariably occurring during October. Some salmon, however, are taken as early as June and as late as February.

The Trask River, third most productive of Oregon's coastal streams, kicks out sport-caught salmon during every month of the year. But fishing activity reaches its zenith during October, when fall coho and Chinook are available. Early November is also a good time to fish the Trask, although salmon are taken in fair quantities from May through September and again in December.

The Umpqua River (and bay) produces large numbers of Chinook and coho. Fishing from its mouth near Winchester Bay to the dam at Winchester, near Roseburg, is best for spring Chinook from about mid-March into June. Brass, nickel, or copper spoons are favored here. Typically, the best salmon fishing for coho occurs during October with fall freshets. Best action is found along the lower river, from Scottsburg to Umpqua. Feathered spoons are used extensively here.

While the south fork of the Umpqua hosts

Widely respected Oregon fishing guide Denny Hannah of Lakeside stands ready to gaff a fish. *Author photo, courtesy of* Salt Water Sportsman.

147

relatively few salmon, the north fork is productive—especially for spring Chinook. Here action peaks during May.

The Wilson River, another top coastal salmon stream, enjoys salmon runs during each month of the year. Best fishing here is during October, when fall Chinook and coho are available in large numbers. The Winchuck is another good salmon river. Although lightly fished, this stream turns out good quantities of fall salmon during November.

The Chetco River (and bay) is termed "the best salmon and steelhead stream south of the Rogue." Large runs of Chinook and coho are found here. Chinook enter the Chetco from September to mid-November, while coho appear from late September through December. By far the best month to fish the Chetco is November. Trolling is the favored technique throughout the brackish waters of the Chetco mouth, but bank casters fare better upstream.

The Elk River is still another good salmon stream. The best fishing here occurs from October through December. Most fish are taken during November.

The Nestucca River is considered by many Oregonians to be the finest fishing stream in the state. Although fewer salmon are taken from this river than many others, the Nestucca provides excellent catches of both Chinook and coho. Spring Chinook show in good numbers in the tidewaters during June and July, and the main fall run follows from August through September. Coho appear about the third week of September and provide outstanding sport into December. In terms of pure catch numbers, October is the best month to fish the Nestucca.

The Little Nestucca River also produces salmon—predominantly coho, which are best sought during October and early November.

The Coquille River hosts runs of both Chinook and coho, with the best fishing taking place in the lower twenty miles of the stream. Boats are used extensively here, although bank anglers score consistently farther upriver. Peak salmon fishing on the Coquille is from mid-September through early December.

The Siletz River supports an excellent Chinook and coho fishery. Typically, the best fishing here is from August through November. For large king salmon, anglers should plan to fish the Siletz during September; coho action peaks during October and early November. Trolling is most popular along the lower river, but casting from the bank farther upstream brings good results.

The Siuslaw River (and bay) yield good salmon catches from late September through early December, and the Sixes and Smith rivers turn out good catches during October and November. The Salmon is a good bet during November and December.

Coos River and Bay enjoy fair salmon runs from about late August until mid-December, with the best fishing occurring during October. Drift Creek is lightly fished but supports fall salmon runs which peak during November.

The Nehalem River and Bay and the north fork of the Nehalem provide top fall angling sport for Chinook and coho. Trolling is the recommended procedure from the river mouth to its intersection with Foley Creek. Chinook show about August and offer topnotch fishing through September, while silvers are available from mid-August to mid-October. Jack salmon appear in large numbers following the first rains of fall. Local anglers take these small fish with salmon roe and light spinning or casting tackle, but spinners with feathered treble hooks enjoy the greatest degree of popularity on the Nehalem.

Tenmile Lakes is a good inland spot for coho. The outlet of the lakes holds fair coho numbers during high water in late October.

The Willamette River and slough from St. Helens to the falls at Oregon City is a freshwater system which receives very heavy angling pressure. Actually a tributary of the Columbia River, the Willamette is the most productive of all individual streams located within Oregon. Here salmon may be found during virtually every week of the year, although the heaviest interest—and indeed the best fishing—typically occurs from March through early May. In fact, in 1976, nearly ten thousand salmon were taken during the month of April, but March and May are also top months.

A number of boathouses may be found stretched along the Willamette, and most of the fishing between Portland and Oswego is done by trolling or anchoring in lines, boats sometimes literally tied to one another and stretching across the width of the river. During June and July, salmon may be found farther upstream. It is during this period that anglers head for the McKenzie and Santiam rivers, where wobbling lures bring strikes.

Other Oregon fresh waters which hold limited numbers of salmon are the Applegate, Beaver Creek, Big Elk Creek (Yaquina system), Floras Creek and New River, Hunter Creek, Illinois River, Kilchis River, Miami River (predominantly chum salmon), Millicoma River, Necanicum River, Neskowin Creek, Rock Creek, Salmonberry River, Siltcoos Lake, Tahkenitch Lake, Tillamook River, Yachats River, and Yaquina River.

California

A number of rivers and streams in northern California hold runs of Pacific salmon. Chinook enter the larger coastal rivers north of San Francisco Bay and sometimes spawn in the smaller tributaries, but coho are found in streams as far south as central Santa Cruz County. The California Department of Fish and Game suggests that the coastal streams from Sonoma County south be "recommended only to local residents. Most of them have sandbars across their mouths for a long period of the year and runs of steelhead and silver salmon are confined to the late fall and winter. The visitor who travels any great distance is apt to find water so low that fish are unable to enter streams or so high that fishing is useless."[1]

The Sacramento River system, of course, accounts for a large number of sport-caught salmon taken from California's fresh waters each year. The main river below Colusa supports large runs of fall Chinook and enjoys heavy angling pressure from late summer to early fall. In general, the best months to fish this section of the Sacramento are September and October, when many brute-sized king salmon fall prey to lucky or skillful anglers.

Fall Chinook are also taken from several Sacramento River tributaries. The main Sacramento is especially productive near the mouths of the American and Feather Rivers, as well as Butte Creek, during September and October. But good catches may also be made near Knights Landing and at other points several miles from the various tributary streams.

The main Sacramento, from Colusa downstream, also produces fresh Chinook during the winter months. Best fishing typically occurs during December and early January. Relatively few spring Chinook are taken here, but one advantage of fishing the main stem of the Sacramento is that anglers always stand a chance of connecting on steelhead trout. Steelhead frequently take the same baits and lures which are used to entice salmon, and fishermen who fail to score on salmon may be fortunate enough to come up with a steelhead as an incidental catch.

That portion of the main Sacramento lying between Redding and Colusa holds salmon during each and every month of the year. Vast numbers of fall Chinook begin to move into the upper Sacramento during the latter half of September. While fish are available into December, the best fishing typically occurs during October and early November. The winter months also provide Chinook angling opportunities here, with action peaking between January and March. That stretch of the river lying above Hamilton City is particularly productive for winter Chinook.

Spring Chinook, although limited in number, are available in the main Sacramento from about March through June. The best fishing usually takes place during April and May. Especially productive are waters lying near the mouths of such tributaries as Deer and Mill creeks. At times, fish appear to concentrate at such points.

A number of resorts line the banks of the Sacramento between Redding and the City of Sacramento. Motels, restaurants, tackle, launching, and boat rentals are available at most of these. While fishing from the bank is popular and productive—especially near the mouths of tributary streams—boat fishing is the generally accepted method of fishing the main Sacramento. Trollers use a variety of lures to take Chinook, but casting from boat may also be extremely effective at times.

Some notable angling opportunities exist in that portion of the Sacramento lying above Redding. Perhaps most significant is the excellent Chinook fishing found below Keswick Dam. Although few fall Chinook are taken here, anglers take impressive catches of winter fish, with action reaching its peak during February and March.

The Klamath River system boasts excellent salmon fishing at certain times of the year. The Klamath is a large coastal river running from Iron Gate Dam to its mouth between Crescent City and Trinidad. Salmon may be taken at virtually any point along the river. While much of the most promising salmon water is inaccessible to foot-bound anglers and may be reached only by white water boaters, salmon must pass through a number of spots which provide easy access.

The Klamath River sees enormous fishing pressure at its entrance to the Pacific. Here boats congregate in vast numbers when salmon begin to mill around the river mouth. Because the number of boats is often so large, most fishermen use heavy tackle. Such gear allows them to bring salmon to net or gaff quickly enough so that lines do not become tangled in the process of playing a fish. While anchoring here is not permitted, boaters are allowed to use their motors and oars to hold their craft in a stationary position, allowing their baits and lures to be worked by the current.

Lighter tackle may be used throughout the lagoon above the Klamath River mouth. Here many fishermen troll or cast from boat. Above Highway 101, both salmon and steelhead are taken in large numbers. Fishing may be done either from boat or bank. Several Klamath River tributaries host salmon runs. Perhaps

149

most significant are the Salmon and Trinity rivers. In fact, some of the best salmon fishing opportunities are frequently found in the main Klamath near such tributary intersections.

The best fishing for king salmon invariably occurs during August and September near the Klamath River mouth. Fall Chinook are also taken from the Shasta and Scott Rivers, as well as the Trinity and Salmon, during late September and October. There is little sport to be found in the Klamath or its tributary streams after October.

Spring Chinook, although relatively few in number, are available to anglers fishing the Klamath and its tributaries. Because water flow of the main river is normally high during the spring, the best fishing usually occurs in the Salmon and Trinity rivers—and in Wooley Creek, which may be reached only by hikers. A relatively small run of coho enters the Klamath during September and October, and the best fishing generally occurs along the lower portion of the river, sometimes as late as November.

The Smith River, California's northernmost coastal stream, enters the Pacific north of Crescent City near the Oregon border. This river is noted for its exceptionally large Chinook; here fish typically run larger than those encountered in many of California's other prime salmon waters, including the Klamath.

Fall Chinook offer the most outstanding angling opportunities. Large kings are taken near the Smith River mouth, with the best fishing usually taking place during September and October.

The Eel River, which empties into the Pacific near Humboldt Bay and the town of Eureka, produces impressive catches of salmon each year. Here trollers ply the expansive tidewater area in search of large king salmon. The best fishing near the Eel mouth occurs from late August through October.

Upriver, the Eel is accessible along its entire length to the mouth of the south fork; for a distance of about fifty miles, the south fork is paralleled by Highway 101. Good salmon catches are taken from both the main stem and the south fork. Access is rather restricted along the main Eel above its confluence with the south fork, however. The middle fork enters the main Eel at the town of Dos Rios.

The Eel River above its mouth is perhaps best noted for its excellent steelhead fishing, but good numbers of salmon are taken upstream during October and November. To a large extent, the time at which Chinook show along the middle and upper reaches of the river depends on water flow volumes. Probably the most productive month for taking coho from the Eel is October.

The Russian River, which enters the Pacific

Ocean at the town of Jenner, just north of Bodega Bay, is yet another California coastal stream better known for its steelheading opportunities than for its salmon fishery. But late spawning Chinook salmon have recently been introduced to the river in order to provide winter action. Limited numbers of coho are also taken here during the fall. The Russian provides good access from its mouth to a point about one hundred miles upstream and is the most significant steelhead—if not salmon—river near the Bay Area.

Salmon are also taken from Central Valley tributaries of the Sacramento River, as well as from the Mokelumne River. Best fishing typically occurs during late September and October. While spring Chinook are relatively scarce, they are found in several Sacramento River tributaries. Among the most productive is Butte Creek, which hosts good runs during March and April.

The California DFG notes: "There is now essentially no salmon or steelhead fishing in the San Joaquin Valley. The Stanislaus and Tuolumne rivers had good salmon runs in 1960 but have had very poor runs ever since. The disaster appears to have been caused primarily by a combination of low stream flows, pollution, an excessive proportion of return irrigation water, and by heavy pumping which reversed the direction of stream flow in much of the Sacramento-San Joaquin Delta, thus destroying the guidelines by which young salmon find the ocean and adults find the rivers."[2] While the DFG hopes to take steps to correct the situation, it will be neither an easy task nor one in which results will become apparent for a number of years.

Alaska

Alaska boasts a plethora of freshwater rivers, streams, and lakes in which Pacific salmon species may be found. Entire volumes could be—and, in fact, have been—written about such "last frontier" fishing opportunities. While it would require a large number of pages to touch even lightly on all of these freshwater salmon areas, following are a number of waters of particular interest to Pacific salmon anglers.

The Ketchikan area, heavily fished by saltwater salmon fishermen, is no less important to freshwater enthusiasts. Here a number of streams and lakes host large runs of the various Pacific salmon species. Silver salmon may be found at Ward Cove Creek lakes, situated only six miles northwest of Ketchikan by road. Pinks and silvers, as well as chum, are taken from Salt Lagoon Creek, twenty-two miles north of Ketchikan by boat, and the Naha River, in the same vicinity, hosts runs of coho, sockeye, pinks, and chum.

Fish Creek, about twenty miles east of Ketchikan by boat and at the head of Thorne Arm, holds coho, pinks, and red salmon (sockeye). And the Unuk River, among the most productive salmon streams in the West, provides plenty of action for coho, pinks, and chum. Silvers are also available at Reflection Lake, forty-six air miles north of Ketchikan above Short Bay, and at McDonald Lake, forty-five air miles north of Ketchikan above Yes Bay. The Karta River, northwest of Ketchikan above Karta Bay, Prince of Wales Island, supports runs of coho, sockeye, pinks, and chum.

Throughout southeastern Alaska, the best fishing for coho typically occurs during July to September. Fish reach a maximum size of about twenty-five pounds, and the favored lure is the salmon spoon. Sockeye fishing here peaks during July and August, and flies account for a large percentage of sport-caught fish. Most red salmon run ten pounds or less.

Small spoons are used extensively to trick pinks or humpies. Throughout the southeast portion of the state, the best humpy action usually occurs during July and August. These fish reach a maximum weight of about seven pounds. Chums, tricked on a variety of salmon spoons, run to about fifteen pounds. Fishing reaches its zenith from July through September.

Near Wrangell, the Stikine River provides an excellent fishery for coho, pinks, and chum. Guides are recommended, and the river is accessible by boat or plane from either Wrangell or Petersburg. Silvers are taken from Pats Creek and Pats Lake, about twelve miles south of Wrangell by road, and from Thoms Lake, situated about eighteen miles south of Wrangell and reached by boat or plane. Silvers may also be found at Kunk Lake, fourteen miles south of Wrangell on Etolin Island.

Coho, pinks, sockeye, and chum are available at both Salmon Bay Lake and Luck Lake on Prince of Wales Island. At the former, there is a boat and cabin present at the outlet of the lake; the latter offers a public cabin.

Salmon are abundant in the fresh waters near Petersburg. One of the most productive waters for coho is the Blind River, sixteen miles southeast of Petersburg by road. Here excellent catches of silvers are made during the fall. Petersburg Creek, located across Wrangell Narrows and accessible from Petersburg by boat, supports good runs of coho, sockeye, pinks, and chum, and Petersburg Lake, four miles by trail up Petersburg Creek, provides

good sport for coho. There is a boat and cabin present at the lake.

Coho, pinks, and chum may also be taken from Falls Creek, about eleven miles south of Petersburg by road. Best fishing here is during the fall. Kah Sheets Creek, twenty miles southwest of Petersburg and accessible by boat, offers one of the most productive and exciting fall coho fisheries. Pinks, sockeye, and chum may also be taken here.

The Castle River, twenty-two miles southwest of Petersburg on the west shore of Duncan Canal, is a fair spot for coho, pinks, and chum, and the same three species are also found at Kadake Creek, about sixty miles by boat or plane west of Petersburg on Kuiu Island.

A handful of Sitka-area streams and lakes support Pacific salmon runs. The two major rivers are the Nakwasina and Katlian. The former hosts only coho and is situated about fifteen miles north of Sitka by boat. The latter provides fishing opportunities for silvers, pinks, and chum and lies only eleven miles northeast of Sitka by boat.

Sitkoh Creek, known for its excellent spring steelhead fishing, also provides coho sport during the fall months. Salmon Lake, at the southeast end of Silver Bay by boat, but requiring a hike of about one mile, and Redoubt Lake, twelve miles south of Sitka by boat, are good spots for four Pacific salmon species—coho, sockeye, pinks, and chum.

Admiralty Island, well endowed with a number of productive saltwater salmon haunts, offers only one freshwater lake in which coho may be taken. Youngs Lake, about fifteen miles south of Juneau by boat or plane, boasts a public cabin and boat.

But there are several other freshwater areas near Juneau which provide excellent salmon angling. Cowee Creek, about forty miles north of Juneau on the Glacier Highway, is a good bet for coho, pinks, and chum, while the Eagle River, about twenty-seven miles north of Juneau on the same highway, offers excellent fall fishing for silvers. Peterson Creek, a few miles nearer Juneau on the Glacier Highway, provides sport fishing for the same species.

Windfall Lake, which requires a four-mile hike from Mile 26 on the Glacier Highway, furnishes coho, chum, pink and red salmon, while Auke Creek, eleven miles north of town on the same highway, offers good late summer and fall fishing for silvers, pinks, and chum. Only pinks and chum are found in Fish Creek, about eight miles north of the Gastineau Channel Bridge on North Douglas Road.

The Chilkat River provides an excellent fall and winter fishery for silvers, pinks, and chum and is located at Mile 16-19 on the Haines Highway.

Sockeye appear in nearby Chilkat Lake. Another top fall-winter fishery is found on the Chilkoot River, ten miles northeast of Haines on Chilkoot Lake Road. Only red salmon and humpies are found here.

Coho are taken during late summer and fall from Thirty-one Mile Slough, located that distance from Haines on the Haines Highway. Dyea Slough, ten miles north of Skagway by road at the head of Taiya Inlet, offers good fall fishing for coho, pinks, and chum.

Near Yakutat, four streams share the sport salmon fishing spotlight. The renowned Situk River is one of the top fishing waters of Alaska and offers good spring and fall fishing. Coho and sockeye, as well as pinks, are abundant from late summer to late fall. But large king salmon are also taken from the Situk. Best Chinook fishing here is from April to July.

Ankau Creek, the only one of these waters accessible by road from Yakutat, hosts good fall runs of coho. The Italio River, twenty-one air miles southeast of Yakutat, holds coho, too—as does the Lost River, accessible by trail or air from Yakutat.

Fishing seasons vary as one moves into the southcentral part of the state. Here the best fishing for king salmon occurs from May through July. Coho provide top sport anytime from July through September, but June and July are typically the best months for sockeye fishing. As in southeastern Alaska, pink salmon angling throughout the southcentral portion of the state hits its stride during July and August; the same two months are normally the best ones for taking chum.

Three fresh waters located along the Chitina-McCarthy Road are of interest to freshwater salmon fishermen. These are the Copper River at Mile 1.1, a productive stream for both Chinook and sockeye, Strelna Lake, at Mile 10.6 and which provides silver sport, and Lou's Lake, at Mile 25.7, in which coho also appear.

The Eyak River and Lake near Cordova are good spots for coho and red salmon. And Afognak Island, accessible by air from Kodiak, boasts several top freshwater salmon spots. Most notable are Afognak River and Lake, Malina Lakes, Portage Lake, and Laura Lake and Creek, each of which holds coho, sockeye, and pinks. The Little Afognak Lake and Kitoi Lakes offer action from only coho and red salmon.

Kodiak Island houses a myriad of freshwater lakes and streams holding Pacific salmon. The Buskin River, five miles south of Kodiak, is productive for coho, pinks, and red salmon, as is the American River, twenty miles south of Kodiak via the Chiniak Road. Pinks are taken from the Russian River, ten miles south of Kodiak, and Mayflower Lake, twenty-two miles south of town on the Chiniak Road, hosts coho. Both pinks and silvers are available on the Olds and Kalsin rivers, accessible on the Chiniak Road and lying about twenty-eight miles south of Kodiak. About thirty miles south of town on the same road is the Roslyn River, productive for coho. A few miles farther south are Twin Forks and Chiniak Creeks, which hold both coho and pink salmon. Nearby Pony Lake offers good fishing for silvers.

Lake Rose Tead and the Pasagshak River, which lie about thirty-six miles south of Kodiak and are reached via the Pasagshak Road, support coho, sockeye, and pinks. Silvers and pinks are available at Lake Miam, a fifteen or twenty minute charter flight from Kodiak.

The Saltery River and Saltery Lake, thirty-six miles southwest of Kodiak via a four-wheel-drive vehicle road to Saltery Cove or a fifteen- to twenty-minute flight from Kodiak, provide good fishing for reds, pinks, and coho. Coho are taken from Woody and Long Island Lakes, two and four miles east of Kodiak.

The Kodiak Wildlife Refuge boasts a half dozen waters which hold sizeable salmon runs. The Uganik River and Lake, thirty-six air miles southwest of Kodiak, hold reds, pinks, and silvers, and the same species are found at the Karluk River and Lake, about seventy-five air miles southwest of Kodiak. The Red River and Lake, about eighty-five air miles from Kodiak, are the most notable Chinook waters on the island, but sockeye, coho, and pinks also abound here. Barbara Lake, twenty-one air miles west of Kodiak, and Akalura Lake, approximately eighty air miles southwest of town, hold both silvers and reds.

Peak fishing times for Kodiak-area salmon are: June and July for Chinook; September-November for coho; July and August for pinks; June and July for sockeye; and July for chum.

Along the western edge of Alaska, peak fishing seasons are somewhat different. Kings are most abundant from May through July, while silvers are most numerous from July through September. June and July are the best months for sockeye, while July and August usually produce the largest numbers of both pinks and chum.

Bristol Bay is among the most productive of all Alaska salmon regions. Here virtually every freshwater lake or stream is home to one or more species of Pacific salmon. Among the more important waters are the Togiak, Igushik, and Wood river systems.

The Togiak System hosts each of the five Pacific species found along the West Coast. The Togiak River itself is the only such waterway to do so. Red salmon are taken from the outlets to Togiak Lake and Pungokepuk Lake, as well as from the outlet to Ongivinuk Lake. Both coho and sockeye, however, may be found in the outlet of Gechiak Lake.

The Igushik River system hosts enormous runs of red salmon only. Included are the Igushik itself, as well as the mouth of the Kathlene River and Amanka Lake.

Both the Togiak and Igushik systems are serviced by air charters operating out of Dillingham. There are no accommodations to be found on site.

The Wood River system is located near Aleknagik Village and may be reached by road during the summer and fall months or via air charters out of either Dillingham or King Salmon. While several fish camps are found in the area, prior arrangements for accommodations are usually necessary. Anglers should inquire at Dillingham or King Salmon.

While kings, pinks, and sockeye are taken from the Wood River itself, only red salmon are found throughout the remainder of the Wood system. These waters include the outlet to Lake Aleknagik, the Agulowak and Agulukpak rivers, Lynx Creek, and the Little Togiak River (Lake Nerka), and the Peace, Wind, and Grant rivers.

The Tikchik Lake system is served by both charter and scheduled aircraft from Dillingham, but accommodations should be arranged in advance. Kings, sockeye, pinks, coho, and chum are all present in the Nuyakuk River, but only sockeye runs are found at the outlet to Tikchik Lake, at the Nuyakuk-Tikchik Narrows, the Chauekuktuli-Nuyakuk Narrows, and the Allen River.

The Nushagak River system is served by charter flights from both Dillingham and King Salmon, although a few spots near villages are served by scheduled flights out of Dillingham. The Nushagak-Mulchatna holds Chinook, sockeye, and chum, although these species—plus pinks—are taken at the mouth of Portage Creek. Kings, silvers, reds, and chum may be found in the Koktuli River. Chinook, sockeye, and silvers are abundant in the Old Stuyahok River and the King Salmon River.

Lake Iliamna is served by scheduled flights from Anchorage, Homer, Kenai, King Salmon, and Iliamna. Prior accommodation arrangements are required, except at Iliamna. A boat is available at Newhalen River and Igiugig.

The Iliamna River hosts vast runs of sockeye salmon. Reds are also taken from Gibraltar Lake, Lake Clark, and the Newhalen River, and the Copper River, but coho show in Lower Talarik Creek.

The Kvichak River system also includes the Igiugig-Kaskanak, which boasts sockeye, chum, and coho.

The Alagnak (Branch) River system holds large runs of Chinook, sockeye, coho, pinks, and chum. All five species are available in the Alagnak itself, but only reds are taken from the Kulik and Battle rivers, and from Funnel Creek. The outlet to Nonvianuk Lake, however, provides angling opportunities for kings, as well as sockeye.

The Naknek Watershed is yet another significant Bristol Bay salmon spawning area. The Naknek River and King Salmon Creek are accessible by foot from King Salmon, where accommodations are available. The outlying areas are reached by charter (and some scheduled) flights from King Salmon, but it is necessary for anglers to arrange for accommodations in advance. There is a fish camp on the Brooks River.

The Naknek River itself holds all five Pacific salmon species. Only sockeye are available from the Brooks, American Creek, the Narrows, and Naknek Lake. Both kings and silvers are taken by anglers fishing Big Creek.

The Egegik River system, accessible by charter flights from Pilot Point and King Salmon, lacks accommondations. Both silvers and sockeye are taken from the Ruth River, Featherly Creek, and other small creeks in the area. The outlet to Becharof Lake holds both species, plus Chinook.

The Ugashik River system, also reached by plane from Pilot Point or King Salmon, is a favorite among Chinook fishermen who take this species from the Meshik River and the outlet to Mother Goose Lake. Both waters also furnish coho sport during the fall. The outlet to Lower Ugashik Lake produces silvers, reds, and pinks, but only silvers are found in the narrows between the lakes. The Sandy River system turns out good catches of both kings and silvers.

The Bear River system, reached by charter flights from Port Moller and Cold Bay, boasts no accommodations. But both Chinook and coho are numerous here.

Several productive salmon waters may be found along the Sterling Highway, which connects Homer to Soldotna. The Kenai River yields large numbers of Chinook, coho, pinks, and sockeye. Coho are found at Centennial Lake and at Lake Tustumena, both located near Mile 110 of the Sterling Highway turnoff. Large numbers of kings and silvers are taken from the Ninilchik River, at Mile 136, at Stariski Creek, Mile 151, and from the Anchor River, Mile 157.

Silvers are found at Skilak Lake, at Mile 7 and 12 access roads on the Skilak Loop Road, and at Rock

Lake, at Mile 5. Salmon are also taken from a number of fresh waters along the Sterling Highway between Seward and Soldotna. Quartz Creek, Mile 41.5, has coho, while the Russian River, Mile 55, holds both coho and sockeye. Upper Jean Lake, Mile 63, produces coho year around, and red salmon are taken during the summer and fall at Sunken Island Lake, Mile 4 of the Swanson River Road. The Swanson River itself is a good producer of coho.

The Seward Highway leading from Anchorage to Seward passes numerous productive salmon waters. Bird Creek, at Mile 27, offers a summer fishery for pinks, while Twenty-Mile River, at Mile 47, is a good bet for fall coho. Pinks are taken during the summer from Ingram Creek at Mile 51 and from Resurrection Creek at Mile 72.

The most productive salmon waters near Anchorage are Campbell Creek, which hosts runs of coho and pinks, Rabbit Creek, from which a "fair to poor" summer-fall fishery of pinks are taken, and Ship Creek, which holds king salmon, as well as coho, pinks, and chum.

The Sport Fish Division of the Alaska Department of Fish and Game also lists numerous other prime salmon waters in its pamphlet, "Alaska Sport Fishing Guide." The Willow-Talkeetna area, for instance, affords good salmon action at several points. Lower Willow Creek (below Canyon Rapids) holds coho, pinks, and chum, but there are no salmon to be found above the rapids. Deception Creek, two miles east of Willow, offers a good July-August fishery for pinks and chum, as well as silvers. Little Willow Creek holds both coho and pinks, and Kashwitna Lake, seven miles north of Willow on the new highway, offers "poor" fishing for small silvers.

The summer and fall months are good for coho, pinks, and chum at Caswell Creek, fifteen miles north of Willow. Sheep Creek, three miles farther from town, holds the same species, as does Montana Creek, twenty-six miles north of Willow. Silvers and reds are found in Birch Creek, a stream offering limited access and which is located five miles south of Talkeetna on the new highway. Both kings and silvers are taken from Moose and Kroto creeks, west of Talkeetna on the Petersville road.

Lower Fire Lake at Mile 17 on the west side of the Palmer Highway holds coho, as does Mirror (Bear) Lake at Mile 22 and on the east side of the highway. Echo Lake, four miles south of Palmer on the Anchorage Highway, Victor Lake, one-half mile by trail, and Wasilla Lake, one-half mile east of Wasilla, provide coho fishing opportunities. Both coho and sockeye are taken from Cornelius Lake, four miles west of Palmer on the Wasilla Highway, while nearby Finger Lake supports only sockeye. Big Lake, at the end of Big Lake Road ten miles west of Wasilla, is a good spot for both silvers and red salmon, and the same two species are present in Barbara Lake, although Alaska DFG officials say fishing here is generally poor.

About the only salmon fishery which is found along the Glenn Highway is at Tex Smith Lake, located at Mile 162. The lake is reported to hold silvers. There are, however, a number of waters which are productive for various Pacific species found between Valdez and Black Rapids along the Richardson Highway. Most notable are the Klutina and Gulkana waterways. Klutina Lake, twenty-five miles of poor road from Mile 101, holds Chinook and sockeye, as does the river itself. The same two species are present in the Gulkana River, situated between Mile 128 and Mile 148.

The Nome area is extremely productive for the various salmon species. The Nome River turns out good catches of kings, silvers, coho, and pinks, in addition to some chum. Best fishing occurs during spring and fall. Salmon Lake, north of Nome on the Kougarok Road, provides a fishery for chum and sockeye. Coho, pinks, and chum are taken from the Pilgrim River, sixty-five miles north of Nome on the Kougarok Road.

Spring and fall are the best times to fish the Snake River, which holds silvers, pinks, and chum and is crossed seven miles west of Nome on the Penny-Sinuk River Road. Pinks and chum are available on the Solomon and Sinuk rivers, the former located between Miles 40 and 50 on the Solomon Highway, the latter reached via the Nome-Teller Highway. The Kuzitrin River, at Mile 68 on the Nome-Kougarok Road, is a fine clear water stream which turns out good numbers of sport-caught Chinook, pinks, and chum. Pinks and chum may also be found on the Fox River, at Miles 60 to 67 on the same road, and on the Niukluk River. The latter is reached via the road to Council and offers outstanding salmon action during July.

The Unalakleet River, one of Alaska's premier salmon waters, is situated on the west side of Norton Sound. There are good accommodations along the lower river, and boats are available. The Unalakleet is a prodigious producer of kings, silvers, pinks, and chum.

Several freshwater salmon areas are found along the Elliott Highway. A good producer of kings is the Chatanika River at Mile 11.4. This river is especially productive during spring and fall. There is a campground along the river, as well as a boat launching ramp. The Chatanika near Miles 29-39 of the Steese Highway offers good fishing for both Chinook and silvers from July through September. Chum are also found along this portion of the river.

Nenana Pond, at Mile 303.7 on the Fairbanks-Anchorage Highway, supports coho, which are available during the fall. Silvers are also found in Bolio and Mark Lakes at Mile 260 of the Richardson Highway, Delta Junction to Fairbanks. Kings may be taken from the Salcha River, along with chum. The Salcha is located at Mile 325.3 on the same highway, but boats are required for the best action.

A handful of fresh waters are found along the Alaska Highway from the boundary to Delta Junction. The Delta Clearwater River, near Mile 1405, is a good bet for coho, but boats are a must. There is a launch site present.

Alaska Department of Fish and Game officials point out that two waters are "excellent"—Lisa Lake, near Mile 1381, and Jan Lake, near Mile 1353.5. Both are outstanding producers of coho. Craig Lakes, near Mile 1383.7, also hold good silver salmon runs.

British Columbia

British Columbia, like Alaska, offers almost innumerable fresh waters in which the various Pacific salmon species may be found. In fact, it is likely that not all the streams which hold salmon—especially coho—have even been catalogued by the government. This is especially true perhaps of the northwest portion of the province, where many small, unsullied streams support good runs of native silvers.

While all five Pacific salmon species may be found in the fresh waters of British Columbia, only two—Chinook and coho—are of interest to river and stream fishermen. This is because *only these two species may be taken from the non-tidal or fresh waters of the province.* It is recommended that anglers check with local fisheries and marine personnel to obtain official regulations pertaining to the various fisheries. Of course, this should be done before fishermen venture forth in *any* area, but it is particularly important to do so throughout British Columbia. Because of a decline in the numbers of certain salmon runs, the government has imposed strict controls on salmon fishing in several areas. It is hoped that the new emphasis on conservation will reverse the dismal shortages of salmon in these specific waters.

Although sport fishermen are allowed to take both Chinook and coho from many of British Columbia's fresh waters, it is the latter species which is the most important. While the waters of the province yield unusually large Chinook at certain times and in certain places (the previous world record sport-caught Chinook, a fish weighing ninety-two pounds, which held the crown for thirty years, came from the Skeenna River), coho are more abundant. At this writing, some 1,800 coho streams have been catalogued!

The largest runs of Chinook and coho are those which occur in the Fraser River system. But these runs have been badly depleted in recent years (especially Chinook), and stabilization efforts are now under way. Much of the information contained in this section was provided through the courtesy of Mr. Lyle Freeman, a district supervisor for the Fisheries Operations Division of the Department of the Environment. Mr. Freeman and other Fisheries and Marine personnel, as well as those associated with the British Columbia Department of Fish and Wildlife, have provided information which will prove invaluable to the sport fisherman interested in taking Chinook or coho from the many rivers in which they abound.

But while Fraser River Chinook and coho runs suffer, other species abound. Pink salmon, which show only during the odd-numbered years in southern British Columbia, also enter the Fraser. In recent years, pink runs have been large. In fact, during 1977, the Fraser System enjoyed the largest escapement of pinks since records have been kept. Unfortunately for the sport angler, humpies—a fine sport fish—may not be taken from the nontidal waters of the province.

But, despite the poor returns of Chinook and coho in recent years, anglers continue to find outstanding action on these two Pacific species. Typically, the best fishing for large Tyee or king salmon occurs during August along the lower Fraser, while excellent fishing may be found during August and September farther upstream. Here anglers use a variety of salmon spoons, spinners, and other artificial lures to trick large Chinook. Natural baits, especially salmon roe, are also effective.

The best coho fishing normally occurs from about early September through mid-October. Tackle employed to trick silvers is often similar to that used for taking steelhead. While many fishermen swear by the old standby, salmon eggs, an increasing number of coho fishermen are enjoying excellent success on artificial lures, the most popular of which are spoons.

Although fishing is good at many points along the Fraser, some of the best sport is found at the mouth of the Bridge River near Lilliwut. This is primarily a bar fishery in which large Tyee salmon are the targets. The Fraser, normally clouded in appearance, is especially productive where clear water streams run into the main river; such a spot is near the mouth of the Bridge River.

A similar fishery exists at the confluence of the Fraser and Thompson rivers. Like the Fraser-Bridge fishery, the Fraser-Thompson is both highly productive and heavily fished.

Coho are also taken from the Fraser but do not occur in the main river above its confluence with the Thompson. One of the most significant coho fisheries occurs in the Fraser Valley at Wing Dam. Here silvers are taken in vast numbers during the fall.

The Thompson River originates at Kamloops and flows westerly some forty-five miles to Ashcroft, then flows southerly for about fifty miles until it joins the Fraser near Lytton. Chinook offer sport along the lower Thompson during August and September, and coho may be taken near the river mouth.

The Harrison River provides an outstanding fishery near its mouth. Here large king salmon are taken during August and September. Coho are available during September and October. Harrison Lake, a large body of water lying between Harrison Hot Springs and Port Douglas, also offers coho and Chinook action when fish pass through during their upstream spawning migrations.

The Skeena River, that record-producing waterway, is well-known for its exceptionally large Tyee. Here the best fishing normally occurs during August and September. Some of the finest fishing for Chinook to fifty or sixty pounds is found at the confluence of the Kalum River near Terrace.

The Nass River is also notable as a producer of exceptionally large king salmon. Here fish are taken during August and September. Perhaps the best fishing is found where the Ishkinish River enters the Nass.

The Nicola River, which runs approximately fifty miles between Nicola Lake and the Thompson River, turns out good numbers of spring salmon, especially near its confluence with the Thompson at Spence's Bridge. And the Quesnel River between the communities of Quesnel and Likely also produces good numbers of Chinook. Fish are taken on flies, as well as a variety of spoons and other artificial lures. Accommodations are available at Likely, and there is public camping nearby.

No rundown of British Columbia sport salmon fishing would be complete without mention of the famed Campbell River. Here anglers fish the river mouth for Tyee—Chinook exceeding thirty pounds. The Campbell is among the most popular and productive of all British Columbia salmon streams and draws anglers from far and near. The area is accessible by road from Nanaimo.

The Nitinat River is still another very productive salmon stream. Large kings are usually the quarry,

and anglers take them on spoons or salmon roe. Best fishing is during August and September. Also near Alberni is the Sproat River, a good spot to try for fall coho. Best fishing here is from about the first of September through about the third week of October.

The Nimpkish, reached via Alert Bay and a favorite of the late Roderick Haig-Brown, now enjoys less prestige as a premier salmon stream than in earlier years but still rates mention as a good producer of salmon. Best fishing is near the river mouth, with action typically peaking during August and September. The Keogh River near Port Hardy is a good bet for coho during the fall. There is good fishing found near the river mouth, with salmon roe or spoons tricking the majority of fish.

Another notable salmon river is the Dean, between Bella Coola and Williams Lake. The Dean supports both Chinook and coho runs. Later summer and fall months provide the best fishing here. The Atnarka River is another stream from which both species may be taken. July, August, and September typically see the best fishing for Chinook; coho afford good angling opportunities during September and October.

Both spring and coho salmon may be taken from the Bella Coola River, and there are excellent accommodations available. Some of the best Chinook fishing is low in the stream. The Squamish River, near the town of the same name, furnishes good angling opportunities during the late summer and fall months, and both springs and silvers are taken from the Ashlu River near Cheekeye. The Cheakamus and Mamquam rivers host both spring and silver runs, too. And the Stawamus is an excellent producer of coho during the fall. The Elaho River, about twenty miles north of Cheekye, supports both Chinook and coho. Here fishing peaks during late summer for kings and during September and October for coho.

The Capilano River near Vancouver is a popular stream for coho. Peak runs appear here from late August into early October. Nearby Lynn Creek also holds coho, with the best fishing found during September and October. Still another good coho stream is the Indian River, near Vancouver. Fall fishing for silvers here can be outstanding. Seymour Creek is another Vancouver-area water which is worth the angler's attention. There are good fall coho runs found near the mouth of the creek.

The Koksilah River, near Duncan, holds salmon, and the Cowichan River, regarded as one of British Columbia's foremost fish producers, is another top salmon bet.

Near Chilliwack, the Chilliwack River and Atchelitz Creek are tempting fall coho streams. The

Jack Bolton, Boise, ventured north to come up with this large king. *Author photo, courtesy of* Salt Water Sportsman.

Sumas River near Abbotsford is still another productive silver stream, and these fish are taken consistently by anglers fishing Hope Slough and Elk Creek after fall freshets have enticed fish into the rivers.

The Skwawka River, at the head of Jervis Inlet in the Powell Lake district, is a good bet for both springs and coho, and the same two species may be taken from the Phillips River, located about sixty miles northwest of Powell River. Best fishing is from July through October. The Brem River, some fifty miles north of Powell River, supports good runs of coho, and peak fishing here is in the fall.

The Salmon River, which empties into Kelsey Bay, is productive for salmon near its mouth. Just north of Nanaimo is the Englishman's River, another stream which hosts salmon runs and is productive near its mouth, and nearby French Creek offers late season coho sport.

Near Haney, the Alouette River (north and south forks) holds coho. These fish are also present in nearby Kanaka Creek. Silvers also frequent the Coquitlam River and lower Pitt River.

Because British Columbia's major population centers are found throughout the southern end of the province, the heaviest angling pressure is concentrated in the same general range. But as new access is opened, rivers and streams which have seen very little angling effort become increasingly popular. Especially throughout the northwest portion of the province, boats and planes provide the only means of travel. Thus, there remain virtually untouched—and certainly untouted—a host of pristine streams which support native coho runs.

Idaho

Idaho is the least productive of Western salmon fishing regions. Because the state does not front the Pacific Ocean and therefore lacks the large number of coastal rivers and streams found from Alaska to California, Idaho does not enjoy the vast salmon runs found elsewhere on this coast.

Idaho's salmon runs enter state waters via the enormous Columbia River system, which separates Washington and Oregon. In fact, the Columbia and its tributary streams provide the *only* means of entrance into Idaho. In order to reach their destination, salmon must travel hundreds of miles up the Columbia—first past the combination of commercial and sport fishermen and, next, past a number of dams. It is no small wonder that Idaho's freshwater sport salmon catch is equal to about three percent of that taken from Washington rivers and streams!

Idaho salmon runs have been severely damaged by the construction of hydroelectric facilities along the Columbia and lower Snake rivers. These dams have caused two distinct sets of problems for Pacific salmon: they not only hamper *upstream* migration by making it difficult for returning adult salmon to negotiate the rivers, but they also bring about a high incidence of mortality in young fish during their *downstream* journeys.

Of the two problem areas, the latter may be more critical to the success or failure of specific salmon runs than the former. Hydroelectric projects are named as the chief culprits, in any event: sport salmon fishing in Idaho was completely closed during 1975 and 1976—thanks, say fisheries biologists, primarily to the dams.

While a restricted sport salmon fishery was permitted during the 1977 and 1978 seasons, the picture is not a bright one at this writing. Biologists note that the 1977 sport catch was a mere 3,500 fish—considerably lower than the annual sport harvests of ten to twenty thousand salmon prior to the early seventies.

Dave Ortmann, Anadromous Fisheries Manager for the Idaho Fish and Game Department, says that some progress is being made, however. Various fisheries management techniques, including dam correction and hatchery production, are aiding the salmon fishery. In fact, as many as seventeen thousand returning adults have been checked at the Rapid River Hatchery. Many upstream migrants are now being transported around blocking dams, and corrective measures are being taken to ensure that young salmon are not destroyed by the various hydroelectric hazards which lie between their native streams and the Pacific.

While there are a few sockeye found in the headwaters of the Salmon River, and while undoubtedly a few coho spawn in Idaho's smaller streams from time to time, the sport fishery revolves almost entirely around the presence of Chinook salmon. By far the most important Chinook waters of the state are those of the Salmon River system.

Spring Chinook provide most of the action, although there are a few summer and fall fish available. Typically, the best fishing in the Salmon River system occurs between mid-June and mid-July (sometimes spring Chinook are taken here as early as May). While fish are found in the Lemhi River, near the town of Salmon, and in the Little Salmon River, most of the angling effort occurs along the Salmon's main stem and middle fork.

Peak angling pressure occurs on the main Salmon between the communities of Challis and Stanley. Here anglers take Chinook running to about twenty-

five pounds (larger fish show occasionally). Most effective are salmon eggs and almost any proven artificial lure designs.

But Idaho Fish and Game officials warn that anglers should not expect to fish in a pristine area and in uncrowded conditions. In fact, the opposite is true: because salmon here are at such a premium and are found in the greatest numbers during a one month period, anglers arriving on the scene are likely to find the river packed elbow-to-elbow with other fishermen.

The Snake River also produces some Chinook, but not many. Some of the best fishing here is found in Hell's Canyon, an area which is extremely difficult to reach but which produces a few fish for anglers with "jet-sleds"—river boats with "jet" attachments substituting for the more commonly used propellers. The upper limit of migration in the Snake River is at Hell's Canyon Dam.

Although salmon runs also occur in other waters, many of the more popular and productive tributary streams have been closed to sport angling for an indefinite period of time. It is hoped that Idaho's efforts to overcome the obstacles detrimental to sufficient salmon escapement will meet with success and that sport salmon fishing in that state's waters will return to the productivity of former years.

Notes

[1]California Department of Fish and Game; *Salmon and Steelhead Fishing Map: Description of the Fishing and What Is Necessary to Maintain It* (Sacramento: California Office of State Printing, 1969), p. 10.

[2]Ibid., p. 12.

PART FOUR
AFTER
THE FACT

10
SALMON CARE AND PREPARATION

THE fortunate fisherman who has successfully hooked, played, and brought a salmon to net to the edge of the streambank is suddenly faced with a number of questions for which prompt answers are required. Is the fish large enough to be kept under local angling regulations? If so, should the fish be kept and used for the table? Or should it be released unharmed? If the catch is particularly large, should it be considered for a mounted trophy? These and other questions flood the angler's mind as he stands admiring his catch.

Of course, the fish should be released immediately if it does not meet local angling restrictions. If it is the proper species and is, in fact, large enough to be kept, the angler may first want to examine the fish to determine if the hooks have damaged it so that its release would be both unwise and wasteful. Perhaps a hook point has penetrated an eye; treble hooks in particular may be difficult to dislodge without severely damaging the jaw structure. The debate continues over whether hooks which are left intact will further injure the fish or will simply rust away in time.

Few fishermen are able to entirely avoid hooking under-sized salmon, especially in salt water where fish of different age groups and sizes may be found in the same area. But anglers who wish to release their catch—regardless of size—may exercise care so that undue injury is avoided.

Using a single hook—rather than tandem, double- or treble-pointed hooks—is desirable if anglers wish to release their catches or if a lot of "shakers" (under-sized salmon) are present. Undoubtedly more fish will be hooked on tandem or multi-pointed hooks than on single ones, but the results may justify that a single hook (with a single hook point) is desirable.

Many moochers have enjoyed considerable success using only a single hook, and such hooks are used extensively in fly casting and trolling techniques. While some anglers may feel that double or treble hooks are more effective, *they are not necessary.*

Once a fish is hooked and brought within sight, the angler should immediately determine if the catch is a legal one. If it is not, contact with the fish is to be avoided if possible. Scale loss is a major cause of mortality among undersized salmon, and fishermen who hook such fish should attempt to free them without letting them come in contact with the hands, net, or boat. It has been demonstrated that a scale loss of twenty-five percent may result in death. Usually, small salmon taken on a single hook may be unleashed without significant contact, but if contact must be made, anglers should grasp the fish *firmly* in one hand while the hook point is drawn free. A fish which loses many of its scales is likely to lose water through its skin and perish of dehydration.

In order to free a fish without handling it, some sort of hook-removing tool is recommended. Many anglers deftly apply needle-nose pliers to this end, but any device which will hold and invert the hook so that the fish may be shaken free is a valuable fishing companion. A coat hanger may be used and fashioned into a release device. The hanger displays a loop-handle at one end and a U-shaped hook at the other.

If stainless steel hooks are used, they should be removed before the fish is freed. Hooks constructed of metals which will corrode may be left in the fish if they cannot be removed. Only hooks which are swallowed or caught in the gills or eye should be left

Results of an unspecified salmon derby. Conservation-minded sportsmen deplore such tournaments, favoring catch-and-release instead. *Courtesy of Washington Department of Fisheries.*

intact. If possible, hooks should always be removed.

If fish are to be kept, they should be killed swiftly with a blow on the head and not left to suffocate. Fish which are left to die slowly may also bruise their flesh by thrashing around on the deck of a boat. A length of hardwood or metal pipe should be carried by salmon anglers at all times. Bleeding salmon by breaking a gill arch immediately after a blow to the head makes for the best product.

Fresh-killed salmon should be kept out of the sun and stored in a cool place as quickly as possible. Like all fish, salmon spoil rapidly, especially under warm conditions. If an ice box or cooler is not available, fish should be placed in a shady spot and covered with water-soaked cloth, grass or moss.

Salmon should be cleaned as soon as possible. A sharp knife—and sharp *knifepoint*—make this an easy task. The knifepoint should be inserted into the anal opening and the knife run toward the head. The fish should be grasped firmly during the initial incision, and the cut should be deep enough only to clear the belly flesh—and not to mangle the entrails. The incision should continue to a point below the

"V" near the gills, where the flesh becomes noticeably firmer. The gills may be cut from the underside of the fish if the head is to be left intact; otherwise, the head and gills may be removed by a single cut from the top of the fish to the bottom.

If the angler wishes to leave the head intact, all gill material should be removed, as this spoils easily. By severing the gullet from the rest of the body and pulling toward the tail, the angler is able to remove the entrails. The "bloodline" which now lies exposed against the upper part of the body cavity is actually the kidney. The knifepoint should be run along the kidney and the dark red material scraped clean. This may be accomplished with one or two fingers, although several fish cleaning knives now on the market have spoon-shaped utensils near their handles for this purpose. Once the body cavity has been cleaned of all entrails, it should be washed thoroughly to remove all blood.

The tail may be severed, and fins may be removed if desired. To remove the fins, make a slit at the base of each side of each fin, then pull the fin toward the head. Scales may be removed by holding the fish firmly while loosening the scales with a knife held at an angle of about forty-five degrees and run from tail to head. Running water is helpful if scales are to be removed in this fashion, and a strong flow from a garden hose directed against the scales at this same angle makes scaling easier. If fish are to be filleted and skinned, scales need not be removed. Some anglers, however, prefer to leave the skin intact when catches are filleted. If charcoal broiled with the skin side down, the fish retains more of its natural moisture. Scaled fish do not keep as well and are prone to freezer burn and loss of juices; thus scaling is not recommended.

While small salmon are best cooked whole, large fish may be either filleted or steaked. The former cutting method results in two long flesh-slabs cut from either side of the fish. The head should be removed before attempting to fillet a salmon.

A sharp filleting knife should be inserted through the flesh along the center of the back and carefully run along the backbone to the tail. The cut should be made slightly *above* the backbone. Using a long-bladed knife, the first fillet may be removed in a single cutting motion. To obtain the second fillet, the knife is run just *below* the backbone and the larger "branch" bones, again from head to tail. To remove the larger bones still left in each fillet, simply cut carefully just beneath the bones so that not too much flesh is wasted.

Filleting a salmon takes some practice but is not essentially a difficult procedure. Special care must be taken that knife cuts are made close to the backbone in order to retain the greatest amount of

To preserve freshness, fish should be cleaned soon after they are caught. Most public ports have fish-cleaning facilities available. *Author photo.*

edible flesh. Fillets may be skinned if desired by placing the fish skin side down and running the knifeblade, the cutting edge slightly downward, along the flat surface. Fillets may be cut into the desired size or cooked whole.

Salmon steaks are obtained easily once the fish has been cleaned. Simply cut into the desired thickness, running the blade completely through the body of the fish. Recommended thickness is about one inch.

Fish may be kept on ice or in the refrigerator if it is to be eaten within a short period of time. If it will not be consumed for some while, it should be frozen or canned.

Salmon which are intended for freezing and later use may be dipped in a solution of water and ascorbic acid (recommended ratio is two tablespoons of ascorbic acid to each quart of water) to prevent darkening. Fish should be immersed in the solution for fifteen to twenty seconds, then wrapped in freezer paper for best results. Frozen fish should be consumed within about three months if properly wrapped and frozen—sooner if flesh shows signs of freezer burn.

Salmon may also be canned. The home canner should first clean and wash the fish, removing all blood, then cut it into can-sized lengths or chunks. The Washington Department of Fisheries recommends that the backbone be left intact (it contains valuable minerals). The agency suggests the following procedure:

The fish should be drained and dried, then packed into cans or jars until even with the rim (but not above it). One-half teaspoon of salt is added, and containers are placed into a pressure cooker, loosely sealed. *Containers should be processed for one hour and fifty minutes at ten pounds (240 degrees) pressure.*

After cooking, the pressure should be allowed to drop to zero before the pressure cooker is opened. Individual container lids should be tightened after cooking.

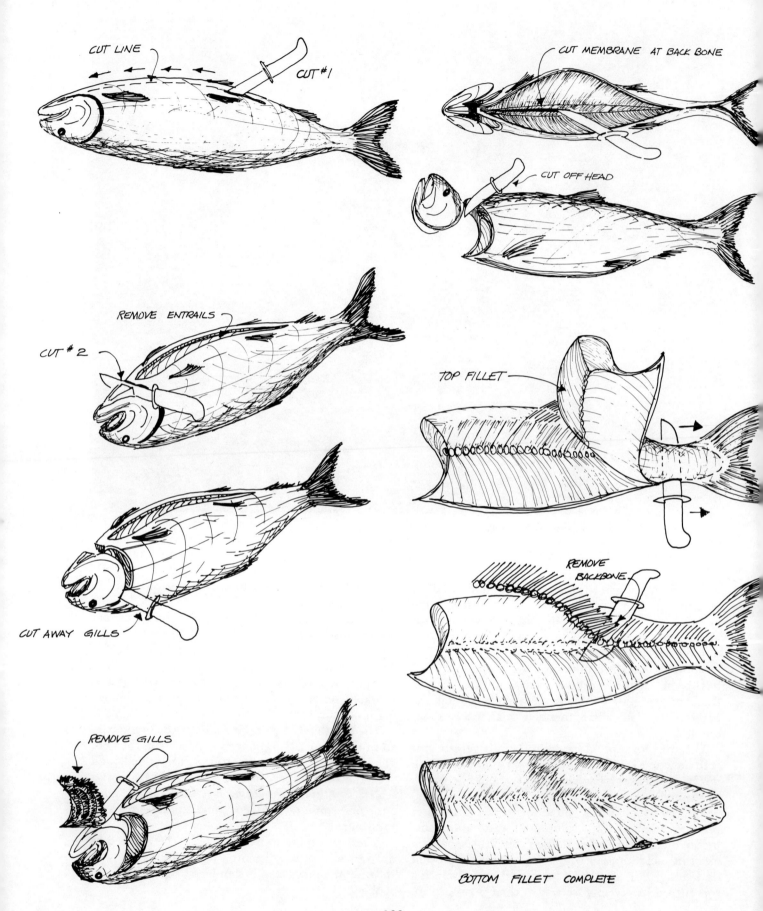

CUT LINE

CUT #1

CUT MEMBRANE AT BACK BONE

CUT OFF HEAD

REMOVE ENTRAILS

CUT #2

TOP FILLET

CUT AWAY GILLS

REMOVE BACKBONE

REMOVE GILLS

BOTTOM FILLET COMPLETE

166

Small salmon like this one are perfect for the smoker.
Author photo, courtesy of Salt Water Sportsman.

It is important that canning jars and lids be clean and free of cracks, dents, rust, or other abnormalities. Only new, clean ring bands should be used. Jar lids should be scalded and kept in hot water until placed on jars.

Salmon may be soaked in a salt brine before canning if desired. Six ounces of salt (three quarters of a cup) should be added to each gallon of water and the fish allowed to soak for at least an hour. (It is not necessary to brine fish if salt is applied directly to the fish once they are placed in jars; if salt is added directly to fish, jars should be filled with water.)

After jars have cooled, ring bands may be removed. At this point, each jar should be checked for leaks (if lid centers stay down when pressed, there is no leakage). Containers may be placed in a dry, cool place for storage.

Salmon may also be smoked at home in a crudely fashioned smoker or in one of several commercial electric smokers now on the market. Luhr Jensen and Sons, Inc., of Hood River, Oregon, manufac-

turers of the popular "Little Chief" Smoker, recommend the following procedure:

Soak fish in a brine solution consisting of two cups of either granulated or brown sugar, one cup curing salt, and one cup rock salt for every quart of water. Fish should be placed skin side up in the solution and submerged with a heavy object, such as a large plate. (It is important that no part of the fish is touched by air.) Fish should be permitted to soak for five to six hours, then rinsed thoroughly and dried for an hour. If fish is not rinsed of all brine solution, it will be far too salty for most palates.

An alternate brine solution may be concocted by adding garlic, liquid onion, lemon juice, or other flavorings (this writer favors adding some of each of those mentioned). Salinometers may be used to test the solution; when eighty degrees is registered, the brine is perfect. Still other variations are available with the addition of dill and the substitution of molasses or honey for sugar.

Once the fish has been brined and rinsed, it is ready for the smoker. Smoking length varies with each individual type of smoker but Luhr Jensen recommends checking for doneness every half hour or so once the fish has been in the "Little Chief" for about six hours. This electric model heats wood chips, which are added every two hours or so. The only way to tell when fish are done is to break open a piece to check that the center is not raw (fish should flake easily). Smoked fish may be wrapped and refrigerated or frozen.

While there are innumerable recipes for preparing fresh or frozen salmon, it is difficult to beat salmon steaks which have been dipped in flour and fried in butter or fillets (or steaks) which have been broiled over charcoal, perhaps with a dash of salt and pepper, and bacon, onion, and lemon slices placed on top of the fish as it cooks. A delicious method of baking salmon (whole or in chunks) is to concoct a mixture of white wine, lemon juice, and chopped onion, into which a dash of rosemary, basil, thyme, and tarragon have been placed. The sauce may be poured over the salmon and the fish allowed to bake at 350 degrees until done (usually about one and one-half to two hours).

The angler who properly cares for and prepares his fish is the one who enjoys it most. While many fishermen thoroughly enjoy catching—but not eating—salmon, even those who relish its flavor are apt to turn up their noses at fish which have been improperly cared for.

11
THE FUTURE

THERE is room for both optimism and pessimism where the future of Pacific salmon is concerned, but those ascribing to the varying schools of thought are in general agreement about one point: regardless of the ultimate outcome, more fishermen will be spending more time in the pursuit of their favorite sport fish. As greater affluence and more leisure time is enjoyed, an increasing number of sport salmon anglers is bound to spend an increasingly greater portion of their time on the various waters in which Pacific salmon species may be found. Angling effort will increase as newer and faster highways facilitate greater ease and speed in moving from home base to more promising fishing grounds, and a greater reliance on both scheduled and light plane transportation is certain to give salmon anglers a wider range of fishing possibilities.

Whether or not the fishery will be able to withstand the pressure is the key question and one around which revolves considerable debate. Already various sport, commercial, and Indian interest groups are jockeying for position with an eye to capturing a significant share of the salmon resource. While the impact of foreign commercial fleets upon the West Coast's salmon populations has been reduced in some measure, there remain a myriad of problems to be solved, questions to be answered, compromises to be made. International negotiations have not always proved successful for the parties involved, and state and federal courts seem to be confusing—rather than clarifying—the issues in several respects. Many believe that certain recent court decisions have hampered fisheries management, and undoubtedly there is some validity to the notion. Indeed Americans may yet see the main questions set-

tled by the U. S. Supreme Court—or Congressional intervention.

But pressures from numerous interest groups are only the proverbial iceberg tip. Such groups contend for greater shares of the *available* resource. What is the current state of health of Pacific salmon populations?

While certain salmon runs appear to be quite healthy, the infirmity of the resource as a whole is apparent. Where salmon once abounded along the Pacific Coast, its inland marine waters, rivers, and streams, they are now less numerous. A century ago, virtually every suitable coastal stream—and many of those situated hundreds of miles inland—harbored extensive salmon runs. But civilization quickly took its toll. Increasing urbanization, the expansion of rural communities, farms, and highways rapidly brought about serious problems for the resource and restricted its natural habitat. In some instances, salmon runs were entirely displaced. The development of hydroelectric power and the rapid expansion of dams, together with a booming timber industry, further harmed natural salmon runs. Pollution, extensive irrigation development, and the diversion of water for domestic use are also to blame.

It is clear that, in light of our ever-increasing quest for progress, we cannot simply allow the resource to follow its present course. Some *positive* steps must be taken to ensure that our salmon runs survive. The goal is to offset the numerous *negative* influences which would otherwise result in the complete decimation of the various species.

Positive management is needed because of the sorry state of certain Pacific salmon runs. Canada's

Seining downstream migrant salmon to mark them and determine their speed of outmigration. Such research allows hatcheries to time their releases to obtain maximum survival under best water conditions. *Courtesy of Oregon Department of Fish & Wildlife.*

salmon runs, for instance, have declined to one-half of what they once were. Idaho has suffered even more: during the 1977 calendar year, only about 3,500 salmon were taken by sportsmen in that state—a far cry from the ten to twenty thousand fish taken annually only a few years before. California's Tuolumne and Stanislaus rivers, which hosted good salmon runs a score of years ago, have enjoyed poor returns since. There are many other examples of declining salmon populations, but the point is clear: salmon enhancement is no longer to be taken lightly. Indeed it is vital—in the literal sense—to the future of the various Pacific species.

Numerous enhancement techniques are employed to reduce the hazards to, and provide more favorable conditions for, Pacific salmon. One of the earliest of fisheries management attempts, and a technique still used extensively today, was artificial propagation. The Washington State Department of Fisheries cites original experiments revolving around the controlled incubation of Connecticut River shad as early as 1867. The following year, similar experiments were conducted on Atlantic salmon on New Brunswick's Miramichi River. In 1872, the U. S. Fish Commission opened the first Pacific salmon hatchery on northern California's McCloud River. Today, numerous salmon hatcheries may be found along the Pacific coast.

Salmon hatcheries, in which eggs are collected, fertilized, and incubated, do not meet all the qualifications required by modern fisheries management, however. Also required are rearing facilities, in which newly-hatched alevins may mature before being released. It has been demonstrated that the larger the fish at the time of their release, the better their chances of survival. Instead of releasing fish as small fry, they are nurtured by a special diet designed to allow them to attain rapid growth. When fish

170

A fisheries specialist captures a lunker Chinook salmon for hatchery spawning. *Courtesy of Washington Department of Fisheries.*

are sufficiently large, they are turned loose to begin their downstream migration. Experimenters found that salmon released at the hatchery at Washougal, Washington, enjoyed a much higher survival rate if they were turned loose as five and one-half inch fish than if they were released when two inches smaller. In fact, fish which were two inches longer than—and about twice as heavy as—the three and one-half inch fry returned in numbers *six times* as great as the smaller, lighter fish.

Salmon hatcheries have proved highly effective as a fisheries enhancement tool, and the results obtained are often astounding. When the Washougal facility was opened in 1957, fewer than five hundred coho arrived there annually. Eleven years later, over *forty-four thousand* silvers arrived at the hatchery! Washington fisheries biologists estimate that, for every coho returning to a hatchery, about six more are taken by sport and commercial anglers (the Chinook catch-to-escapement ratio is even higher!). Using these estimates as a guide, it is apparent that

approximately 240,000 coho, a two year's hatchery release bonus, fell to ocean and river rods and nets.

Fishways are another important resource management tool. They provide passage for upstream migrants through areas which would be otherwise inaccessible. Frequently fishways are placed near dams, waterfalls, strong rapids, and the like. Salmon are able to pass through such areas by negotiating baffled channels or a series of stepped pools which slow the water to a velocity which can be handled by upstream spawners. By easing the progress of spawning fish en route to their normal nesting areas or by allowing fish to reach areas which were previously inaccessible, fishways aid all salmon species but are especially valuable to weak swimming fish such as pinks.

Fisheries managers often transport salmon around obstructions when no other means is available for salmon to continue their upstream migration. This is typically accomplished by trucking fish, by road, around such barriers. Sometimes fish are transported downstream past hazardous areas, in order to insure lower mortality in young fish.

Salmon are also transplanted from one area of a stream to another—or from one waterway to a different one. Transplants can be a very economical means of salmon enhancement, because the natural environment is used as the facility. Transplants may make previously uninhabited waters productive. This technique calls for introducing new stocks or reestablishing former ones into barren streams or portions of streams which are suitable for habitat but which are perhaps obstructed by barriers. Fish are usually introduced as presmolts.

Spawning channels are man-made streams designed to provide an ideal environment for spawning and incubation. Carefully selected gravel is placed in the spawning channels, where water flow is almost invariably controlled. By arranging the channels in a severely curved or zig-zag design, lengthy spawning grounds may be fitted into relatively small areas.

Throughout Canada, spawning channels are used extensively to aid the propagation of sockeye, pink, and chum salmon. Fish spawn naturally in these man-made channels, although biologists closely monitor the situation.

Incubation boxes are sometimes used as substitutes for spawning channels where space is restricted. These are vertically packaged hatcheries or spawning channels in which already fertilized eggs and carefully selected gravel are layered; water is forced up through the gravel. Emerging fry may be collected and transported elsewhere, or they may be released directly into an adjacent stream.

Biologists also employ lake fertilization techniques

171

Oregon Department of Fish & Wildlife's Cole River Hatchery on the Rogue River. This hatchery produces about one million of the 60 million salmon raised in the state each year. *Courtesy of Oregon Department of Fish & Wildlife.*

to enhance salmon runs of lake-spawning sockeye salmon. Here the aim is to make up for a natural deficiency in waters holding substantial sockeye populations. Fisheries managers supply nutrients which are in short supply, namely fertilizer to stimulate the growth of plankton, an important organism in the food chain. Experiments with sockeye in Vancouver Island lakes have demonstrated that the technique is highly effective: the resulting larger sockeye smolts return as adult fish in numbers greater than their undernourished counterparts. Because this enhancement technique requires only the application of fertilizer at regular intervals, it is one of the most economical means of aiding salmon populations.

Water flow is vital to certain salmon runs, and biologists sometimes control the flow by damming streams to create a water storage reservoir and to retain flood waters for release during low water periods. Many streams fluctuate widely in their flows, ranging from near-drought to flood conditions. Low water hampers the progress of upstream spawning fish and sometimes causes young salmon to become cut off from the main channel. This may result in mortality for juveniles. Water which is too low may also bring about the exposure of eggs which have been deposited in the gravel and cause dehydration or freezing of incubating eggs. Flood waters, at the other extreme, also cause severe problems. They may result in cutting new ground channels, causing the original stream to wander, or they may bring excessive siltation which will smother young fry, eggs, and/or food nutrients. Flood conditions may also cause high mortality by causing stream gravel to shift and spawn to be scoured out.

Removal of logjams from streams containing spawning habitat is a continuous project. Hundreds of miles of spawning area are kept available to salmon as a result. *Courtesy of Oregon Department of Fish & Wildlife.*

Incubating eggs may be washed from their redds, and the cutting of new channels may leave spawning salmon without an upstream route. For these reasons, it is sometimes desirable to tamper with natural water flow conditions.

Temperature, too, may be critical to salmon. During extreme heat, cool water may be siphoned from the depths of a lake or reservoir and introduced to the spawning grounds. Or the introduction of warm water may be made in certain areas to promote salmon growth during cold conditions. Temperature control has been used effectively to guard sockeye and pink salmon from disease, which may spread rapidly in warm water conditions.

Stream clearance is yet another technique used to enhance salmon populations. The removal of obstructions or debris which may block certain por-

tions of a stream may aid fish, but sometimes rocks, logs, and the like are placed in certain spots to increase the rearing capacity of open water areas and to create useful resting areas for both upstream and downstream migrants. Gravel which is unsuitable for propogation may be cleaned to provide a desirable water flow, to carry oxygen and nutrients to eggs which are in the incubation stage, or to remove unneeded organic material which may be usurping the oxygen required by the fish. The addition or alteration of streamside vegetation may be desirable to help prevent washouts or to provide new homes for insects upon which young salmon may feed. Stream clearance may include these or other techniques, but the primary goal is to improve or provide a suitable habitat for salmon.

Where stream feed is at a premium, biologists may enrich the diets of juvenile salmon by in-stream feeding, thus causing smolts to grow larger before their downstream migrations. Again, the larger the smolt, the greater the chances of survival.

Biting salmon, taken on hook and line from the Olympic peninsula's Hoh River, are dumped into a makeshift tank truck by Fisheries Department personnel and sportsmen for cross-breeding with hard-to-catch Puget Sound salmon. *Courtesy of Washington Department of Fisheries.*

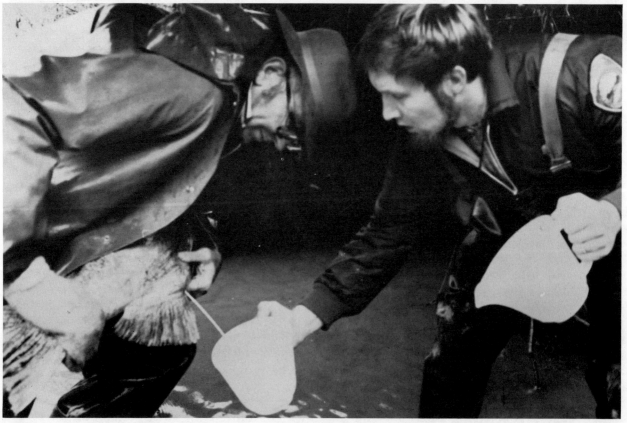

Milking the monsters at Rivers Inlet! Washington Department of Fisheries Assistant Hatchery Chief Dick Noble wrestles a 60-pound *Tyee* salmon. Biologist Ray Buckley holds a beaker to catch precious sperm for cross-breeding Puget Sound salmon with legendary Canadian fish. *Courtesy of Washington Department of Fisheries.*

Research carried on to determine the kill of downstream salmon at various dams has led to screening of intakes and other actions to save these fish. Dams still are major problems to both upstream and downstream migrants. *Courtesy of Oregon Department of Fish & Wildlife.*

Fisheries biologist traps adult Chinook in Washington's Hoh River for transport to nearby salmon hatchery. The project, conducted in the late 1960s and early 70s, was one of the first big efforts to improve the quality of sport salmon fishing in Washington State. *Courtesy of Washington Department of Fisheries.*

While virtually all salmon enhancement techniques at present are directed at fish while they are in their freshwater existence—the likely place, since it is easier to work with salmon in their stream environment—salmon enhancement and fisheries management techniques are apt to include estuarial and ocean research in the future. Such efforts will take considerable time and will be expensive, to be sure, yet as the resource becomes increasingly valuable, salt and brackish water enhancement goals will be set.

It may surprise the reader to learn, however, that we *now* possess the technology to restore Pacific salmon runs to their former numbers. All that is required is the will to do so. As an increasing number of sport and commercial salmon fishermen begin to place greater emphasis on fish management and conservation, as more sport anglers come to learn the immense joy which results from *releasing* a large salmon to do battle again or to proceed to its spawning grounds, and as the concerned citizenry becomes more vociferous about the future of our Pacific salmon, rebuilding efforts will be expanded. Given sufficient funding and the wise use and management of this great resource, we may yet hear the last faint cries of the pessimists.

SUPPLEMENTAL INFORMATION

Sportsmen interested in obtaining information relating to salmon fishing, including seasons and then-current regulations, may contact the following agencies:

Washington:

Washington State Department of Fisheries
115 General Administration Building
Olympia, Washington 98504
Phone: (206) 753-6600

Alaska:

Alaska Department of Fish and Game
Subport Building
Juneau, Alaska 99801
Phone: (907) 465-4100

Oregon:

Oregon Department of Fish and Wildlife
506 S.W. Mill Street
Portland, Oregon 97208
Phone: (503) 229-5403

Idaho:

Idaho Department of Fish and Game
600 South Walnut Street
Boise, Idaho 83707
Phone: (208) 384-3700

California:

California Department of Fish and Game
1416 Ninth Street
Sacramento, California 95814
Phone: (916) 445-3531

British Columbia:

Environment Canada, Fisheries and Marine
1090 West Pender Street
Vancouver, B.C., Canada V6E 2P1
Phone: (604) 666-1583

BIBLIOGRAPHY

Alaska Magazine Editors. *Alaska Fishing Guide*. Anchorage, Ala.: Alaska Northwest, 1976.

——. *The Milepost*. Anchorage, Ala.: Alaska Northwest, 1972.

Bates, Joseph D. *Fishing*. New York: Outdoor Life, n.d.

Bradner, Enos. *Northwest Angling*. Portland, Oreg.: Binford & Mort, 1969.

Brooks, Joe. *Complete Guide to Fishing Across North America*. New York: Harper & Row, 1966.

——. *Salt Water Game Fishing*. New York: Harper & Row, 1968.

Cannon, Raymond. *How to Fish the Pacific Coast*. Menlo Park, Calif.: Lane, 1966.

Colgrave, Bruce, and Gaunt, Jack. *Bucktails and Hoochies*. Sidney, B.C., Canada: Saltaire, 1971.

Davis, Charles. *California Saltwater Fishing*. New York: Barnes, 1949.

——. *Saltwater Fishing on the Pacific Coast*. New York: Barnes, 1964.

Donaldson, Ivan, and Cramer, Frederick. *Fishwheels of the Columbia*. Portland, Oreg.: Binford & Mort, 1971.

Evanoff, Vlad. *How to Fish in Salt Water*. New York: Barnes, 1962.

——. *Fishing Rigs for Fresh & Salt Water*. New York: Harper & Row, 1977.

——. *Surf Fishing*. New York: Harper & Row, 1974.

Farrington, S. Kip, Jr. *Fishing the Pacific*. New York: Coward, McCann, 1953.

Frear, Gordon S. *Northwest Fishing and Hunting Guide*. Seattle, Wash.: Northwest Guides, 1968.

Freer, Blaine, *The Sportsman's Guide to the Pacific Northwest*. Garden City, N.Y.: Doubleday, 1975.

Grundle, Jack, and Broomhall, Pete, eds. *British Columbia Game Fish*. Vancouver, B.C., Canada: Western Fish & Game, 1970.

Haig-Brown, Roderick. *Fisherman's Fall*. New York: Crown, 1975.

Harris, Walter. *Salmon Fishing in Alaska*. South Brunswick and New York: A. S. Barnes, 1967.

Haw, Frank, and Buckley, Raymond M. *Oregon Saltwater Fishing Guide*. Seattle, Wash.: Stan Jones, 1972.

——. *Saltwater Fishing in Washington*. Seattle, Wash.: Stan Jones, 1973.

Holm, Don. *Fishing the Pacific*. New York: Winchester, 1972.

——. *Pacific North!* Caldwell, Idaho: Caxton, 1969.

——. *One-Hundred One Best Fishing Spots in Oregon*. Caldwell, Idaho: Caxton, 1970.

Humphrey, William. *Spawning Run*. New York: Knopf, 1970.

Jones, Stan. *Washington State Fishing Guide*. Seattle, Wash.: Alaska Northwest, 1967.

Lyman, Henry, and Woolner, Frank. *Tackle Talk*. South Brunswick and New York: A. S. Barnes, 1971.

McClane, Al. *McClane's Standard Fishing Encyclopedia*. New York: Holt, Rinehart & Winston, 1965.

McInturff, Roy A. *Wilderness Fishing for Salmon and Steelhead*. South Brunswick and New York: A. S. Barnes, 1974.

Major, Harlan. *Salt Water Fishing Tackle*. New York: Funk & Wagnalls, 1939.

Menke, Frank G. *The Encyclopedia of Sports*. New York: Doubleday-Dolphin, 1977.

Netboy, Anthony. *Salmon of the Pacific Northwest*. Portland, Oreg.: Binford & Mort. n.d.

Rosko, Milt. *Fishing from Boats*. New York: Macmillan, 1968.

Schwiebert, Ernest. *Salmon of the World*. New York: Winchester, 1970.

Thomas, John; Keizer, Milt; Sheely, Terry. *Pocket Guide to Washington Salmon Fishing*. Snohomish, Wash.: Osprey, 1977.

Waterman, Charles F. *Fishing in America*. New York: Holt, Rinehart & Winston, 1975.

White, Charles. *How to Catch Salmon*. Sidney, B.C., Canada: Saltaire, 1971.

Williams, Herb. *Twin Harbors Tales*. Tacoma, Wash.: Herb Williams, 1967.

— —, and Neubrech, Walt. *American Nightmare*. Seattle, Wash.: Outdoor Empire, 1976.

Wolfe, Alfred. *In Alaskan Waters*. Caldwell, Idaho: Caxton, 1943.

Woolner, Frank. *Modern Saltwater Sport Fishing*. New York: Crown, 1972.

Source material also derived from the following:

Washington:

"Angling for Salmon, Shad and Sturgeon in Freshwaters of Washington State," by Frank Haw; Washington State Department of Fisheries.

"A Salmon Angling Program for the Puget Sound Region," compiled and edited by Frank Haw and Peter K. Bergman; Washington State Department of Fisheries.

"Pacific Northwest Marine Fishes"; Washington State Department of Fisheries.

"Salmon Hatcheries"; Washington State Department of Fisheries.

"Tips for the Salmon Salt Water Angler"; Washington State Department of Fisheries.

"Washington State Sport Catch Report—1976" by Gene D. Nye, W. Dale Ward and Lee J. Hoines; Washington State Department of Fisheries.

Oregon:

"Fishing in Oregon"; Oregon State Game Commission.

"Oregon Salmon and Steelhead Catch Data, 1967-76," compiled by R. L. Berry; Oregon Department of Fish and Wildlife, Fish Division.

"Oregon Salmon Fishing"; Oregon Department of Transportation, Travel Information Section.

"Salmon: Estimated Catch by Month by Stream"; Oregon Department of Fish and Wildlife, Fish Division.

California:

"Anadromous Fisheries: 1977 Annual Report"; State of California, The Resources Agency, Department of Fish and Game.

"Salmon and Steelhead Fishing Map: Description of the Fishery and What is Necessary to Maintain It"; State of California, The Resources Agency, Department of Fish and Game.

Alaska:

"Alaska Sport Fish Resorts"; Sport Fish Division, Alaska Department of Fish and Game.

"Alaska Sport Fishing Guide"; Sport Fish Division, Alaska Department of Fish and Game.

British Columbia:

"British Columbia Tidal Waters Sport Fishing Guide—1977"; Canada Department of Fisheries and Environment.

"Department of the Environment Fisheries Operations Statistical Map"; Canada Department of Fisheries and Environment.

"Fisheries Fact Sheet: Fishing Gear and Methods on the Pacific Coast"; Department of the Environment, Ottawa.

"Fisheries Fact Sheet: Otter-Trawling (Dragging)"; Information and Consumer Service, Department of Fisheries of Canada.

"Guide to Salmonid Enhancement"; Canada Department of Fisheries and Environment.

"1976 Salmon Sport Fishing Catch Statistics for British Columbia Tidal Waters"; Department of Fisheries and the Environment, Fisheries and Marine Service.

"Salmonid Fact Sheet Number 1—Fishways: An Enhancement Tool"; Canada Department of Fisheries and Environment.

"Salmonid Fact Sheet Number 2: Lake Enrichment"; Canada Department of Fisheries and Environment.

"Salmonid Fact Sheet Number 3: Enhancement Techniques"; Canada Department of Fisheries and Environment.

"What is Salmonid Enhancement?"; SEP, Canada Department of Fisheries and Environment.

"Where and When to See Salmon"; Canada Department of Fisheries and Environment.

General:

"Basic Salmon Recipes," by Iola I. Berg; Washington State Department of Fisheries.

"The Nitty Gritty of Smoke Cooking," by Dan Stair; Luhr Jensen and Sons, Inc. Hood River, Oregon; and Luhr Jensen and Sons, LTD, Vancouver, British Columbia.

INDEX